ANDREWS UNIVERSITY SEMINARY
DOCTORAL DISSERTATION SERIES
VOLUME XII

JAMES WHITE AND SDA ORGANIZATION:

Historical Development, 1844-1881

by

Andrew G. Mustard

ANDREWS UNIVERSITY PRESS
BERRIEN SPRINGS, MICHIGAN

Christmas 1996

Dearest Jackie,

I think Andy would have wanted you to have this. It represents many hours of blood, sweat and tears, as you know. I don't know whether you'll manage to get through reading the whole thing, but I thought this was something you'd like to have in memory of Andrews, a man we both loved, each in our own special way.

"At the midnight hour, when the sands of the old year are running low, I shall sit and turn the leaves of my Book of Memory. Therein I will find a record of things seen and of friends known, and memories will rise of friendships, some grown deeper for intercourse, others not lessened for silence."

With love,

Thethea

Published August 1988 by
Andrews University Press
Berrien Springs, MI 49104

ISBN 0-943872-46-4

TABLE OF CONTENTS

Chapter
III. (Continued)

Chapter

V. (Continued)

LIST OF ABBREVIATIONS

AH, Advent Herald

AM, Advent Mirror

ASR, Advent Shield and Review

D-S, Day-Star

JS, Jubilee Standard

MC, Midnight Cry

MW, Morning Watch

PT, Present Truth

RH, Advent Review and Sabbath Herald, Advent Review, Second Advent Review, and Sabbath Herald, Adventist Review

ST, Signs of the Times

VT, Voice of Truth and Glad Tidings of the Kingdom at Hand

WMC, Western Midnight Cry

ACKNOWLEDGMENTS

This project could not have been completed without the concern, support, and assistance of many people. I am indebted to the members of my advisory committee, Dr. Raoul Dederen (chairman), Dr. Mervyn Maxwell, and Dr. Russell Staples, who showed genuine interest, provided helpful criticism, and constantly upheld a high standard of excellence. The encouragement of Dr. Roy Graham who, even in the final stages of his illness, took time to advise me is deeply appreciated.

Special recognition is also due to Mrs. Joyce Jones for her editorial expertise; and the library staffs of Andrews University and Newbold College, including those of the James White Library Heritage Room and the respective Ellen G. White Estate Branch Offices, for their ready assistance in my research. My thanks is also extended to the Newbold College Board for providing the opportunity to complete the writing of this dissertation, and to my fellow teachers at the college for their constructive criticism and the opportunity for useful exchange of ideas.

I am grateful, too, for the encouragement of my parents and the unsolicited generosity of my sister-in-law, Esther Haslam. Most of all, I would express appreciation to my wife, Alethea, for her patience in typing this work, her unfailing devotion, and understanding.

vii

CHAPTER I

INTRODUCTION

Addressing the March 1873 General Conference session of the Seventh-day Adventist Church, James White,[1] one of its founders and the driving force behind its organization, declared:

> When we consider the small beginning, and in how obscure a manner this work commenced, the rapidity and soundness of our growth, the perfection and efficiency of our organization, the great work it has already accomplished . . . when we look at these things, and see how God has prospered us, we that are connected with the work can say, "What hath God wrought!"[2]

White's evident satisfaction with the state of the church's organization was expressed ten years after the General Conference was organized. He was clearly convinced that the present state of denominational polity was well suited to the existing needs of a church which at the time had 5,875 members in thirteen conferences and one mission.[3]

---

[1]See below, pp. 9-11, for a biographical sketch. Unless otherwise stated, the White referred to in this work is James White.

[2][James White], "Conference Address," RH, May 20, 1873, p. 184.

[3]"Proceedings of the Eleventh Annual Meeting of the General Conference of S.D. Adventists," RH, March 18, 1873, p. 108.

Aims and Purposes

How well does the present structure of Seventh-day Adventism

serve an international church that operates in 184 countries and

totals approximately 4.5 million members?[1] Reflection on this ques-

tion has stimulated the present writer's interest in the origins and

development of the organizational patterns of the Seventh-day

Adventist Church. In this dissertation, therefore, we have described

the unfolding of church order within Sabbatarian Adventism from the

time of the Great Disappointment[2] of October 1844 until 1881, the

---

[1]For membership statistics as announced at the latest session of the General Conference, see F. Donald Yost, "Membership and Financial Statistics," RH, July 4, 1985, p. 28. Contemporary Seventh-day Adventist sources that have touched on the issue of church structure include a special section, "A Call for an Open Church," Spectrum 14 (March 1984):14-53. It contains the following articles: James W. Walters, "The Need for Structural Change," pp. 14-17; Task Force Reports, "A Call for an Open Church" and "Defining Participation: A Model Conference Constitution," pp. 18-35; George Colvin, "Explaining Participation: A Commentary," pp. 36-39; Raymond F. Cottrell, "The Varieties of Church Structure," pp. 40-53. See also, George W. Reid, "Time to Reorder the Church?" RH, July 28, 1983, pp. 14-15; B. B. Beach, "Windows of Vulnerability," RH, August 2, 1984, pp. 3-5. Cf. also the papers presented at a theological consultation for Seventh-day Adventist Administrators and Religion Scholars, Glacier View, Colorado, August 15-19, 1980. Several of the presentations dealt with aspects of church structure. See especially, Charles E. Bradford, "A Theology of Church Organization and Administration"; Fred Veltman, "The Role of Church Administrators and Theologians."

[2]The failure of Millerite expectations for Christ's Second Advent on October 22, 1844, is described as the "Great Disappointment" or "the Disappointment." For accounts by Millerites of their experiences at that time, see Letter, William Miller to Joshua V. Himes, AH, November 27, 1844, pp. 127-128; Sylvester Bliss, Memoirs of William Miller (Boston: J. V. Himes, 1853), pp. 276-286. Later historical descriptions of the Disappointment may be found in David T. Arthur, "'Come Out of Babylon': A Study of Millerite Separation and Denominationalism, 1840-1865" (Ph.D. dissertation, University of Rochester, 1970), pp. 85-98; P. Gerard Damsteegt,

year of White's death. Our concern has been to record the historical events in the church's growth, with particular attention given to White's role in the development of church organization, and to underline the theological understanding with which Seventh-day Adventist pioneers undergirded the organization of the denomination.

Methodology

Wherever possible, primary materials have been utilized, supplemented by secondary sources where relevant. In the case of the Millerite movement, the numerous periodicals produced between 1840 and 1844 serve as the main source of information. Other primary materials are available on microfilm of rare books and manuscripts.[1] The dissertations of David T. Arthur,[2] Everett N. Dick,[3] and David L.

Foundations of the Seventh-day Adventist Message and Mission (Grand Rapids, Mich.: William B. Eerdmans Pub. Co., 1977), pp. 100-117; L. E. Froom, The Prophetic Faith of Our Fathers: The Historical Development of Prophetic Interpretation, 4 vols. (Washington, D.C.: Review and Herald Pub. Assn, 1946-1954), 4:822-833; Francis D. Nichol, The Midnight Cry (Washington, D.C.: Review and Herald Pub. Assn, 1944), pp. 263-276; Clyde E. Hewitt, Midnight and Morning: An Account of the Adventist Awakening and the Founding of the Advent Christian Denomination, 1831-1860 (Charlotte, N.C.: Venture Books, 1983), pp. 159-202. See also below, pp. 69-74.

[1]The Millerites and Early Adventists, microfilm collection (Ann Arbor, Mich.: University Microfilms International, 1978). The collection is based on a bibliographic essay by Vern Carner, Sakae Kubo, and Curt Rice originally published in The Rise of Adventism, ed. Edwin S. Gaustad (New York: Harper & Row, 1974), pp. 207-317. The bibliography in Damsteegt's dissertation, Foundations, pp. 314-334, also proved an invaluable guide to the primary sources.

[2]Arthur, "'Come Out of Babylon'" (1970).

[3]Everett N. Dick, "The Adventist Crisis of 1843-1844" (Ph.D. dissertation, University of Wisconsin, 1930), pp. 29-55.

Rowe[1] have served as useful guides to the study of Millerite separatism and organization.

The most important primary source for the history of Seventh-day Adventist church organization is the Advent Review and Sabbath Herald between 1850 and 1881.[2] In the absence of separately published bulletins of General Conference proceedings until 1888, the pages of the Review were used to record debates engaged in and actions taken at church councils. The letters to the editor served as a useful forum for open and vigorous discussion on a wide range of subjects, including church order, to which White, as an editor, responded with equal forcefulness. The willingness of Sabbatarian Adventists to engage in free give and take over sometimes controversial and sensitive issues is a boon to the modern researcher. As the bibliography of this dissertation indicates, a constant stream of articles on organization appeared from the pens of Seventh-day Adventist pioneers including, most notably, White, Ellen G. White, Joseph Bates, J. B. Frisbie, R. F. Cottrell,[3] Uriah Smith,[4]

---

[1]David L. Rowe, "Thunder and Trumpets: The Millerite Movement and Apocalyptic Thought in Upstate New York, 1800-1845" (Ph.D. dissertation, University of Virginia, 1974), pp. 189-226.

[2]The Advent Review and Sabbath Herald is the general church paper of the Seventh-day Adventist Church. Published continuously from the summer of 1850 to the present, it has been issued under various titles such as Advent Review, Second Advent Review, and Sabbath Herald, and the Adventist Review. We shall cite it hereafter simply as the Review (RH).

[3]Unless otherwise stated, the Cottrell referred to in this work is Roswell F. Cottrell.

[4]Unless otherwise stated, the Smith referred to in this work is Uriah Smith.

J. N. Andrews, J. N. Loughborough, and G. I. Butler.[1] Other sources include the first Sabbatarian Adventist periodical Present Truth,[2] the extant private letters of White, and the published books, letters, and manuscripts of his wife, Ellen G. White.[3]

Of the historical accounts that have been published on the development of Seventh-day Adventist church order, perhaps the most significant is by Loughborough, as it was based upon the author's personal memories of the events in which he participated after his conversion to Seventh-day Adventism in 1852.[4] Unfortunately, its value is limited due to the fact that in the main it is a collection of quotations selected from Review articles or books by White and his wife. Frequently only the briefest comment links one section of the book with another. The same shortcoming is to be found in later histories of Seventh-day Adventist church organization by Clarence C. Crisler[5] and Oliver Montgomery.[6] None of the above three works

---

[1]Unless otherwise stated, the Butler referred to in this work is G. I. Butler.

[2]Published July 1849-November 1850.

[3]James White's letters, together with his wife's published and unpublished letters and manuscripts, are available at the Ellen G. White Estate Branch Offices at Andrews University, Berrien Springs, Michigan and Newbold College, Bracknell, Berkshire, England.

[4]J. N. Loughborough, The Church: Its Organization, Order, and Discipline (Washington, D.C.: Review and Herald Pub. Assn, 1907).

[5]Clarence C. Crisler, Organization: Its Character, Purpose, Place, and Development in the Seventh-day Adventist Church (Washington, D.C.: Review and Herald Pub. Assn, 1938).

[6]Oliver Montgomery, Principles of Church Organization and Administration (Washington, D.C.: Review and Herald Pub. Assn, 1942).

seeks to examine critically the biblical or theoretical grounds on which Seventh-day Adventists built church order. Carl D. Anderson's dissertation concentrates primarily on organizational developments from 1888 to 1901 and as he also does not examine the conceptual bases of denominational polity his work is not relevant to the present study.[1]

In order to lay out the development of Seventh-day Adventist church order as fully as possible, chapters two to four have been written from a descriptive point of view, intermingling interpretative and analytical comments with the historical account. Chapter two provides a brief outline of the background for the emergence of Seventh-day Adventism, namely, the socio-political and religious situation in North America during the first half of the 19th century. Particular attention has been paid to the Millerite movement from 1840 to 1844 as the milieu out of which Sabbatarian Adventism arose and which was a possible source of some of the patterns of organization used by Seventh-day Adventists.

Chapter three traces the experience of the former Millerites after the Disappointment. In the first place, an account is given of events and theological discussions immediately after 1844. The attempts of non-Sabbatarian Adventists to hold together the splintering Millerite movement are included in order to provide a point of contrast with the development of Sabbatarian Adventism. Second, the early days of Sabbatarian Adventism are described, as a few small

---

[1]Carl D. Anderson, "The History and Evolution of Seventh-day Adventist Church Organization" (Ph.D. dissertation, American University, 1960).

groups of believers moved toward consolidation of what came to be the distinctive doctrines of Seventh-day Adventism.

Chapter four describes the emergence of Seventh-day Adventist church order from 1850 to 1881. The account follows events from the earliest references to organizational concerns to the formation of the General Conference in 1863, and beyond that date to the development of the church into an international body marked by the sending out of the first official overseas missionary of Seventh-day Adventism in 1874. Since White played a significant role in discussions on church order throughout his lifetime, 1881, the year of his death, has been chosen as an appropriate milestone to mark the end of foundational developments in Seventh-day Adventist organization.

The fifth chapter is an evaluation of the theological bases of White's and other Seventh-day Adventists' positions concerning church order. These beliefs are considered in light of their accordance with stated methods of biblical interpretation as expressed in Sabbatarian Adventist writings and in articles and tracts of Millerite authors. White's interaction with his associates is also assessed. We have sought to determine if his views changed in reaction to others, if there was progress or regression in his thinking, and if he was consistent with his own stated presuppositions. The impact of his own personality on the form of church organization that was consolidated during his lifetime is another factor taken into consideration.

Finally, some suggestions are made which may serve as pointers in current expressions of the Seventh-day Adventist doctrine of church order.

Scope and Delimitations

In view of the extensive literature on church order throughout the period in question, the present writer has excluded a detailed examination of later significant events. The reorganization of the General Conference in 1901, for instance, was no doubt equally important in the evolution of Seventh-day Adventist structure; but it would seem logical to investigate first the earlier formative episodes and leave to a later study subsequent changes or developments.[1]

It should also be pointed out that this study has described and evaluated the historical development and theoretical foundations of Seventh-day Adventist organization, but has not inquired into the practical administrative conduct of church business. Further limitations have been required by lack of unpublished primary sources, apart from the letters and manuscripts of James and Ellen G. White available at the Ellen G. White Estate Branch Offices. Consequently, this work has confined itself to the historical data and expressed opinions of Seventh-day Adventist pioneers. It has not sought to discover how Seventh-day Adventist church order was perceived by other denominations or by off-shoots of Seventh-day Adventism.

---

[1]Apart from Anderson's dissertation, "SDA Church Organization" (1960), which fails to make adequate use of primary sources, no significant monograph has appeared on organizational developments around the turn of the century. For useful general historical accounts, see Richard W. Schwarz, Light Bearers to the Remnant (Mountain View, Calif.: Pacific Press Pub. Assn, 1979), pp. 267-281; Arthur L. White, Ellen G. White, vol. 5: The Early Elmshaven Years (Washington, D.C.: Review and Herald Pub. Assn, 1981), pp. 70-83; C. Mervyn Maxwell, Tell It to the World, rev. ed. (Mountain View, Calif.: Pacific Press Pub. Assn, 1977), pp. 251-261.

Biographical Sketch of James White

A brief biographical account of White is provided to aid in
defining his role in the founding of the Seventh-day Adventist
Church.[1]

Born August 4, 1821, in Palmyra, Maine, the fifth of nine
children, White suffered as a boy from physical disability,
especially weak eyesight, which prevented him from attending school
until he was nineteen. He then entered an academy in St. Albans,
Maine, where by studying eighteen hours a day for twelve weeks he
attained a certificate as a school teacher. After teaching the next
winter he attended school for another seventeen weeks. This was the
extent of his formal education.

White was baptized into the Christian Connection[2] at the age
of fifteen. After hearing William Miller and Joshua V. Himes preach
in September 1842[3] he decided to join in the proclamation of the
Millerite message of Christ's imminent Second Advent. Apparently,
his preaching was effective as more than a thousand accepted Christ
as a result of his work.[4]

---

[1]For further biographical information, see Virgil Robinson,
James White (Washington, D.C.: Review and Herald Pub. Assn, 1976);
"White, James Springer," SDA Encyclopedia (1976), 10:1598-1604. Cf.
also White's autobiographical account, Life Incidents, in Connection
With the Great Advent Movement, As Illustrated By the three Angels of
Revelation XIV (Battle Creek, Mich.: Seventh-day Adventist Pub.
Assn, 1863), pp. 9-25, 72-120, 264-373.

[2]Cf. below, pp. 29-32.

[3]For a further account of the work of William Miller and
Joshua V. Himes, see below, pp. 33-44.

[4]White, Life Incidents, pp. 72-120. Cf. also Robinson, James
White, p. 26.

Following the Disappointment in October 1844, White soon parted company with most former Millerites, believing them to be mistaken in denying the validity of their past experience.[1] In seeking to encourage other former Millerites to maintain their faith he came into contact with Ellen G. Harmon with whom he worked to encourage Adventist believers. Despite initial misgivings because of the supposed shortness of time before Christ's return, they were married on August 30, 1846, in Portland, Maine.

Soon after their marriage they adopted the seventh-day Sabbath, which had been introduced to them by Bates who, along with the Whites and others, was to become another prominent figure in the early days of Sabbatarian Adventism.

White participated in the important formative conferences of Sabbatarian Adventism in 1848 and soon afterward began to publish a periodical, Present Truth, which in time gave way to the Review. The work of publishing and writing remained one of White's major activities for the rest of his life. In view of his limited formal education, his success as a writer, editor, and publisher is remarkable. His writing style was simple as one might expect, but he was able to express himself quite forcefully and effectively.

From approximately 1850 to 1863, White was the leading figure in promoting church order, his work coming to fruition in May 1863 when the General Conference of the Seventh-day Adventist Church was organized in Battle Creek, Michigan. Because he had been the leading advocate of church organization, he declined the invitation

---

[1]On the parting of the ways between Sabbatarian Adventists and the other former Millerites, see below, pp. 67-91.

to serve as the church's first president. In future years he did serve as president of the General Conference (1865-1867, 1869-1871, 1874-1880).

In addition to his administrative, publishing, and preaching responsibilities, White led out in the establishment of Seventh-day Adventist medical and educational institutions. The pressure of overwork may well have led to a severe stroke in August 1865, followed by several minor ones in 1871 and 1873. In spite of the obvious need for rest, he continued to carry heavy administrative responsibilities which no doubt contributed to his premature death at the age of sixty on August 6, 1881.

CHAPTER II

THE BACKGROUNDS FOR THE FORMATION OF ADVENTISM

The 19th century was a time of diversity and change in the social, political, and religious spheres of American life.[1] Thus, the religious upheavals of the period that we are interested in--the time of the Millerite movement of the 1830s and 1840s--were influenced by the social and political situation; while the religious upheavals, in turn, had a profound and lasting effect on all aspects of American life. The religious history of this period has been well documented by numerous authors.[2] We will attempt to set the 19th-century scene in which Adventism developed by providing a general description of this context, progressing from universal to more specific religious conditions.

---

[1]For a comprehensive study of American culture that not only deals with political events, but also a broad array of subjects from science to religious movements, see Daniel J. Boorstin's three-volume work, The Americans. The second of the three volumes (The National Experience [New York: Random House, 1965]) deals with the early decades of the 19th century. See also Jacob E. Cooke, "The Federalist Age: A Reappraisal," in American History: Retrospect and Prospect, ed. George A. Billias and Gerald N. Grob (New York: Free Press, 1971), pp. 85-153; Alice F. Tyler, Freedom's Ferment: Phases of American Social History to 1860 (Minneapolis: University of Minnesota Press, 1944), pp. 1-22. Tyler's work is still regarded as the classic study of American revivalism and reform although it is now somewhat dated in its interpretation. A valuable recent work on the same subject is Ronald G. Walters's American Reformers, 1815-1860 (New York: Hill and Wang, 1978).

[2]General accounts of the religious history of the first half of the 19th century may be found in Winthrop S. Hudson, Religion in

The Socio-political Milieu

Fundamental to the great changes taking place in society at the time, both in Europe and North America, was the vast increase in human knowledge. The improved understanding of the physical universe enabled the Western world to invent new machines which greatly facilitated travel, communication, and the industrialization of society. An essential ingredient of these advances was the development of the scientific method. This method did more than encourage the growth of human knowledge; it also stimulated an attitude of individuality and freedom of thought that extended to all areas of human endeavor and investigation.[1]

Not all the consequences of these developments were positive. The industrial revolution brought about a great shift in population

America: An Historical Account of the Development of American Religious Life, 2nd ed. (New York: Charles Scribner's Sons, 1973) pp. 109-204; Sydney E. Ahlstrom, A Religious History of the American People (New Haven, Conn.: Yale University Press, 1972), pp. 385-669; Edwin S. Gaustad, A Religious History of America (New York: Harper & Row, 1966), pp. 132-153; Kenneth S. Latourette, A History of the Expansion of Christianity, vol. 4: The Great Century, A D. 1800-A.D. 1914, (London: Eyre and Spottiswoode, 1941), pp. 1-21. One may also wish to consult Samuel E. Morison, The Oxford History of the American People (New York: Oxford University Press, 1965), pp. 400-430, 516-537. For Seventh-day Adventist perspectives on the same era see Schwarz, Light Bearers, pp. 13-23; Froom, Prophetic Faith, 4:429-442.

[1]On the impact of the scientific method on 19th-century thought, see John H. Randall, Jr., The Making of the Modern Mind (Cambridge, Mass.: Houghton Mifflin Co., 1940), pp. 282-307; Franklin L. Baumer, Modern European Thought: Continuity and Change in Ideas, 1600-1950 (New York: Macmillan Pub. Co., 1977), pp. 302-323. For further study of the experimental method in America, see Morton White, ed., Documents in the History of American Philosophy, from Jonathan Edwards to John Dewey (New York: Oxford University Press, 1972), pp. 191-251; Morton White, Science and Sentiment in America: Philosophical Thought from Jonathan Edwards to John Dewey (New York: Oxford University Press, 1972), pp. 71-119.

from rural to urban, resulting in a notable shift in social and economic problems. Increased wealth and prosperity on the part of a few bred discontent among those less fortunate or less enterprising. Reformers sounded calls for the reorganization of society, thus precipitating a struggle between conflicting ideologies such as capitalism, individualism, and laissez faire economics on the one hand and socialism on the other.

The political arena in America was marked by a sense of national destiny and buoyant optimism concerning America's future. Thus, the period from 1789 to 1829 (marked by the inauguration of George Washington as president and the election of Andrew Jackson, the popular hero of the masses) became known among later "Jacksonian" historians as the "era of good feeling." Some interpreters have characterized the years of Jackson's administration (1829-1837) as an age in which the common man came into his own and the principles of equality, fuller participation in the affairs of government, universal public education, and extension of the right to vote emerged.[1]

The optimism of the age is well expressed in the following statement by Andrew Johnson, an enthusiastic follower of Jackson:

> I believe man can be elevated; man can become more and more endowed with divinity; and as he does he becomes more God-like in his character and capable of governing himself. Let us go on elevating our people, perfecting our institutions, until

---

[1]See, e.g., the Pulitzer prize-winning work on the Jacksonian era, Arthur M. Schlesinger, Jr., The Age of Jackson (New York: Book Find Club, 1945), pp. 350-368. See also the bibliographical essay in Glyndon G. Van Deusen, The Jacksonian Era, 1828-1848 (New York: Harper & Bros., 1959), pp. 267-283.

democracy shall reach such a point of perfection that we can acclaim with truth that the voice of the people is the voice of God.[1]

More recently, historians have questioned the characterization of Jackson as the hero of the masses. Instead, the suggestion has been made that the influence of Jackson on the politics of the period has been exaggerated and that "Jacksonian Democracy gave power not to Tom, Dick, and Harry but to the shrewd, ambitious, wealthy, and able politicians who knew best how to flatter them."[2]

The Religious Situation in the Early Decades of the 19th Century

In describing the religious situation in the first half of the 19th century we shall attempt to give emphasis to its outstanding features, the influence of which may be distinguished in the Millerite movement. These features are revivalism, perfectionism, Puritanism, Congregationalism, and denominationalism. We shall also sketch the organizational modes of the three denominations (the Methodists, Baptists, and the Christian Connection) whose members joined the Millerite movement in the greatest numbers and had the most impact on attitudes toward organization within Adventism.

In spite of (if not because of or in reaction to) the challenges posed to the Christian faith by the socio-political developments sketched above, the 19th century was a time of expansion

---

[1]Andrew Johnson, quoted by Winthrop S. Hudson, "A Time of Religious Ferment," in The Rise of Adventism, p. 2.

[2]The most notable reinterpretation of the Jacksonian era is Edward Pessen, Jacksonian America: Society, Personality and Politics, rev. ed. (Harewood, Ill.: Dorsey Press, 1978), pp. 1-32, 324-327. Pessen provides a useful bibliographical essay on recent Jacksonian scholarship (pp. 329-367).

for Christianity that was unprecedented, at least since the days of
the early church. The increased wealth of society and easier means
of travel and communication helped to provide an environment
favorable to the spread of Christianity. This, however, does not
fully explain the geographical and numerical growth of Christianity.
Indeed, we must agree with Kenneth Scott Latourette that the primary
explanation for this phenomenon lies in an "upsurging creative
impulse within Christianity itself."[1]

What was true of 19th-century Christianity in general was
also true of Christianity in its American form, and to a greater
degree. In common with its European counterpart, American
Christianity's new vitality was partly a reaction against the
atheistic or agnostic philosophies of the age, as well as the result
of a desire to restore the original simplicity and purity of the New
Testament faith.[2] Many Americans also regarded their new nation as

---

[1]Latourette, The Great Century, p. 22. Our intention in
using Latourette's depiction of an "upsurging creative impulse"
within European and American Christianity is to point out that no
account of the political, social, and religious factors behind the
expansion of Christianity in the 19th century can adequately account
for its growth. One must also take into consideration the influence
of the religious faith of the people.

[2]The attempt to pattern doctrine and praxis after Scripture,
especially in the New Testament Church, reveals the influence of
Puritan ideals on 19th-century American evangelicalism and revivalism
in particular. Cf. Richard Hofstadter's statement concerning the
evangelicals of the 19th century: "The objective was to return to
the pure conditions of primitive Christianity, to which Scripture
alone would give the key" (Anti-intellectualism in American Life
[New York: Alfred A. Knopf, 1963], p. 83). Cf. also Alan Simpson,
Puritanism in Old and New England (Chicago: University Press, 1955),
p. 6; Peter Toon, Puritanism and Calvinism (Swengel, Penn.: Reiner
Publications, 1973), p. 9; William A. Clebsch, From Sacred to Profane
America: The Role of Religion in American History (New York: Harper
& Row, 1968), pp. 21-27; cf. below, pp. 21-22.

having a part to play in a grand divine plan. Thus, the United States as a nation of destiny was expressed in religious terms as well. It was seen as the appropriate ground for revival, the perfection of human institutions, even as the redemptive instrument for the entire world.[1] This theme was later adapted and developed by Seventh-day Adventist writers who saw the emergence of the United States as a fulfillment of Rev 13:11-18 and who believed the new nation to be the divinely ordained springboard for missionary expansion and the proclamation of the imminent return of Christ.[2]

Revivalism and Perfectibility

In the religious sphere, optimism was also reflected in the numerous evangelical revivals that flourished all over the frontier. These revivals as a group have most commonly been named "The Second Great Awakening," or "The Great Revival." While convenient, such descriptions should not lead one to suppose that the Second Great Awakening was a homogeneous movement or that its starting, ending, and common characteristics can be readily identified. However, it did flourish from approximately the beginning of the 19th century until the 1830s or 1840s. The most prominent name associated with it

---

[1]Perhaps the best account of this sense of destiny in the United States is in Tyler, Freedom's Ferment, pp. 1-22. See also Damsteegt, Foundations, pp. 3-6; Hudson, "A Time of Religious Ferment," pp. 1-17; Religion in America, pp. 110-114.

[2]See, e.g., L. E. Froom, Movement of Destiny (Washington, D.C.: Review and Herald, 1971), p. 45; Ellen G. White, The Great Controversy (Mountain View, Calif.: Pacific Press Pub. Assn, 1888), pp. 439-440.

is that of Charles G. Finney, who led its greatest thrust in the decade following 1825.[1]

Allied to the view of America as the redemptive instrument of the world was the prevailing post-millennialism, the view that a thousand years of peace and prosperity were at the door and could be achieved by human effort. This type of optimism was epitomized in a sermon preached by Eliphalet Nott, president of Union College, Schenectady, New York, from 1804 to 1866, in which he claimed that the millennium was at the door and would be "introduced BY HUMAN EXERTIONS."[2] This belief in the perfectibility of man and his institutions resulted in numerous movements of a humanitarian or reform nature.[3] The beginning of the 19th century saw the formation of numerous missionary societies. Other closely allied groups sought

---

[1]For descriptions of this type of revivalism, see Bernard A. Weisberger, They Gathered at the River: The Story of the Great Revivalists and Their Impact Upon Religion in America (New York: Harper & Row, 1965); Whitney R. Cross, The Burned-over District: The Social and Intellectual History of Enthusiastic Religion in Western New York, 1800-1850 (New York: Harper & Row, 1965). An account of the influence of Finney's revivals may be found on pp. 156-158. See also William G. McLoughlin, Jr., "Revivalism," in The Rise of Adventism, pp. 119-150.

[2]Eliphalet Nott, A Sermon Preached Before the General Assembly of the Presbyterian Church in the United States of America; . . . May 19, 1806 (Philadelphia: Printed by Jane Aitken, 1806), pp. 13-14, quoted by Froom, Prophetic Faith, 4:90. Throughout this study, unless otherwise indicated, emphasis in quotations is in the original.

[3]We are not suggesting that reform societies were the exclusive province of post-millennialists. Reformers appeared from a variety of religious persuasions. Nevertheless, post-millennialism provided the main thrust to moral reform. In the words of Hudson: "The revivals provided the impetus, summoning men and women to battle against sin; and the reform movements were the implementation of the thrust toward the coming kingdom of righteousness" (Hudson, Religion in America, p. 198).

to promote Christian knowledge and education through the publication
of countless tracts, magazines, and Bibles. Thus, in 1816 the
American Bible Society was organized and in no less than four years
had distributed nearly 100,000 Bibles.[1] Other societies attacked
the moral conditions of the time. The most prominent of these
organizations were the temperance societies, though other groups also
crusaded against such improprieties as Sabbath-breaking and profan-
ity, and in favor of dress and dietary reform. Humanitarian concerns
that grew out of this time of religious revival included prison
reform, better treatment of the handicapped and the insane, and the
abolition of slavery.

As P. Gerard Damsteegt has pointed out, such stress on the
improvement of society by human effort reflected a theology that
emphasized man's freedom and minimized his depravity.[2] Finney, for
example, although he denied that he was a Christian perfectionist,
taught that "entire obedience to God's law is possible on the ground
of natural ability."[3] The distinction in his mind was that a
perfectionist boasted of his own self-righteousness while one who
believed in entire sanctification attributed his righteousness wholly
to the grace of Christ which provided man with the power to overcome

---

[1]Ahlstrom, A Religious History, pp. 422-428. See also
Hudson, Religion in America, pp. 145-157; Timothy L. Smith, "Social
Reform," in The Rise of Adventism, pp. 18-29.

[2]Damsteegt, Foundations, p. 9.

[3]Charles G. Finney, Lectures on Systematic Theology,
originally published in 1878 (South Gate, Calif.: Colporter Kemp,
1944), p. 407. See pp. 402-481 for a full exposition of his views on
sanctification and perfection. Cf. also, Charles G. Finney, Views of
Sanctification (Oberlin, Oh.: James Steele, 1840).

sin.[1] Finney's theology coincided well with the optimism of the

post-millennialist position which expected the creation of a perfect

society before the return of Christ.[2]

Belief in the perfectibility of man also exposed strong

Methodist and Pietist influences on the revivalism of the age.

Timothy L. Smith suggests four main types of thought on the nature of

man that existed in 19th-century America. These are traditionalism

as taught among Episcopalians and old Lutherans, orthodox Calvinism

as found in the Presbyterian churches, the almost Arminian position

of revivalistic Calvinism, and evangelical Arminianism as believed

largely by Methodists and freewill Baptists.[3] The growth of the

Methodists and freewill Baptists in the first few decades of the 19th

century and the simultaneous decline of the traditional and

Calvinistic denominations illustrate the success of revivalism and

the prevalence of the Arminian position on the nature of man.[4]

---

[1]Finney, Lectures on Systematic Theology, p. 461. Finney
believed that Christians could reach perfection on earth by means of
a second "baptism of the Holy Ghost" or a "second blessing" (Charles
G. Finney, Lectures to Professing Christians [Oberlin, Oh.: James
Steele, 1880], pp. 358-359). Cf. William G. McLoughlin, Jr.,
Modern Revivalism (New York: Ronald Press Co., 1959), pp. 103-104.

[2]On the post-millennial expectations in the first half of
the 19th century, see Froom, Prophetic Faith, 4:391-392; Diedrich H.
Kromminga, The Millennium in the Church (Grand Rapids, Mich.:
William B. Eerdmans Pub. Co., 1945), pp. 232-235.

[3]Timothy L. Smith, Revivalism and Social Reform: American
Protestantism on the Eve of the Civil War (New York: Abingdon Press,
1957), pp. 32-33.

[4]Hudson, in Religion in America, pp. 116-130, indicates the
change in denominational membership figures in the post-Revolutionary
War period. Besides showing that Methodism and other freewill
churches grew at the expense of the Old World churches, he also
points out that church affiliation increased as a result of the many

The success of revivalism among the freewill churches also had a significant influence on attitudes toward the nature of the church. Membership was reserved for those who had experienced conversion and followed a consistent Christian lifestyle. Methodists required a period of probation for many converts, and such religious exercises as attendance at worship services and missionary and benevolent activities were required of the believers.[1]

Puritanism

The strong influence of 19th-century American Puritanism on Adventism deserves special mention. Puritanism was able to hold in balance a marked emphasis on learning and rational thought with a proper regard to religious feelings. "Puritanism had always required a delicate balance between intellect . . . and emotion, which was necessary to the strength and durability of Puritan piety."[2] Thus, the revivals that swept through American religion in the 19th century should not be regarded as unrestrained outpourings of emotion. While

---

revivals from approximately one in 15 to one in 8 of the total population (pp. 129-130). It should be noted that "regular" Baptists, who were by no means Arminian in their theology, also grew rapidly as a result of the religious awakenings. Hudson attributes this growth to the stress placed by Baptists, whether "freewill" or not, upon the importance of a "conversion" experience as a necessary pre-requisite for believers' baptism and their appeal to Scripture as a final authority (p. 121).

[1]Cf. Timothy Smith, Revivalism and Social Reform, p. 18.

[2]Hofstadter, Anti-intellectualism in American Life, p. 64. Some basic works on American Puritanism include: Edmund S. Morgan, Visible Saints: The History of a Puritan Idea (New York: University Press, 1963); Darrett B. Rutman, American Puritanism: Faith and Practice (Philadelphia: J. B. Lippincott Co., 1970); Herbert W. Schneider, The Puritan Mind (Ann Arbor, Mich.: University of Michigan Press, 1958); Simpson, Puritanism in Old and New England; and the several works of Perry Miller.

appeals to the emotions were made by 19th-century revivalists, converts were also expected to make intelligent decisions.[1]

One may identify other Puritan characteristics within the American revivalism of the 19th century. William A. Clebsch, for example, suggests that the Puritan's genius was his use of the Bible "as a reliable, yet flexible and varied, charter of the divine will for every human circumstance."[2] Sydney E. Ahlstrom identifies three main features of Puritan theology, each of them reflected in 19th-century revivalism. They were the stress on the importance of regeneration in the life of the believer, along with the assumption of the rationality of God's dealing with man and the integration of one's personal, social, and political life with one's religious experience.[3]

---

[1] On the relationship between intellect and emotion in the revivalism of the 19th century, see Hofstadter, Anti-intellectualism in American Life, pp. 55-116; Cross, The Burned-over District, pp. 3-13; Timothy Smith, Revivalism and Social Reform, pp. 15-33; Tyler, Freedom's Ferment, pp. 33-45. On the nature of the camp meetings which came into prominence about the turn of the 19th century and were particularly popular with Methodist revivalists, see Charles A. Johnson, The Frontier Camp Meeting: Religion's Harvest Time (Dallas: Southern Methodist University Press, 1955), pp. 81-121. Johnson challenges "the legend that the camp meeting was nothing but one long orgy of excitement" (p. 4). Dick ("The Adventist Crisis" [1930], pp. 56-58) described the Millerite camp meetings which were part of the same revivalistic movement and noted the fanaticism which occurred at some of these meetings; he also pointed out that it was quickly suppressed by the Millerite leaders.

[2] Clebsch, From Sacred to Profane America, p. 24.

[3] Sydney E. Ahlstrom, "Theology in America: A Historical Survey," in Religion in American Life, 4 vols., ed. James W. Smith and A. Leland Jamison (Princeton: University Press, 1961), vol. 1: The Shaping of American Religion, p. 242.

Congregationalism

One may also see the influence of Puritanism in the congregational form of church organization adopted by several American denominations. As Williston Walker has pointed out, this system of church polity was much more widespread than the Congregational name.[1] Baptists, Disciples of Christ, the Plymouth Brethren, Unitarians, and some sections of the Lutheran Church were congregationally governed. The term came into common usage in England about the time of the English Civil War and contemporaneously among the Puritans of New England.

Churches organized according to the congregational system were local associations of experiential Christians. Each church regarded Christ as its only head and was completely self-governing. The members joined together by signing a covenant expressive of their common faith. The only offices of the church were those for which there is a precedent in the New Testament, i.e., pastors, teachers, elders, deacons, and helpers. The pastor's responsibility was chiefly exhortation and proclamation of the Word, while the teacher's role was primarily doctrinal instruction. The elder was the disciplinary officer, who was answerable to the pastor and the church board and was not permitted, independently of the ordained pastoral ministry, to administer the sacraments. Ordination, being the charge of a particular church, was repeated on each fresh entry into office, and until 1648 was carried out by the local congregation. This custom was changed in that year by the Cambridge Platform, on which

---

[1]Williston Walker, "Congregationalism," Encyclopaedia of Religion and Ethics (1914), 4:19-25. See also below, pp. 233-241.

occasion ordination became the act of the ministry.[1]

Denominationalism

Numerous reasons have been given in an attempt to explain the vast array of religious groups characteristic of the 19th century, a phenomenon which seems to have been, at that time at least, almost exclusively American. This multiplication of religious groups reached a high point in the 1830s and 1840s.[2]

One attempt to explain the causes of denominationalism is an essay by Sidney E. Mead tracing the origin of Protestant diversity to the Reformation, which broke up the unity of Christendom.[3] The Reformers insisted that each group or even each individual should be free to interpret Scripture. This self-sufficient attitude among American Protestants was reflected in the phrase "we will accept no creed but the Bible."[4] Each group sought to justify its own interpretations and practices by the teaching of the New Testament. Under Puritan influences, as has already been mentioned, it was

[1]See Philip Schaff, The Creeds of Christendom, 3 vols. (New York: Harper & Brothers, 1877), 1:836. American Congregationalists have from time to time expressed their acceptance of the Westminster Confession of Faith with the exception of the sections relating to synodical church government. Some of the more notable statements of congregational order include, in addition to the work of the Cambridge Synod, the Declaration of the Savoy Conference (1658), the Synod of Boston (1680), and the Synod of Saybrook (1708); cf. Schaff, The Creeds of Christendom, 1:835-837.

[2]Hudson, "A Time of Religious Ferment," p. 7. He points out that upstate New York, "the burned-over district," saw more new movements arise in the 1830s and 1840s than any other area.

[3]Sidney E. Mead, "Denominationalism: The Shape of Protestantism in America," Church History 23 (December 1954):291-320.

[4]Cf., e.g., John W. Nevin, "The Sect System," Mercersburg Review 1 (1849):499.

assumed that God's will for man was clearly indicated in Scripture, and that man could understand the Bible and should pattern his life and his church after it. In the minds of the "free" churches it was not individualism that was the cause of the splintering of Christendom but the failure of many church leaders to follow the teachings of the Bible and trust instead in human creeds.[1] Augmented by the move to the New World, which shook off some of the civil and ecclesiastical restraints that still remained in Europe, this independent spirit also resulted in an upsurge in the membership of the "free" churches and a corresponding decline in denominations closely patterned after Europe's state churches.[2]

The Denominational Makeup of the Millerite Movement

As has been noted above,[3] the freewill churches benefited the most in terms of rapid growth from the revivals of the Great Awakening. These denominations, in turn, contributed the greatest number of adherents and preachers to the Millerite movement.[4] We shall attempt to describe the organizational methods of these churches and to discover what influence, if any, their practices had upon the Millerite movement.

---

[1]Cf. below, pp. 30-31.

[2]Mead, "Denominationalism," p. 294.

[3]Cf. above, p. 20.

[4]Dick's study of 174 Millerite preachers showed that 44.3 percent were Methodists, 27 percent Baptists, 9 percent Congregationalists, and 8 percent members of the Christian Church, to name the better represented denominations. See Dick, "The Adventist Crisis" (1930), p. 232.

The Methodist Church

According to Dick, the Millerite movement appears to have attracted more preachers from the Methodist Church than from any other denomination.[1] This may explain why the Millerites adopted several Methodist practices. For instance, in Methodism's early years preachers were circuit riders with no settled pulpit or church. They travelled from town to town seeking converts, leaving responsible laymen in charge of worship and discipline.[2] They viewed organizational matters pragmatically, fitting the character of the leadership and discipline of the church to the task at hand. As John Wesley, Methodism's founder, said: "Church or no Church, we must save souls."[3]

The practical nature of Methodism soon resulted (even within Wesley's lifetime) in a very strong organizational structure so that it became the "most hierarchical of the Nonconformist Churches in England."[4] What was true of England was also the case for American Methodism. As William Warren Sweet has pointed out, the basic features of Methodism's organizational structure (always notable for its efficiency) have persisted from its early days. While the

---

[1]Ibid.

[2]Donald G. Mathews, "The Second Great Awakening as an Organizing Process, 1780-1830: An Hypothesis," American Quarterly 21 (1969):36.

[3]Quoted in M. L. Scudder, American Methodism (Hartford, Conn.: S. S. Scranton and Co., 1867), p. 101. For a more extended study of the Methodist economy, see below, pp. 252-257.

[4]E. R. Taylor, Methodism and Politics (New York: Russell & Russell, 1975), p. 197. It is understandable that a faith that prescribed strict regulation of every part of one's life should also become noted for its organizational efficiency.

Methodist Church in America, led by Francis Asbury and his successors, used the title and office of bishop,[1] other main features--such
as the conference system of organized Methodism which Wesley began in
1744 when he called the first conference in England--persisted on
both sides of the Atlantic, the first American conference being
called in 1773.[2] The term "conference" implied both an area of
jurisdiction and a regularly-called meeting (usually annual).
Meetings were designated as district conferences if local in nature,
and general conferences if they represented an entire area.[3]

M. L. Scudder, an American Methodist contemporary to the
events being described, identified several other characteristic
features of the "Methodist economy." They included field preaching
(that is, holding meetings wherever there was a crowd, whether in a
field, on the street, or in a home), the erection of plain, functional chapels (not churches) designed so that ordinary people would
feel at home, the proper supervision (not surveillance) of the flock,
the principle of caring for one another as fellow members of one
sanctified church, and a system of rules "so simple, so strict, so
broad, so comprehensive, that no one could obey them, and not become
a consistent Christian."[4] The most distinctive feature of the

---

[1]It should be noted that Wesley always objected to the use of
the title and office of bishop in American Methodism (see John Wesley
to Francis Asbury, September 20, 1788, in The Letters of the Reverend
John Wesley, A.M., 8 vols., ed. John Telford [London: Epworth Press,
1931], 8:91).

[2]William Warren Sweet, Methodism in American History
(Nashville, Tenn.: Abingdon Press, 1961), pp. 432-433.

[3]Ibid.

[4]Scudder, American Methodism, pp. v, 103-111.

economy, he added, was "its organized effective missionary work."[1]

The Baptist Church

Baptist representation among Millerite preachers was second only to Methodist, apparently amounting (according to Dick) to some 27 percent of the total number of lecturers whose denominational affiliation is known.[2] Both Calvinist and Freewill Baptists were represented—by such men as Elon Galusha, N. N. Whiting, J. B. Cook, F. G. Brown, and Miller himself.[3]

Baptist church organization was characterized by "determined efforts to reestablish the New Testament pattern for the church."[4] It recognized that in the primitive church organizational structures were simple and functional, the exact structure depending on the needs of the local situation. This meant that Baptist organization was less centralized and hierarchical than Methodist, the

---

[1]Ibid., p. 29. For further information on the history of American Methodism and its "economy" during the first half of the 19th century, see two contemporary works: Charles C. Goss, Statistical History of the First Century of American Methodism (New York: Carlton and Porter, 1866), pp. 144-186; Matthew Simpson, A Hundred Years of Methodism (New York: Phillips & Hunt, 1881), pp. 210-236. See also the standard work on American Methodism, Emory S. Bucke, ed., The History of American Methodism, 3 vols. (New York: Abingdon Press, 1964). Of special interest for our study is chapter 10, "Methodism on the Frontier," by Theodore L. Agnew (1:488-545); and chapter 26, "Structural and Administrative Changes," by Nolan B. Harmon (3:1-58).

[2]Dick, "The Adventist Crisis" (1930), p. 232.

[3]Arthur, "'Come Out of Babylon'" (1970), p. 14. In the same place he indicates the denominational affiliation of most of the prominent Millerites.

[4]L. Russ Bush and Tom J. Nettles, Baptists and the Bible (Chicago: Moody Press, 1980), p. 26. Cf. also below, pp. 249-252.

independence of the local church being "practically unquestioned."[1]
Ahlstrom indicates that the desire for local autonomy was
particularly strong among the Freewill Baptists, especially among
those who had experienced an emotional conversion such as occurred
during the revivals of the Great Awakening.[2]

Church organization and discipline were predicated upon a
basic presupposition among Baptist churches--one shared with the
Methodists--that the basic nature of the church is spiritual and the
members, therefore, should consist of the regenerate only.

> Baptists have always contended that the church is not a worldly,
> but a spiritual body--spiritual, not in the sense of lacking a
> local organization or visible identity, but because organized on
> the basis of spiritual life. In other words the church should
> consist of the regenerate only. . . . [3]

The Christian Connection

Henry C. Vedder included the Christian Connection (or
Christian Church as it was also called) in his history of the
Baptists.[4] Many of the ministers of the "Christians" were ordained

---

[1]Henry C. Vedder, A Short History of the Baptists
(Philadelphia: American Baptist Publication Society, 1907), p. 417.
See also Bush and Nettles, Baptists and the Bible, pp. 17, 26.

[2]Ahlstrom, A Religious History, pp. 321-322. Other sources
on the history and church polity of American Baptists in the first
half of the 19th century include, O. K. Armstrong and Marjorie
Armstrong, The Baptists in America (Garden City, N.Y.: Doubleday &
Co., 1979), pp. 171-184; William G. McLoughlin, Jr., New England
Dissent, 1630-1833: The Baptists and the Separation of Church and
State, 2 vols. (Cambridge, Mass.: Harvard University Press, 1971),
2:723-750; Edwin S. Gaustad, "Baptists and the Making of a New
Nation," in Baptists and the American Experience, ed. James E. Wood,
Jr. (Valley Forge, Penn.: Judson Press, 1976), pp. 39-53.

[3]Vedder, A Short History of the Baptists, p. 410.

[4]Ibid., p. 393.

by the Freewill Baptists, and at the beginning of the 19th century
the two groups did consider merging in view of the similarity of
their doctrines at the time as well as the fact that they both
practiced open communion. Eventually, however, no union of the two
churches occurred, mainly because of the increasingly Unitarian
tendencies among the "Christians," which alienated the Baptists.[1]

The Christian Connection began with three independent
movements in North Carolina and Virginia, Kentucky, and Vermont. The
group most directly involved with the Millerite movement was the one
originating in Vermont and later spreading to the rest of New England
and New York State. This section of the Christian Connection was
sometimes called the Eastern Church, and was founded by Abner Jones
and Elias Smith.[2] Although the Christian Connection joined with the
Southern groups in 1808, it maintained some distinctive features. In
ecclesiology the Bible was its only creed, "Christian" its only name.
The Eastern Church practiced open communion and was congregational in
structure. The following quotation is typical of its viewpoint:

> There were many . . . who never had and never could submit to
> human dogmas. Therefore when asked "of what sect they were?"
> the reply was "None." "What denomination will you join?"
> "None." "What party name will you take?" "None." "What
> will you do?" "We will continue as we have begun--we will

---

[1]See Ahlstrom, A Religious History, p. 446.

[2]Milton V. Blackman, Jr., Christian Churches of America:
Origins and Beliefs (Provo, Utah: Brigham Young University Press,
1976), pp. 141-148. For additional information on the Christian
Church see N. Summerbell, History of the Christian Church
(Cincinnati: Office of the Christian Pulpit, 1873); Milo T. Morrill,
A History of the Christian Denomination in America, 1794-1911 A.D.
(Dayton, Oh.: Christian Pub. Assn, 1912); J. J. Summerbell,
"Christians," The New Schaff-Herzog Encyclopedia of Religious
Knowledge (1909), 3:45-46.

be Christians. Christ is our leader, the Bible is our only creed, and we will serve God free from the trammels of sectarianism."[1]

In practice, their anti-organizational stance did not last very long. Central organization of the New England branch of the Christian Church was particularly rapid. As early as 1805, ministers' conferences were conducted for the "itinerant ministry."[2] From 1820 on, annual general conferences were held which, after 1834, became quadrennial.[3] At these conferences, a standing committee was elected to transact the business of the church between sessions, and by 1836 a strong organizational foundation was being laid by the leaders of the church. According to Milo T. Morrill, the conference system of organization was adopted by "Christians" because an unsupervised church "laid laity and ministry open to endless imposition, loss of prestige, and charge of abetting charlatans."[4] In addition, ministers were ordained and provided with letters of commendation, and church discipline was administered at these conferences. The conferences also carried on a very strong publishing program. Their periodical, The Herald of Gospel Liberty, has been termed "the first religious newspaper."[5]

In proportion to its size, the Christian Connection produced

---

[1]N. Summerbell, History of the Christian Church, p. 519.

[2]Morrill, A History of the Christian Denomination, p. 106.

[3]Ibid., p. 379.

[4]Ibid., p. 121. Conference organization was viewed with some trepidation by many who feared loss of independence, "but safeguarding the ministry and churches outweighed all fears" (p. 126).

[5]Ibid., p. 150.

the largest number of Millerite adherents, and some of the most prominent leaders of the Millerite movement--including Himes, Timothy Cole, Lorenzo D. Fleming, Joseph Marsh, and Henry Plummer--came from a Christian Connection background.[1]

Direct links can easily be observed among the Methodist, Baptist, and Christian Connection churches and the attitudes of the Millerites toward church organization. The basic structure of regional and General Conferences, the pragmatic approach to church order, and the camp meeting system were taken over directly from the Methodists.[2] The Baptist Church contributed a less centralized and hierarchical approach than the Methodists, while the influence of the Christians may be seen in the extensive publishing program of the Millerites and in their growing antipathy to formal creeds and sectarianism. The Baptists and Christians contributed a desire to follow the New Testament pattern of church order.

The Development of the Organization and Separatism of the Millerite Movement

One of the products of the religious ferment of the 19th century was the Millerite movement. Interest in eschatology was stimulated by the political and social upheavals of the time, revivalistic preaching, and a growing interest among evangelical Christians in the biblical prophecies alluding to the Second Advent.

---

[1]Arthur, "'Come Out of Babylon'" (1970), p. 14.

[2]The camp meeting, a distinctive feature of frontier religious life, was first developed by the Presbyterian minister James McGready in Kentucky, beginning about 1796. Within little more than a decade, however, "the camp meeting had become almost exclusively the property of the Methodists" (Hudson, Religion in America, p. 140).

The most prevalent form of millennialism,[1] especially in the early decades of the 19th century, was post-millennialism.[2] However, the optimism of the age was cooled by socio-political events such as the financial depression of 1837 and the ineffectiveness of some of the reform movements.[3] The conviction also arose among some of those studying the Scriptures that the return of Christ and the Day of Judgment were imminent and would precede rather than follow the millennium.[4]

In this description of the growth and increasing popularity of the Millerite movement in the early 1840s, we shall concentrate on the rising separatism and independence of the movement immediately preceding the Great Disappointment of 1844,[5] and the Millerites' rationale for leaving the established churches.

The Career of William Miller

One of the principal exponents--perhaps the principal exponent--of pre-millennialism in America during this time was

---

[1]On the millennialism debate see Ernest R. Sandeen, The Roots of Fundamentalism: British and American Millenarianism, 1800-1930 (Chicago: University Press, 1970), pp. 42-58. A more concise account may be found by the same author in "Millennialism," in The Rise of Adventism, pp. 104-118. Cf. also Damsteegt, Foundations, pp. 6-16; Froom, Prophetic Faith, 4:330-426.

[2]Cf. above, pp. 19-20.

[3]Reuben E. E. Harkness, "Social Origins of the Millerite Movement" (Ph.D. dissertation, University of Chicago, 1927), pp. 111-130.

[4]Cf. Damsteegt, Foundations, p. 13.

[5]The "Great Disappointment" refers to the experience of the Millerites whose expectation of the return of Christ on October 22, 1844, was unfulfilled.

Miller (1782-1849).[1] Born in Pittsfield, Massachusetts, the oldest in a family of sixteen children, he was raised in a religious atmosphere at Low Hampton, New York. Lacking extensive formal education, he became well informed through his own personal study, gaining in time a position of respect and prominence in the community, as is indicated by the fact that he served for a time as a deputy sheriff and justice of the peace. While living, after marriage, at Poultney, Vermont, his pursuit of knowledge led him into association with a group of Deists whose ideas he accepted. His years of service as a lieutenant and captain in the second war between Britain and the United States (1812-1814) contributed to a growing disillusionment with Deistic principles as he observed the sinful nature of man. As a result, he resumed attendance at the Baptist church and experienced conversion in 1816. This led him to an intensive period of Bible study, partly to meet the challenges to his faith presented by his former Deist associates. After some two years of study Miller was convinced that the Bible could withstand Deist criticisms.[2] His contemplation of human nature and Bible study

---

[1]For more biographical information see William Miller, Wm. Miller's Apology and Defence (Boston: J. V. Himes, 1845); Bliss, Memoirs of William Miller; Robert Gale, The Urgent Voice (Washington, D.C.: Review and Herald Pub. Assn, 1975); Nichol, The Midnight Cry pp. 17-289; Froom, Prophetic Faith, 4:455-527. A recent history of the Millerite movement commissioned by the Advent Christian Church includes a biographical account of Miller's life, although it adds little to the information available in the biographies cited above. See Hewitt, Midnight and Morning, pp. 1-33, 67-111.

[2]Miller describes a meeting with a former Deist friend who asked him how he could believe in Christianity in light of his previous arguments against the Bible. Miller replied "that if the Bible was the word of God, everything contained therein might be understood, and all its parts be made to harmonize; and I said to him

contributed to his pre-millennial views. He was convinced that there would be no world conversion before Christ's Second Advent and that the Second Coming would occur within his lifetime. Not wishing to be precipitous in announcing his conclusions, he continued his study for a further thirteen years until 1831. At this time, his conviction that Christ would return about 1843 became so strong that he was impressed that it was his duty to tell the world. Finally, even though conscious of his lack of training and experience as a public speaker, he accepted an invitation to present his views to a nearby Baptist congregation in August 1831.[1]

In the course of his study, Miller produced fourteen rules of biblical interpretation, one of which stated that "nothing revealed in Scriptures can or will be hid from those who ask in faith, not wavering."[2] The most striking and significant of these rules were those dealing with his method of integrating biblical prophecies that he believed culminated in the literal return of Christ.[3] It was the harmonious system of the biblical time prophecies which covered the

---

that if he would give me time, I would harmonize all these apparent contradictions to my own satisfaction, or I would be a Deist still" (Miller, Apology and Defence, pp. 5-6). Miller reported the success of his undertaking thus: "I was satisfied that the Bible is a system of revealed truths, so clearly and simply given, that the wayfaring man, though a fool, need not err therein" (ibid., p. 6).

[1]Nichol, The Midnight Cry, pp. 41-43.

[2]Bliss, Memoirs of William Miller, p. 70. All fourteen rules may be found in Bliss's work (pp. 69-70). They were originally published in William Miller, Views of the Prophecies and Prophetic Chronology Selected from Manuscripts of William Miller; With a Memoir of His Life, ed. Joshua V. Himes (Boston: Moses A. Down, 1841), pp. 20-24.

[3]The significance of these principles of prophetic interpretation has been discussed at length elsewhere. See, e.g., Froom,

whole sweep of human history with precise accuracy that was his ultimate defense against Deistic attacks upon the Bible.[1]

This aspect of Miller's teaching needs to be clearly understood. Miller shared with the free churches of America, under their common Puritan heritage, a conviction that the Bible provided a comprehensive guide to every facet of the Christian life. His basic method, of comparing one part of the Bible with another until all were satisfactorily harmonized, lay at the foundation of the whole Millerite movement.[2] Without the application of this method to prophetic interpretation and the general acceptance of its validity by Miller's audiences, Adventism would hardly have come to prominence.

The failure of various preachers to explain the seeming inconsistencies of the Bible had been one important factor in Miller's drift toward Deism in the first place.[3] In his view, the Bible was so clear in its teaching that the blame for sectarian differences lay with the churches of Christendom whose past had been nothing but "a history of blood, tyranny, and oppression, in which

---

Prophetic Faith, 4:462-475; Damsteegt, Foundations, pp. 16-20; Sandeen, "Millennialism," pp. 112-116; Don F. Neufeld, "Biblical Interpretation in the Advent Movement," in A Symposium on Biblical Hermeneutics, ed. Gordon M. Hyde (Washington, D.C.: General Conference of Seventh-day Adventists, 1974), pp. 109-125.

[1]He had not, therefore, changed his reasonable, common-sense approach toward the Bible, that it could only be the Word of God if it could be proven empirically to be a consistent, harmonious whole, not just in its basic theme but in all its parts (cf. Rowe, "Thunder and Trumpets" [1974], p. 27).

[2]Cf. Froom, Prophetic Faith, 4:462, who described Miller's approach as "the tried and true Protestant method."

[3]Miller, Apology and Defence, pp. 2-3.

the common people were the greatest sufferers. I viewed it as a system of craft, rather than of truth."[1] Understandably, Miller had little use for the theological debates that raged in his day such as Universalism, church order, and Transcendentalism.[2] For example, speaking in the context of the Calvinist-Arminian debate over man's free will and election, he said: "It is in the use of terms not found in Scriptures that disputations arise."[3] Individuals from varied denominational and theological backgrounds were able to unite on the one all-important truth--the imminent, literal return of Christ. The first General Conference of Christians expecting the Advent of Christ, held at the Chardon Street Chapel in Boston, October 14-15, 1840, only required those who attended to declare their faith in the near approach of Christ.[4]

Throughout his Christian life Miller was disturbed by the scandal of a divided church and believed that a return to the plain statements of Scripture would end the sectarian strife plaguing the religious world of mid-19th-century America. In what has become known as "Miller's Creed" he wrote in 1822: "I believe that before Christ comes in his glory, all sectarian principles will be shaken,

---

[1]Joshua V. Himes, "Memoir of William Miller," MC, November 17, 1842, p. 1.

[2]Cf. Hudson, Religion in America, pp. 158-180; Cross, The Burned-over District, pp. 40-51.

[3]Miller, Apology and Defence, p. 27.

[4]The First Report of The General Conference of Christians Expecting the Advent of the Lord Jesus Christ. Held in Boston, Oct. 14, 15, 1840 (Boston: J. V. Himes, 1841), p. 7; "The Conference," ST, September 1, 1840, p. 84; David T. Arthur, "Millerism," in The Rise of Adventism, p. 156.

and the votaries of the several sects scattered to the four winds."[1]
This dissatisfaction with the state of the churches led in time to
the call to "Come Out of Babylon." Yet, Miller was far less radical
in his attitude toward the churches than were many of his followers.
He never wished to separate himself from his own Baptist church.[2]
An example of his irenic spirit is reflected in his statement, made
in 1845 after conflict between the Millerites and the established
churches in 1843 and 1844, that he shared "all the essential
doctrines of the Bible" with the Christians of all ages.[3]

The Increasing Momentum of the
Millerite Movement

The period 1831-1839 saw a gradual increase of interest in
Miller's preaching, aided by the additional publicity generated by
the publication of his ideas in 1832 and 1833 in the Vermont
Telegraph and collections of his sermons in book form.[4] His
lectures were presented primarily in the small towns and rural
communities of New England and New York State.[5] During this time,
he found general approval of his work among the churches of the

---

[1]Bliss, Memoirs of William Miller, p. 79. Miller's creed
may also be found in Froom, Prophetic Faith, 4:466-467.

[2]Arthur, "Millerism," p. 155. Cf. Froom, Prophetic Faith,
4:761, 770.

[3]Miller, Apology and Defence, p. 27.

[4]See Vermont Telegraph (Brandon, Vt.), November 6, 1832-
March 12, 1833; William Miller, Evidences from Scripture and History
of the Second Coming of Christ about the Year A.D. 1843, and of His
Personal Reign of 1000 Years (Brandon, Vt.: Vermont Telegraph
Office, 1833).

[5]For more details on these years see Bliss, Memoirs of
William Miller, pp. 97-143.

various denominations, as indicated by the fact that he was invited to speak from so many of their pulpits. In addition, on its own initiative, the local Baptist church gave him a license to preach.[1] Not until about the year 1840 did ecclesiastical opposition to Miller's message begin to arise.[2]

A pivotal year, 1840[3]

On November 11, 1839, Miller began a series of meetings at Exeter, New Hampshire. Several ministers of the Christian Connection were present, most notably Himes, who was especially impressed by Miller's presentations. Himes extended an invitation for Miller to preach at his Chardon Street Chapel in Boston. Miller accepted, thus beginning a productive association between the two men. This was a major step forward for the Millerites, as Himes used his promotional talents to give the Adventist message an impetus that took it from the villages to the cities and made it front-page news.[4]

---

[1]Ibid., p. 109.

[2]The first church on record for closing its doors to Miller was the Congregational Church in Westfield, Mass., on December 17, 1839 (ibid., p. 141). No reason is given by Bliss for the closing of the Westfield church. Certainly at this stage Miller and his associates had no intention of proselytizing among the established churches. On the reasons for later opposition, see below, pp. 45-66.

[3]Numerous writers have rightly identified 1840 as an important turning point in the Millerite movement. See, e.g., Arthur, "'Come Out of Babylon'" (1970), pp. 7-22; Dick, "The Adventist Crisis" (1930), pp. 30-37; Rowe, "Thunder and Trumpets" (1974), pp. 92-111; Froom, Prophetic Faith, 4:502-554.

[4]On Himes's role in the Millerite movement see David T. Arthur, "Joshua V. Himes and the Cause of Adventism, 1839-1845" (M.A. thesis, University of Chicago, 1961). Other accounts of the first meeting between Himes and Miller may be found in Bliss, Memoirs of William Miller, pp. 139-141; Rowe, "Thunder and Trumpets" (1974), pp. 92-111.

The publishing work of the Millerites, which prospered under Himes's leadership, was an important factor in the rapid spread of Millerism. As a minister in the Christian Connection, Himes drew upon his familiarity with the latter's publishing activities in launching and spreading a vast array of Millerite publications between 1840 and 1844.[1] One of the first steps toward some form of organization for the Millerites occurred when provision was made at the first Millerite General Conference held on October 14 and 15, 1840, at Himes's chapel in Boston, for the continuing support of the Signs of the Times, the first weekly Millerite publication, of which Himes was the editor.[2] The journal was appropriately described by L. E. Froom as the parent of an "unrivaled battery of Millerite periodicals."[3] Not only did the publishing activities of the Millerites play an important part in bringing their ideas before the public but they also helped to maintain a spirit of unity among the widely scattered followers.[4]

The apparent fulfillment of Josiah Litch's prediction that

---

[1]Himes himself claimed that by May 1844, five million periodicals had been circulated (quoted by Froom, Prophetic Faith, 4:624-625). Maxwell, Tell It to the World, p. 18, estimates that by October 22, 1844, the number had reached eight million. For a more detailed account of Millerite publishing activity see Dick, "The Adventist Crisis" (1930), pp. 89-123.

[2]"Proceedings of the Conference on the Second Coming of Our Lord Jesus Christ, Held in Boston, Mass., October 14, 15, 1840," ST, November 1, 1840, p. 115.

[3]Froom, Prophetic Faith, 4:621-641.

[4]Arthur speaks of the Signs of the Times as the first influence in creating a "sense of community" and a "bond of union" among the Millerites (Arthur, "Millerism," p. 151).

the end of the supremacy of the Turkish or Ottoman empire would occur on August 11, 1840, gave "an important boost to the missionary enthusiasm of the Millerite movement."[1] Basing his calculations on the prophecy of the seven trumpets (Rev 8 and 9),[2] Litch published his conclusions on August 1, 1840. When the fall of the Turkish empire was perceived to have happened on the very day, the precision of such a forecast was seen by many as an impressive vindication of the entire historicist system of prophetic interpretation followed by Miller and his associates. In an article which accompanied Litch's original exposition Himes, quoting Rev 10:7, even suggested briefly that human probation would close on August 11, 1840, the day the Ottoman Empire was expected to fall.[3]

In addition to Himes's joining the Millerite movement and the fulfillment of Litch's prediction, a third 1840 event of considerable importance, one to which we referred earlier,[4] was the first General Conference of Christians expecting the Advent of the Lord Jesus

---

[1]Damsteegt, Foundations, pp. 26-27.

[2]Josiah Litch, "Fall of the Ottoman Power in Constantinople," ST, August 1, 1840, p. 70. He added a more complete exposition later (Litch, "The Nations," ST, February 1, 1841, p. 162). See Damsteegt, Foundations, pp. 26-29, for a more complete explication of Litch's position.

[3][Joshua V. Himes], "The Closing Up of the Day of Grace," ST, August 1, 1840, pp. 69-70. Himes does not seem to have maintained his idea concerning the close of probation very long. Miller was not willing to set a specific date for the end of probationary time at this point, although he accepted Litch's basic method of interpreting the prophecy of the seven trumpets (cf. Letter, William Miller to Joshua V. Himes, ST, September 1, 1840, pp. 81-82). The fact that both Himes and Miller considered that the time of opportunity for sinners to repent was soon to finish lent urgency to their missionary endeavors.

[4]See above, p. 37.

Christ, held on October 14 and 15.[1] This meeting was called, as
Henry Dana Ward stated in the keynote address, "not to contend with
opposers, not to dispute among ourselves, not to raise the banner of
a new sect; but out of every sect to come into the unity of the faith
as it is in Jesus."[2] Even differences as to the time and manner of
Christ's Second Advent were not considered important enough to
exclude anyone.[3]

Ward's spirit was admittedly one of the most irenic of those
present, but the following excerpt from his address reflects the
non-antagonistic attitude of the meeting in general toward organized
Christianity.

> We neither condemn, nor rudely assail, others of a faith
> different from our own nor dictate in matters of conscience for
> our brethren, nor seek to demolish their organizations, nor build
> new ones of our own; but simply to express our convictions like
> Christians, with the reasons for entertaining them, which have
> persuaded us to understand the word and promises, the prophecies
> and the gospel of our Lord, as the first Christians, the
> primitive ages of the church, and the profoundly learned and
> intelligent reformers, have unanimously done, in the faith and

---

[1]Contemporary reports on this Conference may be found in
[Joshua V. Himes], "The General Conference," ST, November 1, 1840,
p. 113; Henry Dana Ward, Henry Jones, and Philemon R. Russel,
"Circular: The Address of the Conference on the Second Advent of the
Lord, Convened at Boston, Mass., October 14, 1840," ST, November 1,
1840, pp. 116-117; "Proceedings of the Conference," pp. 113-116;
[Joshua V. Himes], "Our Course," ST, November 15, 1840, pp. 126-127;
[Josiah Litch], "The Rise and Progress of Adventism," ASR, May 1844,
pp. 46-93. Additional information is available in I. C. Wellcome,
History of the Second Advent Message and Mission, Doctrine and People
(Yarmouth, Me.: I. C. Wellcome, 1874), pp. 176-180; Dick, "The
Adventist Crisis" (1930), pp. 30-37; Arthur, "'Come Out of Babylon'"
(1970), pp. 7-22; Froom, Prophetic Faith, 4:559-569.

[2]"Proceedings of the Conference," p. 114. Miller was unable
to attend this conference, being indisposed with typhoid fever
(Froom, Prophetic Faith, 4:561).

[3]"Proceedings of the Conference," p. 113.

hope that the Lord will "come quickly," "in his glory," to fulfil all his promises in the resurrection of the dead.[1]

Any desire "to rail at the office of the ministry, and triumph in the exposure of the errors of the secular and apostate church" was explicitly denied.[2] Even Himes, in line with the anti-sectarian attitude of the Christian Connection of which he was a member, declared that "our fellow laborers are among the choicest of the faithful in Christ among all denominations. We know no sect or party as such, while we respect all."[3]

Still, the very nature of the language in these two statements implied that, in the minds of the Millerites, there was indeed much wrong with the various sectarian churches. While at this time their only thought was to reform the churches from within, the conference, no doubt unconsciously, laid the groundwork for later separation. As Arthur has pointed out, the conference did not produce a creedal statement, but it did set forth certain points of belief.[4] While not in agreement on the exact year of Christ's return the members of the conference concurred that it was near. They also set out to refute such ideas as the temporal millennium, the invisible reign of Christ, the return of the Jews to Jerusalem, and the conversion of the whole world.[5] A chairman and secretary were appointed to lead out in and record the business of the conference and a Committee of Correspondence was appointed to promote

---

[1]Ward, Jones, and Russel, "Circular," p. 116.

[2]Ibid.   [3][Himes], "Our Course," p. 126.

[4]Arthur, "Millerism," p. 156.

[5]First Report of the General Conference, 1841 ed., pp. 21-22.

the activities of the Advent believers after the conference. Thus, a "rudimentary organization" was formed which was to lead more and more to a separate identity being formed.[1] As time passed, membership in the Adventist movement became for many a passion that consumed most of their time and energy. Thus, participation in the Millerite organization, "rudimentary" though it was, eventually came to compete with the established denominations and became inconsistent with church membership.

In comparison, membership in one of the numerous inter-denominational reform societies which were formed in America in the first half of the 19th century was not at all incompatible with membership in one of the established denominations and was not perceived by them to be a threat.

Millerite conferences

After the first general conference held by the Millerites, several general conferences met in the next two years.[2] The practice of holding general meetings appears to have died out by the spring of 1843, numerous local conferences being convened instead.[3] The conferences, both local and general, seem to have played an important part in the developing self-awareness of the movement. The second general conference, held in Lowell, Massachusetts, June 15-17, 1841, eight months after the first, reflected a noticeable change in

---

[1]Arthur, "Millerism," p. 157.

[2]Arthur, "'Come Out of Babylon'" (1970), p. 26.

[3]Froom, in Prophetic Faith, 4:557, estimates that more than a hundred local conferences were held between January 1842 and October 1844.

attitude, an increasing independence that tended toward separatism. It was reported that those attending the conference, from nearly all the evangelical denominations in the land, were in "perfect harmony."[1] This amity of spirit reflected the intentions of those who had announced the convening of the conference. It was declared that they would engage in no controversy, sectarianism, or attacks against the church and its teachings at the meeting.[2]

In spite of these intentions, the Millerites reported that they were meeting increasing opposition in their work. The advice given to the participants was that they should stay in their churches, although it was recognized that this might not always be possible.[3] This counsel was reiterated in a circular, produced at the conference, which set forth nine resolutions under the heading "Our Work." The seventh recommended "remaining within and working within existing churches to 'bring the church to a better mind' rather than withdrawing from them and/or forming a new church."[4] Some of the other resolutions, however, tended toward separatism.[5]

---

[1]"Second Advent Conference," ST, July 15, 1841, p. 61.

[2]Miller et al., "General Conference of Christians Expecting the Second Advent of Our Lord Jesus Christ," ST, April 15, 1841, p. 12.

[3]Proceedings of the Second Session of the General Conference of Christians Expecting the Advent of Our Lord Jesus Christ, Held in Lowell, Ms., June 15, 16, 17, 1841, Second Advent Tracts, No. VIII [Boston: J. V. Himes, 1841].

[4]Josiah Litch, Joshua V. Himes, and William Clark, "Circular. Address of the Second General Conference on the Second Appearing of our Lord Jesus Christ, convened at Lowell, Mass., June 15, 16 and 17, 1841," ST, August 2, 1841, pp. 69-70.

[5]This is Arthur's view ("' Come Out of Babylon'" [1970], pp. 23-24).

Thus, the formation of Bible classes and the convening of "social meetings"[1] for prayer and exhortation were not intended to, but did, compete with the religious services of the churches. It was just a small step from these prayer meetings to the formation of Second Advent associations. One of the first of these was organized in New York City on May 18, 1842.[2] These associations were formed wherever there were sufficient numbers of Advent believers, so that they might gather together for mutual encouragement and support, although even these were not regarded by their members as separatist. Before the end of 1843, associations existed "in almost every city of any size in the North."[3]

Another suggestion of the circular encouraged believers to question ministers, asking them "to explain those portions of scripture relating to the second advent." Such questions, if pressed insistently, had the potential of embarrassing the ministers concerned. Finally, the document made provision for the circulation of books and pamphlets and the allocation of funds for this purpose.[4]

---

[1]Meetings held for prayer, fellowship, and especially testimonies of faith.

[2]See Letter, E. H. Wilcox to Joshua V. Himes, ST, July 6, 1842, p. 110. The purpose of such an association was to be for mutual encouragement, to make provision for the dissemination of information and the payment of dues; and finally, it was to be governed by the Golden Rule.

[3]Dick, "The Adventist Crisis" (1930), p. 46.

[4]Arthur, "'Come Out of Babylon'" (1970), p. 24. See also Dick, "The Adventist Crisis" (1930), pp. 30-47, on the organizational importance of the general conferences and the Second Advent associations.

In the same year as the second general conference, Miller recommended the creation of a committee to screen and appoint lecturers for the Millerite movement, which if implemented would have been a step toward the establishment of a properly qualified ministry. Apparently, the proposal was never acted upon.[1]

Millerite camp meetings

At a general conference held in Melodion Hall, Boston, in May 1842, a resolution was passed adopting camp meetings as a means of advancing the Millerite message.[2] More than one hundred of these were held in the years 1842 and 1843.[3] These open-air or tent meetings, says Froom, "began first to augment and then to supplant their meetings in the denominational churches."[4]

During the year 1842, the conferences, camp meetings, and local Second Advent associations brought increasingly frequent references in Millerite periodicals to the question of separation.[5] After one conference held in October 1842, for instance, it was reported that "no hostile opposition has been manifest," but the

---

[1]Letter, William Miller to the Second Advent Conference held at Portland, Me., October 12, 1841, ST, November 1, 1841, p. 117.

[2]Editorial, "Boston Second Advent Conference," ST, June 1, 1842, p. 68. See Dick, "The Adventist Crisis" (1930), pp. 56-85, for a detailed account of these camp meetings.

[3]Froom, Prophetic Faith, 4:448.

[4]Froom, Movement of Destiny, p. 69. Cf. Dick, "The Adventist Crisis" (1930), pp. 44-45.

[5]See, e.g., D., "More Ultraism," ST, July 20, 1842, p. 126; "Look at Facts," D-S, repr. in ST, October 19, 1842, p. 34; Joshua V. Himes, "The Crisis Has Come!" ST, August 3, 1842, pp. 140-141. Cf. Damsteegt, Foundations, pp. 78-79.

pastor and deacons of the local Congregational church called it "all delusion and fanaticism."[1]   The advice   of the Millerite leaders, however, remained the same--to stay   within   the churches.[2]   This remained their position until the rise of the "Seventh Month movement" during the summer of 1844.[3]

"Come Out of Babylon"

If 1840 was a pivotal year, the year 1843 was equally significant and perhaps may best be described as a year of crisis for the Millerite movement.[4]   In the mid-19th century,   there was a strong anti-Roman Catholic sentiment throughout the United States of America, partly in reaction to the rising tide of immigration from predominantly Roman Catholic nations in Europe, partly a result of the historicist hermeneutic of many Protestants which identified the Roman Catholic Church with Babylon,[5] and partly from the oppressive history of Catholicism in lands from which the Americans had fled.

---

[1]D. H. Hamilton,   "Result of the Second Advent Conference in Prospectville," ST, October 19, 1842, p. 38.

[2]Editorial, "Our Duty," ST, November 30, 1842, p. 86.

[3]Reasons for the call to separate are developed below, pp. 61-66.   The Seventh Month movement was so named because S. S. Snow was convinced from his study of the Mosaic tabernacle and Jewish festival types that Christ would return on the Jewish day of Atonement--the tenth day of the seventh month.   Basing his calculations on the calendar of the Karaite Jews, Snow concluded that the day of Christ's coming would be October 22, 1844.   His arguments appeared in a periodical, the True Midnight Cry, August 22, 1844. Cf. also Damsteegt, Foundations, pp. 93-100; Froom, Prophetic Faith, 4:810-826; Nichol, The Midnight Cry, pp. 206-216.

[4]Cf. the title of Dick's dissertation, "The Adventist Crisis of 1843-1844."

[5]On the   anti-Catholicism   of the 19th century, particularly the 1840s, see Gaustad, ed., The Rise of Adventism, pp. xii-xiii,

The Millerites shared in this attitude toward Catholicism. Litch, for example, in his interpretation of prophecy (in particular Rev 13:1-10; 14:8; and 18:1-24), reflected the widely held view of the time in identifying the Roman Catholic Church as the power that "made war with the saints" and as mystical Babylon.[1]

The event that marked the most significant new development in the Millerites' interpretation of Babylon was a sermon preached by Charles Fitch in Cleveland, Ohio, in July 1843. Entitled, "Come Out of Her, My People" and based on Rev 18, it identified Babylon not merely with the Roman Catholic Church, but with "the mass of Protestant Christendom" as well.[2] The chief evidence of

---

128, 140; Damsteegt, Foundations, pp. 46-47; Hudson, Religion in America, p. 128; Tyler, Freedom's Ferment, pp. 374-385. A more general account of American antagonism toward immigrants (including Roman Catholics) may be found in John Higham, Send These to Me: Jews and Other Immigrants in Urban America (New York: Atheneum, 1975), pp. 68-77. See Froom, Prophetic Faith, 4:114-124, 148-152, on the historicist interpretation of the Roman Catholic Church as Babylon.

[1]Josiah Litch, "Babylon's Fall--the Sanctuary Cleansed," ST, July 26, 1843, pp. 165-166. See also Josiah Litch, The Probability of the Second Coming of Christ about A.D. 1843. Shown by a Comparison of Prophecy with History, Up to the Present Time, and an Explanation of Those Prophecies Which Are Yet to Be Fulfilled (Boston: David H. Ela, 1838), p. 186. Numerous other examples of this interpretation are cited in Froom, Prophetic Faith, 4:114, 121-122, 124, 148, 150, 189, 248, 259, 280, 342, 353, 1075, 1191. See also Damsteegt, Foundations, p. 47; and Jonathan M. Butler, "Adventism and the American Experience," in The Rise of Adventism, pp. 180-181.

[2]Charles Fitch, "Come Out of Her, My People," MC, September 21, 1843, p. 35. The entire sermon appeared on pp. 33-36 and was later published as a pamphlet under the same title in Rochester, New York, by Himes. A point of clarification is perhaps needed here. The identification of Protestantism with Babylon was not a new idea when expressed by Fitch in 1843. Several interpreters in Britain and America had done so in the 18th century (see Froom, Prophetic Faith, 4:767-770). Such a view did not become common among the Millerites, however, until after Fitch had made such an application.

Protestantism's downfall was the fact that <u>all</u> the churches had
rejected the message of Christ's personal appearing. The logical
conclusion drawn by Fitch was that "to come out of Babylon is to be
converted to the true scripture doctrine of the personal coming and
kingdom of Christ."[1] The sermon made a "tremendous impact" and
Fitch's call was soon taken up by others.[2]

How comprehensive and categorical was Fitch's condemnation
can be seen from the following excerpt:

> Come out of Babylon or perish. If you are a Christian, stand for
> Christ, and hold out unto the end. I do not undertake to say how
> many in these professed Christian sects will be saved or lost,
> but I hesitate not to say that every individual among them, who
> is found a true child of God in the end, will cease his
> opposition to Christ's personal reign, and be found at last
> faithfully defending the truth. No one that is ever saved can
> remain in Babylon.[3]

Introducing the sermon, the editors of the Millerite

---

[1]Fitch, "Come Out of Her," p. 34.

[2]Arthur, "'Come Out of Babylon'" (1970), p. 66. Arthur
says that the call for separation was felt more strongly in the West
(Ohio and Western New York) than in New England (p. 57). Arthur's
account of the "Come Out of Babylon" message is the most detailed
(see especially pp. 42-83). Others who allude to the importance of
Fitch's sermon are Dick, "The Adventist Crisis" (1930), pp. 48-52,
124-153; Rowe, "Thunder and Trumpets" (1974), pp. 221-226; Froom,
Prophetic Faith, 4:544; Damsteegt, Foundations, pp. 78-84. Madeline
Warner in "The Changing Image of the Millerites in the Western
Massachusetts Press," Adventist Heritage 2 (Summer 1975):5-7, has
helped to demonstrate the significance of the events of 1843. They
mark, she says, a "distinct change in press attitude." Revivals
conducted by Miller in the area in 1842 had actually increased church
attendance and very little anti-Millerite feeling was noticeable in
the press until about 1843.

[3]Fitch, "Come Out of Her," p. 36. Fitch based his reasoning
on Rev 18:2, 4: "And he cried mightily with a strong voice, saying,
Babylon the great is fallen, is fallen, and is become the habitation
of devils, and the hold of every foul spirit, and a cage of every
unclean and hateful bird. . . . And I heard another voice from
heaven saying, Come out of her, my people, that ye be not partakers
of her sins, and that ye receive not of her plagues" (KJV).

periodical The Midnight Cry inserted the following qualification:
"We should make a different application of the Scriptures relating to
the fall of Babylon, but that does not affect the excellence of the
main doctrine of the sermon."[1]   Obviously, there was "no immediate
united acceptance of Fitch's interpretation of symbolic 'Babylon' to
include Protestantism."[2]   The Protestant churches in Cleveland, to
be sure, were not too pleased, as Cook indicated when he spoke of a
"torrent of opposition" against the preaching of Fitch.[3]

Among those who adopted Fitch's emphasis were Luther
Caldwell, David Plumb, George Storrs, Marsh, and even (for a time)
Miller himself. Caldwell claimed that the nominal churches had
rejected the message of the immediate return of Christ and that this
fact was evidence of their fallen condition and reason enough to
leave them.[4] In the following year, as the date set for Christ's
expected return grew nearer, the condemnation of Protestantism became
stronger and the call "to come out of her" more insistent.

Plumb was quite explicit in his identification of Babylon and
gave numerous evidences of its fallen state. He characterized it as
an anti-Christian church, an ecclesiastical body which has existed in
every age of the Christian dispensation. Historically, he said, its

---

[1]Editorial, MC, September 21, 1843, p. 33.

[2]Nichol, The Midnight Cry, p. 160.

[3]Letter, J. B. Cook to George Storrs, MC, November 23,
1843, p. [120].

[4]Luther Caldwell, "I Will Spue Thee Out of My Mouth," MC,
December 14, 1843, p. 149.

organized existence had been in the form of the Papacy, but all of this was preliminary to his main point: "The Babylon of the present period includes the great body of the Protestant churches, especially of the churches in America."[1] Among the evidences he mentioned of the fallen condition of these churches were: (1) Babylon means "confusion," and the divisions within Protestantism attested to its confused state, (2) many "heterogeneous elements" were brought together within one organization, such as rich and poor, and advocates of temperance and "drunkards," (3) the churches were full of worldliness, covetousness, pride, and luxury, (4) the "ease loving ministry" with its "salary system" revealed the fallen state of the leaders of Babylon, and (5) most importantly, the clearest identifying mark of Babylon was the pro-slavery stance of these churches. Consequently, he declared, the call must be issued to come out from "these worldly-minded, pro-slavery and anti-Christian bodies."[2]

Two weeks after the publication of Plumb's article, Storrs expressed similar sentiments in The Midnight Cry.[3] Like Plumb, he identified Babylon as "the old mother and all her children,"[4] distinguished by the divisions and confusion within the churches. But whereas Plumb regarded slavery as the key issue, Storrs held that

---

[1]David Plumb, "Babylon," MC, February 1, 1844, p. 218.

[2]Ibid., p. 219.

[3]George Storrs, "Come Out of Her My People," MC, February 15, 1844, pp. 237-238.

[4]Ibid., p. 237.

the existence of competing and conflicting creeds was what led to the churches' Babylonish state.[1]

Storrs proceeded from his condemnation of differing creeds to a blanket disapproval of organization itself. His statement that "no church can be organized by man's invention but what it becomes Babylon <u>the moment it is organized</u>,"[2] is emblematic of the anti-organizational stance of many Millerites and may be the most frequently quoted statement from Millerism.[3] As we shall see in chapter four, Storrs's stance became the rallying cry of all opposed

---

[1]Storrs denounced the confusion among the churches as follows: "It is done by the manufacturing of creeds, whether written or oral, and endeavoring to organize a party; the test of fellowship being now, not love to God and each other, but assent to these creeds. . . . Now look for the loving Church of God; where is it? All is 'confusion'--rent and torn into as many parties as there are agents of sects to carry on the Babylonish work. Instead of the Church of God, a loving, united, brotherly body, delighting to meet each other, you now have Baptists, Methodists, Presbyterians, &c., &c., down to the end of the list of divisions; and the so called churches are each making war on the others, not because they do not live as holy as themselves, but because their <u>creeds differ</u>; and hence 'confusion' or <u>Babylon</u> is truly their name" (ibid.).

[2]Ibid., p. 238. Storrs apparently did not see any contradiction between labelling the churches as Babylon on the basis of their confusion <u>and</u> of their organization! Not all Millerites accepted Storrs's extreme position, however. J. N. Loughborough reflected many years later: "A gathering of Adventists at Boston, Mass., seemed to realize that there was danger in taking too 'extreme' a position in the matter, so they issued an address, signed by William Miller, Elon Galusha, N. N. Whiting, Apollos Hale, and J. V. Himes. Among other excellent advice they cautioned against the dangerous 'yielding to a spirit of revenge against the churches on account of their injustice against all such <u>organizations</u>.' This advice was given a few weeks after Brother Storrs's strong statement against any form of organization. It seemed designed of the Lord to hold the people from assuming too ultra ground on the subject of church order" (Loughborough, "Anarchy or Order--Which?" <u>RH</u>, May 28, 1901, p. 347).

[3]See, e.g., Damsteegt, <u>Foundations</u>, p. 83; Arthur, "Millerism," p. 168; Schwarz, <u>Light Bearers</u>, p. 47.

to the organization of the Seventh-day Adventist Church.[1]

The sentiments of Marsh, editor of The Voice of Truth, although they grew out of the Seventh Month movement of 1844, reflected those first expressed by Fitch more than a year earlier. Babylon, he said, is not exclusively papal Rome but "it IS THE NOMINAL CHURCH." He also decried the confusion of "names, creeds, doctrines, worship, ordinances, practices and so forth."[2] In fact, the major portion of the September 11, 1844, issue of The Voice of Truth was devoted to the question of Babylon, and ten thousand extra copies were printed in order to extend the call to "Come Out of Babylon" as far as possible.[3]

One individual who did not join in the specific condemnation of Protestantism was Sylvester Bliss, who developed a broader view of the identity of Babylon as he reviewed its history from Babel to his own time. Mystical Babylon, he said, represented (1) all human supremacy, (2) the embodiment of Satan's kingdom, (3) King Nebuchadnezzar himself, who represented the height of Babylon's blasphemous claims, (4) the City of Rome, (5) the papal horn that succeeded it,[4] and (6) in the present age "everything that is Antichristian in its tendencies."[5] Even though this gave wider scope

---

[1]See below, p. 143.

[2]Joseph Marsh, "Come Out of Babylon!" VT, September 11, 1844, pp. 127-128.

[3]Arthur, "'Come Out of Babylon'" (1970), p. 70.

[4]This terminology is based on Dan 7:8, 20-26.

[5][Sylvester Bliss], "The Downfall of Great Babylon," ASR, May 1844, pp. 112-120.

to the meaning of Babylon, papal Rome was still identified as part of
this historic apostasy.

As has been mentioned earlier, even Miller, perhaps stung by
the rising tide of opposition, on more than one occasion denounced
the spirit of the established churches. He spoke of Galusha, a
prominent Baptist minister who joined the Millerites, as one who
suffered persecution "from the proud and scoffing ministry and
worldly professors."[1] Miller compared the "defamation" of the
Millerites by the Protestant churches to the treatment Protestants
had received at the hands of the Catholics at the time of the
Reformation. He identified the Roman Catholic Church with the mother
of harlots (Rev 17:5) and the Protestant churches of his day as her
daughters. Miller's justification of this application of Scripture
is reported in the Advent Herald: " . . . therefore that portion of
the Protestant churches that imitate and partake of the spirit of the
old mother must be the daughters referred to."[2]

Even though Miller joined with his associates in denouncing
the persecuting spirit of the fallen churches, he never went so far
as to make a blanket condemnation of organized Protestantism. This
stance is clarified in his Apology and Defence, written in the year
following the Disappointment. Decrying the formality and persecution
of Adventists by the fallen churches, he nonetheless criticized those

---

[1]Letter, William Miller to Joshua V. Himes, MC, December
14, 1843, p. [145].

[2]Editorial, "The Conference," AH, February 14, 1844, p. 9.
Cf. also letter, William Miller to N. Southard, MC, November 23,
1843, p. [117].

of his followers who called the churches Babylon and insisted that it was still possible that some churches might "love the Lord in sincerity."[1]

Such statements as the ones quoted above from Fitch, Plumb, Storrs, and Marsh[2] must have later proved to be an embarrassment to Miller, not being typical of his own attitude. In reflecting on the past experience of the Millerites, Miller declared:

> The calling of all churches, that do not embrace the doctrine of the advent, Babylon, I before remarked, was a means of our not being listened to with candor; and also, that I regarded it as a perversion of Scripture.[3]

One finds in the 1843 Millerite periodicals growing concern over whether or not to remain in the churches. Several individuals wrote for advice as to the proper course of action. Usually, the answer given stopped short of telling all their readers to leave, but the implication was that to remain in fellowship with those who opposed the Advent message was inconsistent and spiritually hazardous.[4]

The Seventh Month movement

In a February 1844 article, Miller declared that "he had ever and at all times advised Adventists to stay in their respective

---

[1]Miller, Apology and Defence, p. 32.

[2]See above, pp. 48-54.

[3]Miller, Apology and Defence, p. 30.

[4]See, e.g., Editorial, "To Correspondents," ST, August 23, 1843, p. 5; Editorial, "You Are Breaking Up the Churches," MC, December 14, 1843, p. 148. Cf. also the similar advice of L. D. Fleming in "Enquiry," MC, February 8, 1844, p. 228.

churches."[1] Why therefore, he asked, were Adventists being cut off from the churches? Was not belief in the Second Coming of Christ something taught by all church creeds? Surely the fact that Millerites said that Christ would come in that year, or that they studied the Bible for themselves, was insufficient reason for such action, he claimed. Even here, in the face of enforced severance, he protested against rather than advocated separation.[2]

During the early months of 1844, the editors of the Millerite periodicals received several inquiries from correspondents about the duty of Millerites in regard to church membership.[3] Fleming's reply was typical. In the case of ministers engaged in preaching Christ's imminent return, he advised them in most instances to relinquish their pastoral duties, in order to engage full time in the task of giving "the word of warning." As far as the rest were concerned, Fleming concluded that it was not necessary for a person to withdraw from his church as long as he was free to speak out of his faith in the Second Coming.[4] Fleming's answer reflects the attitude of most

---

[1]William Miller, "An Address to the Believers in Christ of All Denominations," AH, February 14, 1844, p. 9. Also to be found in William Miller, "An Address to the Believers in Christ, of All Denominations," MC, February 22, 1844, pp. 420-421.

[2]Ibid.

[3]The editors of the Signs of the Times reported that they had received several letters seeking advice as to whether or not to remain in the "nominal" churches (Editorial, "To Correspondents," p. 5).

[4]Fleming, "Enquiry," p. 228. Articles advocating separation written in the first half of 1844 include: Himes, "Editorial Correspondence" (1844), p. 399; Editorial, "The Church at the First Advent," MC, April 25, 1844, p. 326; [C. S. Minor], "Life from the Dead, No. 3," MC, April 11, 1844, pp. 309-310; Hiram Munger, "Affairs at Chicopee," AH, June 19, 1844, pp. 158-159; S. C. Chandler,

Millerites, who always considered themselves to constitute an unsectarian movement. In view of their disapproval of the dividing walls of Christendom, they had no wish to add to that confusion. Their task was clear--to warn the world of Christ's return, a return so imminent that, in the view of the editor of the Voice of Truth, no ecclesiastical organization was necessary.[1]

One of the clearest statements of the rationale behind the exodus from the established churches was written by Himes in June 1844. He was positive that the blame for the separation was brought about, with but few exceptions, entirely by the antagonism of the old organizations. We quote a portion of his article to show the tone Himes uses, which is typical of Millerite leadership at this late time.

> We found that the friends and supporters of the Advent cause, had as a general thing left their respective churches, and declared themselves free and independent of all associations that stood opposed to the Advent at hand, whether they professed friendship or hostility. . . . They have regretted the necessity of this step. But it was a case of life and death; certain death, if they remained in the old organizations.
> It has been said, that this movement was got up and carried forward, by indiscreet men; disorganizers, come outers, etc. that there may be some such persons among us, we will not deny; but that the great body of the Advent believers, who have left the churches, are such, we do deny.
> The churches have taken such a course in relation to the advocates of "the faith once delivered to the saints" that they could not honestly live with them: and notwithstanding the remonstrances against leaving the churches, heretofore, God has led his people out into a large place, and into rich pasture; and

---

"Conference at Jamaica, Vt.," MC, June 20, 1844, p. 391; Letter, S. S. Snow to N. Southard, MC, June 27, 1844, p. 397.

[1]Cf., e.g., Joseph Marsh's response to the question of what the Millerites should do if they left their churches: "You have no time for conferring with flesh and blood; the case is urgent . . ." (Marsh, "Come Out of Babylon!" p. 127).

we believe the hand of God is in the matter; although, we never anticipated such a result, in the commencement of our labors.

We cannot give up our faith, or hope. If it sever us from the church, friends, and all that is dear, we shall give them up cheerfully.[1]

According to Damsteegt, "only during the late summer of 1844 did the Millerite leaders support separation with any degree of unanimity."[2] It was the urgency and excitement of the Seventh Month movement that brought the question of separation from the churches to its most critical stage. S. S. Snow made the suggestion that Christ's return would take place in the autumn of 1844,[3] eventually fixing on an exact date--October 22, 1844, the tenth day of the seventh month (the day of Atonement) in the Old Testament ceremonial system. His proposal received little attention at first, but at a camp meeting in Exeter, New Hampshire (August 12-17, 1844), his presentation on the subject stirred the Millerites to great enthusiasm and urgency.[4] For the first time, there was virtual

---

[1]Joshua V. Himes, "Editorial Correspondence," MC, June 27, 1844, p. 399.

[2]Damsteegt, Foundations, p. 81.

[3]Letter, S. S. Snow to N. Southard, MC, February 22, 1844, pp. 243-244. See also Damsteegt, Foundations, pp. 89-96; Froom, Prophetic Faith, 4:813-814, for details on the bases of his conclusion. Cf. Letter, S. S. Snow to N. Southard, MC, June 27, 1844, p. 397. Attached was a disclaimer by the editors stating that they did not necessarily agree with all of the textual expositions in the letter.

[4]White, in Life Incidents, pp. 153-168, discusses the importance of the Exeter camp meeting and describes the impact of Snow's sermon. Wellcome, in History of the Second Advent Message, pp. 356-366, cites statements by other Millerite leaders who accepted the "Seventh Month." See also Damsteegt, Foundations, pp. 96-99; Schwarz, Light Bearers, pp. 49-50; Froom, Prophetic Faith, 4:818-826.

unanimity on the date of the Second Coming, and the result was a movement--the "Seventh Month movement"--to issue the "true midnight cry," the final warning to the world.[1] Miller himself accepted Snow's interpretation early in October, and wrote to Himes that on October 22 "the door will be shut" and "the next will be the last Lord's day [October 13] sinners will ever have in probation."[2]

The excitement of the Seventh Month movement crystallized in the minds of the Millerite leaders the need and the reasons for separation. Shortly before the climax of the movement, Himes spelled out his reasons for severing ties with established Christendom:

1. Suppression of the subject of the Second Advent by the churches which are "none other than the daughters of mystic Babylon";

2. Ridicule and oppression;

3. Being cut off from former privileges and enjoyments;

4. Lack of "meat in due season."[3]

We conclude this survey of the attitude to separation in the final months of the Seventh Month movement with reference to Marsh who was equally unequivocal in his call to leave Babylon. Repeating earlier Millerite interpretation of Rev 17, which identified Roman Catholicism as the mother of harlots and the Protestant churches as

---

[1]Based on the cry, "Go ye out to meet him," in Christ's parable of the ten virgins, Matt 25:1-13.

[2]Letter, William Miller to Joshua V. Himes, MC, October 12, 1844, p. 122.

[3]Joshua V. Himes, "Editorial Correspondence. Separation from the Churches," AH, September 18, 1844, p. 53. Cf. catalog of reasons for separation by F. G. Brown, although it was written before the Seventh Month movement came to prominence. His list of causes for

her daughters, he concluded: "The church with which you are connected has become an 'harlot'. . . . Hence it is plain that duty calls you to dissolve all connection with her. God requires it."[1]

Evolution of Millerite Attitudes Toward
Separation and Organization

Analysis of Millerite attitudes toward separation and organization reveals a clear change of mood as time passed. The expressions of 1844 were much more urgent and passionate than those of four years earlier. It is also clear that among the individual Millerite leaders there were differences of degree in the strength of their condemnation of those churches opposed to the Second Advent message. It seems that the most important factor was opposition to the idea of Christ's imminent return. In part, this opposition may be attributed to the Millerites' time setting of a specific year, or even day. But included in the underlying antagonism to Miller and his associates was disagreement over a far more fundamental issue-- pre-millennialism. As Dick has indicated, Miller's ideas ran

---

the departure of the Millerites from the churches may be summarized as follows: (1) the abandonment by the churches of the simplicity of the gospel; (2) their denial of the doctrine of the resurrection of the body; (3) their denial of the pre-millennial Second Coming of Christ; (4) ridicule by the churches directed against the Millerites; (5) the association of the churches with the world; (6) persecution, including "excommunication," of Advent believers practiced by the churches; (7) the Laodicean state of the "nominal church"; (8) membership in an apostate church hindering the work of evangelism and ministry (Brown, "Reasons for Withdrawing from the Church," MC, April 4, 1844, p. 301). It should be noted that Brown cites reasons other than persecution for leaving the churches. Eschatology holds an important place, but there is no mention by him of opposition to date setting.

[1]Marsh, "Come Out of Babylon!" p. 127.

contrary to the widely prevalent post-millennialism of the age.[1] As early as the first General Conference on the Second Advent in 1840, it was observed that the creeds of all the Protestant churches supported a pre-millennial view of the Second Advent and that the churches of the Reformation had, therefore, forsaken their first love by holding "to the doctrine of the kingdom in this world" (i.e., post-millennialism).[2] Two other reasons for separation given prominence in Millerite literature were sectarianism and the making of human creeds. We have seen, for example, that the former was given by Miller as a factor in his disenchantment with Christianity when he became associated with Deism.[3]

An extensive list of reasons for leaving the Protestant denominations may be placed under the general heading of the Babylonish state of the churches. Included in this category were such things as the hierarchical nature of their organization, complex liturgies, wealth and pride of the clergy, their support of slavery,

---

[1]Dick, "The Adventist Crisis" (1930), p. 48. Miller's pre-millennialism, he suggested, "resurrected from the primitive church, was new and radical for his day." Cf. also above, p. 18. Wellcome, in History of the Second Advent Message, pp. 326-327, lists the major post-millennialist arguments against Millerite preaching.

[2]Ward, Jones, and Russel, "Circular," p. 116. On the same issue see Letter, William Miller to Joshua V. Himes, ST, October 15, 1841, p. 105, where he expresses the view that the "deplorable state" of the divided body of Christ was such that there was no hope of union before the Second Coming and therefore was a strong argument against a temporal millennium. Cf. L. S. Stockman, "Ecclesiastical Trial," AH, February 14, 1844, p. 13, who reports that at an annual conference of the Methodist Episcopal Church in Maine he and other Millerite sympathizers were instructed to refrain from preaching a spiritual millennium.

[3]See above, pp. 34-36. Miller was a Deist for twelve years (1804-1816) according to Bliss, Memoirs of William Miller, p. 25.

their intemperance, and the confusion and competition caused by the vast number of sects and parties.[1] Evidence that these churches did indeed constitute "Babylon" lay in their low spirituality. As Miller said:

> Among all the churches where the doctrine of the Second Advent is shut out, I have not heard of one case of revival; and where they have excluded their members for their connection with the Adventists, they are, to all appearance, cursed of God.[2]

A final major cause of separation given by the Millerites was persecution. This involved sarcasm and ridicule directed against the idea of Christ's imminent return, the lack of freedom to express their ideas within the confines of church membership, and the lack of spiritual nourishment from the nominal preachers. Almost without exception, then, the blame for severing ties with the churches was placed on the denominations themselves. In almost every instance, the Millerites felt forced to leave the churches. If some left of their own accord it was only because it was "death" to remain.

An examination of the interpretation of the call to "Come out of Babylon" by later writers reveals several diverse explanations. Arthur states more emphatically than anyone else that the Millerites were the aggressors.[3] While he recognizes that what he calls their censorious spirit was no doubt unintentionally disruptive, he suggests that as they became more certain of their position "their

---

[1]Dick, "The Adventist Crisis" (1930), p. 30, has provided a similar list of reasons for "coming out of Babylon." Cf. Damsteegt, Foundations, pp. 79-84.

[2]Letter, William Miller to Joshua V. Himes, MC, February 1, 1844, p. 221.

[3]Arthur, "'Come Out of Babylon'" (1970), p. iv.

denunciations of the church, the clergy, indeed of all who refused to adopt their message grew more strident and reckless."[1]

Seventh-day Adventists have regarded the Millerites as their spiritual forefathers and therefore their accounts of the movement have tended to be apologetic. White (1821-1881) was a young Millerite preacher who participated in the events leading to the Disappointment of 1844. Looking back on that experience, he said:

> But of all the great religious movements since the days of the first apostles of our Lord, none stand out more pure and free from the imperfections of human nature, and the wiles of Satan, than that of the autumn of 1844.[2]

Loughborough[3] delineated the evidences of the fall of the Protestant churches and the resultant separation by the Millerites in the Rise and Progress of Seventh-day Adventists (1892), the first hard-back denominational history of the church, later revised and published as The Great Second Advent Movement.[4] He described the mockery by church leaders of the Millerites and the corrupt practices of the churches, such as "donation parties" which included "ring guess-cakes, ten-cent kissing bees, donkey shows, crazy socials, holy lotteries."[5] In such an environment, he explained, it would have been just as impossible to preach Adventism's distinctive truths as it was for the apostolic church to proclaim the gospel as a Jewish

---

[1]Ibid., pp. 36-37.   [2]White, Life Incidents, p. 171.

[3]For biographical details see "Loughborough, John Norton," SDA Encyclopedia (1976), 10:815-816.

[4]J. N. Loughborough, The Great Second Advent Movement: Its Rise and Progress (Washington, D.C.: Review and Herald Pub. Assn, 1905), pp. 171-181.

[5]Ibid., pp. 151-152.

sect.[1] Nevertheless, he expressed surprise at the "unaccountable
opposition" of the churches against the message of Christ's return.[2]

Froom echoed Loughborough's sentiments in identifying the
cause of separation. Sometime around 1843, he wrote, "the tide of
spiritual fervor, and paralleling reforms, definitely began to
recede," and, as a result, "first there was an aloofness, then a
suspicion, and last a hostility" toward the Millerites.[3] Consequently, those expecting the Advent of the Lord felt constrained to
issue a "reluctant call" to leave the churches.[4]

Little acknowledgement has been given by Seventh-day
Adventist authors to the fact that Millerism must have been seen as a
great distraction and threat to the churches. Dick is one writer who
has recognized this side of the question. He admitted that the
fervent missionary activity of the Advent believers resulted in
neglect of their church duties, as the "opposition" saw them.
"Obviously," in Dick's view, "the church members began to exert some
pressure on the zealous fanatics, as they were thought to be."[5]

In conclusion, it is not our purpose to apportion blame in
this matter, but to demonstrate that Millerism became increasingly

---

[1]Ibid., p. 178.   [2]Ibid., p. 175.

[3]Froom, Movement of Destiny pp. 68-70.

[4]Froom, Prophetic Faith, 4:770. See pp. 761-783 for details
on attitudes by the Millerites toward separation and the formation of
a new sect. Similar interpretations may be found in M. Ellsworth
Olsen, A History of the Origin and Progress of Seventh-day Adventists
(Washington, D.C.: Review and Herald Pub. Assn, 1925), pp. 144-146;
Nichol, The Midnight Cry, p. 157; "Millerite Movement," SDA
Encyclopedia (1976), 10:892-898.

[5]Dick, "The Adventist Crisis" (1930), p. 49.

separatist, often "in spite of itself."[1] We would suggest that there were several factors in the reluctance of the Millerites to make provision for the establishment of a permanent organization among the Adventists. Many Millerites, including their leaders, retained the connection with the established churches almost until the time of the Disappointment and saw no need to create another organization. Not only was there seen to be little time before Christ's expected return, but there was, in the view of the Advent believers, a clear-cut task to be accomplished; namely, to proclaim the message of Christ's imminent return. They foresaw, therefore, no time and perceived no need for anything but the most rudimentary form of organization. In the words of Litch:

> All . . . have agreed to work together for the accomplishment of a certain object; and the organization to which this has given rise, so far as there is anything which may be called an organization, is of the most simple, voluntary and primitive form.[2]

---

[1]Ibid., p. 76.

[2]Quoted in White, Life Incidents, p. 151.

CHAPTER III

THE POST-DISAPPOINTMENT YEARS:

THE SPLINTERING OF ADVENTISM

The time immediately after the Great Disappointment[1] was
marked by varied attempts to come to terms with and explain the
failure of Millerite hopes. Strenuous efforts were made by the
leaders to hold the movement together in the face of fanaticism in
some quarters and dying interest in others.[2]

The material under consideration in this chapter falls
naturally into two main sections. First of all, the situation among
the non-Sabbatarian Millerites will be described leading up to the
pivotal Albany Conference, which was convened by these Adventists on

---

[1]Hereafter the experience of the Millerites on October 22,
1844, is referred to as "the Disappointment." Eyewitness accounts of
the Disappointment by Seventh-day pioneers include White, Life
Incidents, pp. 168-191; Ellen G. White, Life Sketches of Ellen G.
White (Mountain View, Calif.: Pacific Press Pub. Assn, 1915), pp.
54-63. Another contemporary account is in Wellcome, History of the
Second Advent Message, pp. 356-366. Other more recent accounts
include Damsteegt, Foundations, pp. 93-100; Nichol, The Midnight Cry,
pp. 247-260; Froom, Prophetic Faith, 4:822-826.

[2]Extreme beliefs and fanatical practices that emerged after
the Disappointment included "spiritual wifery," the theories that
Christ's return would be spiritual or that He had already returned in
the flesh and was to be found in the true believer, and the belief
held by some that they had already entered Christ's thousand-year
Sabbath and therefore should do no secular work. For accounts of
these fanatical elements see Arthur, "'Come Out of Babylon'" (1970),
pp. 101-123; Schwarz, Light Bearers, pp. 55-56.

April 29, 1845, to end the growing divisions in their midst.[1] An important part of this portion of the account is the emergence of certain "Shut Door" theories which taught, with varying levels of severity and exclusiveness, that the door of salvation (or door of mercy) had been closed at the end of the 2300 days, the Seventh Month movement had been valid, and prophecy had indeed been fulfilled on October 22, 1844.[2]

Second, we shall devote the rest of our attention to the emergence of Sabbatarian Adventism,[3] which was to culminate in the organization of the Seventh-day Adventist Church in 1863. However, this chapter will trace developments only from 1844 to 1851, during which time the distinctive doctrines of Sabbatarian Adventism were consolidated and its theology of mission gradually developed.[4] The experience of the non-Sabbatarian Adventists serves as a useful point

---

[1]Miller wrote after the Albany Conference: "It was convened . . . if possible to extricate ourselves from the anarchy and confusion of Babylon in which we had so unexpectedly found ourselves" (William Miller, "The Albany Conference," AH, June 4, 1845, p. 129). "Fanatical" practices condemned at the meeting were: "Jewish fables" (probably a reference to observance of the seventh-day Sabbath), "the act of promiscuous feet-washing and the salutation kiss," and acts of voluntary humility such as sitting on the floor or shaving one's head ("Mutual Conference of Adventists at Albany," AH, May 14, 1845, p. 107).

[2]The biblical rationale for the Shut Door was based upon a combination of texts, including Matt 25:10; Rev 22:10-12. An account of the Shut Door concept appears below, pp. 74-79, 103-109.

[3]The terms "Sabbatarian Adventists" and "Sabbatarians" hereafter denote the former Millerites who came to accept the Sabbath and eventually formed the Seventh-day Adventist Church.

[4]See Damsteegt, Foundations, pp. 103-164, for a comprehensive account of the development of the Seventh-day Adventist concept of mission.

of contrast in the study of the earliest stages of Sabbatarian Adventist organization.

The Aftermath of the Disappointment Among Non-Sabbatarian Millerites

Immediate Reactions

The Millerites experienced more than one "disappointment." Many, for example, had expected the Second Advent by the spring of 1844.[1] However, no disappointment equalled the intensity of October 22, 1844, when their hopes for the return of Christ on that day were dashed. None of the previous date setting had been so closely attached to an exact day. It is difficult to imagine the depth of their feelings immediately after October 22. Millerite periodicals which resumed publication shortly thereafter were restrained in their public statements, but the sentiments revealed in print hid a deep despondency. For example, the two most prominent Millerite periodicals, the Advent Herald[2] and The Midnight Cry,[3] resumed publication on October 30 and 31, respectively. The main articles and correspondence had been written before October 22, and the only reference to the failure of the expectations appeared in the editorial columns of the two papers. In the Advent Herald, the editors merely stated that

---

[1]For example, an editorial in Signs of the Times (June 21, 1843, p. 123) suggested that Christ might return on or before April 18, 1844, the last day of the Jewish year as calculated by the strict and precise Karaite Jews. A significant number of Millerites apparently looked for Christ's return by that date and were disappointed when their expectations failed. Cf. also Froom, Prophetic Faith, 4:796-797; Schwarz, Light Bearers, pp. 48-49.

[2]Edited by Himes, Bliss, and Apollos Hale.

[3]Edited by N. Southard, published by Himes.

Christ's non-appearance was "contrary . . . to our wishes and expectations."[1] Even so, they declared that "we have found the grace of God sufficient to sustain us, even at such a time."[2] Moreover, confidence was expressed in the fact that it was God who had led them throughout their recent experience.[3] The Midnight Cry expressed similar feelings.[4]

One might compare the above with the personal descriptions that Bates and the Whites provide of their situation immediately after the Disappointment. Bates wished that the earth "could have but opened and swallowed me up."[5] White wrote the following later:

> The disappointment at the passing of the time was a bitter one. True believers had given up all for Christ, and had shared his presence as never before. They had, as they supposed, given their last warning to the world, and had separated themselves, more or less, from the unbelieving, scoffing multitude. . . . And now to turn again to the cares, perplexities, and dangers of life, in full view of the jeers and revilings of unbelievers who now scoffed as never before, was a terrible trial of faith and patience. When Elder Himes visited Portland, Me., a few days after the passing of the time, and stated that the brethren should prepare for another cold winter, my feelings were almost uncontrollable. I left the place of meeting and wept like a child.[6]

---

[1]Editorial, "The Advent Herald," AH, October 30, 1844, p. 92.

[2]Ibid., p. 93.

[3]Editorial, "To Those Who Are Looking for the Appearing of Our Lord Jesus Christ, in His Glory," AH, October 30, 1844, p. 96.

[4]See, e.g., Joshua V. Himes, "Provision for the Destitute," MC, October 31, 1844, p. 140.

[5]John O. Corliss, "The Message and Its Friends--No. 2: Joseph Bates As I Knew Him," RH, August 16, 1923, p. 7. Cf. also Bates's own account in his Autobiography (Battle Creek, Mich.: Seventh-day Adventist Pub. Assn, 1868), p. 300.

[6]White, Life Incidents, p. 182. Cf. Ellen G. White's similar sentiments: "It was hard to take up the cross of life that

It would seem that White's statement reflects more accurately the feelings of the majority of Millerites who had accepted the "tenth day of the seventh month," than the comments printed for public consumption in the Millerite periodicals. Furthermore, we would suggest the impact was stronger on the average believer who had accepted wholeheartedly the message of a precise time than on the most prominent of the Millerite leaders, such as Himes, who had accepted the date of October 22 only about two weeks beforehand and did not cancel a proposed trip to Europe later in that year until approximately the first of October.[1] By virtue of the nature of their work, these leaders were more familiar with the many objections to their belief and hinted in their own statements that they were swept along on a tide of enthusiasm rather than being convinced by the force of the arguments originally presented by Snow. Himes and Bliss, in lending stronger support than earlier to a definite time, wrote: "The hand of the Lord is manifest in the spread of this doctrine, and in the effect it produced."[2] After the Disappointment, Himes expressed the same confidence in the "irresistible power

---

we thought had been laid down forever. It was a bitter disappointment that fell upon the little flock. . . ." (Testimonies for the Church, 9 vols. [Mountain View, Calif.: Pacific Press Pub. Assn, 1948], 1:56).

[1]One can gain an insight into the development of Himes's thinking on this question by reading the last few issues of the Advent Herald prior to October 22. See, e.g., Editorial, "Mission to Europe," AH, October 2, 1844, p. 68; Joshua V. Himes and Sylvester Bliss, "The Time of the Advent," AH, October 9, 1844, p. 80; Joshua V. Himes, "The Advent Herald," AH, October 16, 1844, p. 81.

[2]Editorial, "The Scale Turned," AH, October 9, 1844, p. 76.

attending its [a definite time] proclamation."[1] This is not to say
logical argument and biblical evidence were not important, but the
thing that finally swayed them, according to Himes and Bliss, was the
spiritual power and experiential results of the movement. The same
was true of Miller who, in reflecting on the recent Disappointment,
said, "And those of us who have been familiar with the fruits and
effects of the preaching of this doctrine, must acknowledge that he
[God] has been with us in so doing. . . ."[2]

Thus, thousands of people[3] experienced a shattering and
baffling failure of their expectation. In seeking to understand his
own experience, Miller's position at first was that the Millerites
had indeed been right in the matter of time, and prophecy had been
fulfilled in some way in the autumn of 1844. He stated his position
quite clearly:

> I feel confident that God will justify his word, and the time
> which we have preached; for we cannot have varied far from the

---

[1]Joshua V. Himes, "The Advent Herald," AH, October 30, 1844,
p. 93.

[2]Letter, William Miller to Joshua V. Himes and Sylvester
Bliss, AH, December 18, 1844, p. 147. Cf. also his statement, "I am
sure I never experienced a more holy and benificent [sic], effect in
my life than then." Letter, William Miller to the Second Advent
Brethren, JS, April 17, 1845, p. 42.

[3]Miller (Apology and Defence, p. 22) estimated that some
50,000 expected Christ's advent on October 22, 1844. Dick ("The
Adventist Crisis" [1930], p. 234) has attempted to estimate the
number of Millerite adherents based upon the rise and fall of the
membership of mainline churches during the peak of the Millerite
movement. He considered Miller's estimate to be a conservative one.
Froom, in Prophetic Faith, 4:686, quotes a much higher figure
(150,000-200,000) from the Proceedings of the American Antiquarian
Society.

truth in our own views of the seven times, the 2300 days, the 1335 days. . . .[1]

Generally speaking, historians have divided the post-Disappointment Millerites into three main categories. Bliss, for example, named the groups as follows:

1. Those who still believed in the imminent Advent, but who assumed that there had been an error in time calculations. (Bliss included himself in this group.)

2. Those who ascribed to the Seventh Month movement a satanic influence and gave it (and in some cases all religion) up entirely.

3. Those who "contended that it [the Seventh Month movement] was all ordained and ordered of God." Bliss included Sabbatarian and other Shut Door Adventists in this category and labelled them extremists.[2]

Many of the ones who maintained position three (as described above) believed that the door of probation was closed in October 1844 and that those who had rejected their message on the matter of definite time were eternally lost. The hatred and scoffing of those who had opposed the message confirmed them in their belief that these

---

[1]Letter, William Miller to Joshua V. Himes, AH, November 27, 1844, p. 128. Himes and Bliss were more careful than Miller in their editorial statements in the Advent Herald. They agreed that the Millerite message had "served to draw a line among the professed followers of Christ" (Editorial, "The Late Movement," AH, November 6, 1844, p. 102), but did not claim that the time that they had proclaimed had been fulfilled or that those who had rejected their preaching were forever lost. Cf. Editorial, "Address to the Public," AH, November 13, 1844, pp. 108-112.

[2]Bliss, Memoirs of William Miller, p. 293. Cf. similar analyses by Cross (The Burned-over District, pp. 309-313) and Arthur, ("'Come Out of Babylon'" [1970] pp. 85-108).

people had passed the point where repentance was possible. Brown's comment illustrates this point of view:

> We closed up our work for the world some time ago, that is my conviction: and now God has given us a little season for self-preparation, and to prove us before the world. . . . The world and the nominal church know nothing at all of your hope--they cannot be made to understand us. Let them alone.[1]

Miller's Views on the Shut Door[2]

There is no doubt the opinion Brown espoused was shared for a time also by Miller. In an extensive discussion of the Disappointment and the Shut Door, written on the eleventh of November and published a month later, Miller declared:

> We have done our work in warning sinners, and in trying to awake a formal church. God in his providence has shut the door; we can only stir one another to be _patient_; and be diligent to make our calling and election sure.[3]

He continued that the separation between the just and unjust immediately prior to the Second Coming was prophesied in Rev 22:10-12, and that never was the distinction between the righteous and the wicked so distinct as around October 22, 1844. The mocking the Millerites were presently experiencing only served to emphasize this

---

[1]Letter, F. G. Brown to Sylvester Bliss, _AH_, December 4, 1844, p. 135.

[2]The Shut Door theory was based primarily on the parable of the ten virgins (Matt 25:1-13). Some Millerites maintained for a time after the Disappointment that Christ had arrived as the Bridegroom in October 1844, and accepted the wise virgins with Him into the wedding. At that time He also shut the door after them leaving the foolish virgins outside. This door they referred to as the door of mercy. Cf. below, pp. 103-109.

[3]Letter, William Miller to Joshua V. Himes, _AH_, December 11, 1844, p. 142.

fact.[1] In two later letters, Miller added that he was convinced they were correct on the matter of chronology and were then in the "tarrying time," and that the Disappointment could never have been foreseen or avoided.[2]

Miller maintained this position on the Shut Door until about February 1845. In a letter to Bliss on the twelfth of that month, he gave evidence that his thinking was undergoing revision.

> I did believe, and I must honestly confess that I do now, that I have done my work in warning sinners and that in the seventh month. I know my feelings are no rule for others; therefore, let every one who feels he has a duty to do to sinners, let him do it. I will have no hard feelings. But I must be honest; when I am inquired of, I must state my own conviction honestly. I have done it, and given my reasons from the word of God. And now let me say, Brethren, we will have no contention on this point, for we be brethren.[3]

This statement indicates that considerable discussion on the time of the close of probation had been going on. Miller personally felt he had no need to continue to warn sinners, but was not willing to denounce as traitors to the movement those who believed otherwise and had resumed their work. He continued that the question of the Shut Door "if handled at all, it ought to be done very wisely." Because this was such a sensitive issue, care must be taken above all not to hurt the faith of the believers.[4]

---

[1]Ibid.

[2]Letter, William Miller to Joshua V. Himes and Sylvester Bliss, AH, December 18, 1844, p. 147; Letter, William Miller to I. E. Jones, AH, December 25, 1844, pp. 154-155.

[3]Letter, William Miller to Sylvester Bliss, AH, February 12, 1845, pp. 2-3.

[4]Ibid.

That his thinking was in a state of flux at the time is shown by comparing the statements in his letter to Bliss cited above, and a comment by Miller published in the Voice of Truth on February 19, 1845:

> Has Christ come in the sense of Matt. 25:10? I think he has. Was the contract finished, and when? My opinion is, that it was on or about the 10th of the seventh month. . . . There was a division line drawn then. . . . I have not seen a genuine conversion since. . . . If I am correct, you will see a general and powerful struggle among our nominal sects, for revivals in a short time; but it will prove a failure, no one will be made truly pious. They will knock and say, Lord! Lord! open unto us. They will make many pharisaical prayers, but will not be heard. And soon the Savior will come in person.[1]

Within three weeks of the publication of the latter statement, Miller changed his mind. Writing on March 10, 1845, he declared, "I think at present the evidence is strong against the idea of the door being shut." The reason given for his new opinion was the fact that reports had been reaching him of conversions.[2] He even claimed:

> I have ever been of the opinion, that my first and last view of that parable, as given in my lectures, is the true exposition. That parable was never given to show the exact order or time of marriage and shutting of the door.[3]

----

[1]Letter, William Miller to Joseph Marsh, VT, quoted in D-S, March 11, 1845, p. 13. Presumably Miller was influenced by the ridicule he and his associates had faced after the Disappointment. The opposition the Millerites faced from the churches apparently convinced them that any show of piety by members of the "nominal" sects was not genuine.

[2]Letter, William Miller to My Dear Brother, MW, March 20, 1845, p. 91.

[3]Ibid. Cf. William Miller, Evidence from Scripture and History of the Second Coming of Christ, About the Year 1843: Exhibited in a Course of Lectures (Troy, N.Y.: Kemble & Hooper, 1836), pp. [189]-207.

A few days later, he pleaded with those who had supposed the door to be shut to yield their position in order to avoid conflict with their brethren and the guilt of denying the working of the Holy Spirit.[1] It would seem he was also later reluctant or embarrassed to admit he had ever held the Shut Door position himself.[2]

The change in Miller's thinking serves to demonstrate the struggle that took place in the minds of some of the Millerite leaders to come to terms with the Disappointment. In contrast to Miller, it seems that Himes and Bliss opposed the Shut Door concept from immediately after the time of the Disappointment. As they assumed that they had been mistaken on the exact time of the Advent, it and the close of probation must still be future, they reasoned. Thus, in the editorial columns of the Advent Herald, December 1844, they wrote:

> Already our friends are sending in new subscribers . . . [and] we are happy to know that the efforts of our enemies to destroy us have gained the sympathy of many who had been indifferent, have made us many new friends, and greatly strengthened our old ones.[3]

---

[1]Letter, Miller to "My Dear Brother," MW, March 20, 1845, p. 91.

[2]Cf. Himes's statement concerning Miller's opinions: "For a little time, he cherished some views, relating to the door of mercy, and the coming of the Bridegroom, that were not in strict accordance with the above principle of exposition. The peculiar, and the striking circumstances of the time, led him into the view. But, the fact of souls being converted, in different places, as formerly, at once showed the mistake which he readily and cheerfully corrected" (Joshua V. Himes, "Editorial Correspondence," MW, April 3, 1845, p. 110). According to Rowe, "Thunder and Trumpets" (1974), pp. 224-276, Miller's change of mind came about in part as a result of pressure from Himes and Bliss to renounce the Shut Door.

[3]Editorial, "The Tide Turning," AH, December 11, 1844, p. 141. Hale is also on the masthead as co-editor, but as he also shared editorial duties of the Advent Mirror with Joseph Turner,

At the Low Hampton Conference of Adventists, held December
28-29, 1844, Himes recognized three ways the Millerites could
properly carry on gospel labor:

> 1. Comforting the saints who are still looking for the kingdom
> at hand. 2. The arousing once more of the professed Christian
> world to the examination and preparation for the advent. 3. The
> full and free proclamation of salvation to the lost and perishing
> sinner.[1]

Obviously, until the moderates had come to the conclusion
that salvation was still available to all, there would have been no
need in their minds to continue, establish anew, or even discuss an
organizational structure suited to missionary activity. Those who
maintained some form of Shut Door theory for a longer period would
have been even less disposed to any thought of organizing for future
evangelism.[2] Thus, Himes argued that the Shut Door inhibited plans
for current gospel work. He wrote: "The idea that our work is done,

---

which advocated Shut Door ideas in its January 1845 edition (see
Apollos Hale and Joseph Turner, "Has Not the Savior Come As a
Bridegroom?" AM, January 1845, p. [3]), we cannot associate Hale's
name with Himes's and Bliss's opinions expressed the month before.
By the time of the Albany Conference, Hale had changed his position,
claiming that the 2300 days had not expired, and he continued to set
further dates for the Second Advent (Apollos Hale, "Editorial Correspondence," AH, September 10, 1845, p. 10). On the Albany Conference,
see below, pp. 83-89.

[1]Editorial, "Low Hampton Conference," AH, January 15, 1845,
p. 182.

[2]One can only estimate what proportion of the Millerites
remained with the Advent movement after the Disappointment or how
many followed the leading of the "moderates" such as Miller and Himes
on the Shut Door. Arthur ("'Come Out of Babylon'" [1970], p. 88)
suggests that the majority remained with the Advent movement as the
humiliation would have been too strong to return to the established
churches, and because they were assured by the leaders that the basis
for their faith was sure. An index to the situation may be obtained
by determining the editorial positions of the various periodicals in
the immediate post-Disappointment period. The Advent Herald and
Morning Watch, the most widely circulated, had rejected the Shut Door

prevails to some extent, which has prevented united and energetic labors for the spread of light and truth."[1]

The Parable of the Ten Virgins

Jesus' parable of the wise and foolish virgins had long been a prominent part of Millerite theology, and repeated attempts were made to historicize the details of the parable and identify them with specific events associated with the expected Advent. As early as 1836, Miller associated the shutting of the door (Matt 25:10) with the close of human probation, also implicit in Rev 22:11. The closing of this door, he said, would take place shortly before Christ's return.[2] Miller's reasoning was based upon Rev 10:5-7 which describes an angel who swore "that there should be time no longer." Identifying this angel with Christ,[3] Miller argued that the end of time spoken of by the angel was the moment when "the gospel or mediatorial time should cease." At that moment, Miller continued, there would be

> no more time for mercy . . . for Jesus has sworn by himself . . . that your day of probation "should be no longer." For "he that is filthy shall be filthy still" [Rev 22:11]. The bridegroom has come and shut to [sic] the door.[4]

---

by December 1844, or early in 1845. Damsteegt (Foundations, p. 109) lists the papers which promoted the Shut Door, 1844-1846. The Day-Star was the most outspoken supporter of the Shut Door (and hence the validity of the Seventh Month movement). The others were the Jubilee Standard, Hope of Israel, Hope Within the Veil, Voice of the Shepherd, Advent Testimony, and the True Day Star.

[1]Joshua V. Himes, "Editorial Correspondence," AH, February 5, 1845, p. 205.

[2]Miller, Evidence from Scripture and History (1836), pp. 193-207.

[3]Ibid., p. 97.   [4]Ibid.

Storrs and other Millerite leaders also applied the parable to the experience of the Millerites _before_ the Disappointment. Unlike Miller, who had identified the ten virgins with mankind in general,[1] Storrs said that they symbolized the professed believers in the Advent in 1843.[2] After the first disappointment, he maintained, the believers entered a time of waiting (the tarrying time of the parable) and were awakened from their sleep by the True Midnight Cry which was associated with the Seventh Month movement.

The parable continued to play an important role in Millerite theology after the Disappointment and became one of the primary tools used to explain their error.[3] The classic extant exposition of the parable in this way was written by Apollos Hale and Joseph Turner under the title "Has Not the Bridegroom Come?"[4] We may summarize the intent of their article in two main points: (1) they admitted "a very natural mistake" in their preaching prior to October 22, 1844, but the mistake was _not_ one of time; (2) basing their interpretation on Luke 12:35-37 and Dan 7:9-14, they proposed that on October 22 Christ went to the Ancient of Days as the Bridegroom to receive the kingdom. Thus, on that day Christ experienced a "change in his heavenly state" shortly before "returning from the

---

[1]Ibid.

[2]George Storrs, "'Go Ye Out to Meet Him,'" Bible Examiner, September 24, 1844, p. [1].

[3]For detailed information on the many nuances in post-Disappointment interpretations of the parable see Damsteegt, Foundations, pp. 44, 96-98; "Open and Shut Door," SDA Encyclopedia (1976), 10:1034-1037.

[4]Hale and Turner, "Has Not the Savior Come?" pp. [1-4].

wedding" in glory.[1] Furthermore, they said, "our history is a perfect fulfillment of the parable."[2]

The Shut Door Among Non-Sabbatarian Millerites

An integral part of Hale's and Turner's "Bridegroom come" theory was a statement in the parable, "and the door was shut" (Matt 25:10). "By this act," they wrote, "is undoubtedly denoted the exclusion from all further access to saving mercy, those who have rejected offers during their time of probation."[3] It was therefore concluded that the possibility of further conversions no longer existed and to continue to work for sinners was worse than useless-- it would evince a rejection of the Seventh Month movement. In the words of J. D. Pickands, another earnest supporter of the Shut Door, Adventists were faced with the dilemma either "to deny the reality of sound conversions, as reported by our brethren, or to deny the whole history of Adventism."[4]

The contemporary religious situation (that is, religious indifference or opposition to their message) only strengthened their opinion that "spiritual death" had followed for all who had rejected the Seventh Month movement. Even the apparent conversions, the reports of which turned Miller and others away from the Shut Door,

---

[1]Ibid., p. [1].   [2]Ibid., p. [2].

[3]Ibid., p. [3].

[4]Letter, J. D. Pickands to S. S. Snow, JS, June 19, 1845, p. 120. Other enthusiastic supporters of the Shut Door included Enoch Jacobs, editor of the Day-Star; J. B. Cook; Snow and B. Matthias, editors of the Jubilee Standard; and Marsh, editor of the Voice of Truth.

were put down to external changes only.[1] Hale's and Turner's position denied the possibility of conversion, not only for those who had consciously rejected the True Midnight Cry but for the whole world. The two following excerpts from the article make this clear:

> But can any sinners be converted if the door is shut[?] Of course they cannot.
> But to think of laboring to convert the great mass of the world at such a time, would be as idle as it would have been for the Israelites, when they were down by the Red sea, to have turned about to convert the Egyptians.[2]

Turner claimed, therefore, that preaching to "a fallen church and a rejected world" is like "preaching in the tombs."[3]

It is important to note that the thinking of these individuals was in a state of flux during the last part of 1844 and, for some, throughout 1845. We have observed that Miller relinquished his Shut Door ideas by March 1845. Marsh and Hale also gave up their positions on the matter by the time of the Albany Conference in April 1845. Enoch Jacobs, on the other hand, at first opposed the Shut Door but later was convinced, by the lack of interest in spiritual things he observed in Christian circles, that the door had indeed been shut.[4]

---

[1]Hale and Turner, "Has Not the Savior Come?" pp. [3-4].

[2]Ibid., p. [4].

[3]Hope of Israel, January 24, 1845, as quoted in Wellcome, History of the Second Advent Message, p. 398.

[4]For details on the positions of these and other individuals on the Shut Door, see Arthur, "'Come Out of Babylon'" (1970), pp. 106-111. Cf. [Joseph Marsh], "Door of Mercy," VT, February 26, 1845, p. 19; William Miller, Sylvester Bliss, and Apollos Hale, "Advent Conference in Boston," MW, June 19, 1845, p. 198. The Morning Watch account of an Advent Conference held May 26-29, 1845, refers to a statement by Hale denying that he had ever believed that the Bridegroom had come and shut the door! (cf. above, pp. 77-78). On

It is not necessary for our purpose to develop further the question of the Shut Door as it affected the attitudes of the non-Sabbatarian Adventists. From the evidence cited above, it would seem that several former Millerites, who did not renounce their faith entirely, held for a short time some concept of an end of human probation in relation to the tenth day of the seventh month. Those who maintained this position believed their work for "a wicked world, and a corrupt, apostate, world-loving church"[1] was done, and it simply remained for them as they awaited the Second Coming "to comfort one another."[2]

The Albany Conference

Faced with the threat of the complete disintegration of Millerism, the leaders called an Advent Conference, which opened in Albany, New York, on April 29, 1845. The meeting was convened, as Miller stated after the event, "to deliberate respecting, and if possible to extricate ourselves from the anarchy and confusion of BABYLON in which we had so unexpectedly found ourselves."[3]

Jacobs's position see [Enoch Jacobs], "The Time," WMC, November 29, 1844, p. 20. Jacobs's editorial policy was to publish a variety of viewpoints including the Shut Door. His own position was not a dogmatic one. As an example of his point of view, see [Enoch Jacobs], "Intolerance," WMC, December 30, 1844, p. 30.

[1][S. S. Snow], "The Laodicean Church," JS, June 12, 1845, p. 108.

[2]Ibid.

[3]Miller, "The Albany Conference," p. 129. One can imagine how disconcerting it must have been for those who had issued the call to "come out of Babylon" to find themselves wrangling in much the same way as the "nominal" churches over doctrinal issues. The attempted solution to the problem was to convene a series of conferences, the one at Albany, New York, in April 1845 being the most

A ten-point statement of "Important Truths" was produced, which it was hoped would end the splintering of the movement and terminate the fanatical practices springing up among them.[1] Included in the ten propositions was an affirmation that according to prophetic chronology Christ's coming is "emphatically nigh." They also declared that the Advent message must continue to be preached, explicitly denying the idea of the Shut Door.[2] There were other positions taken that had particular relevance to the question of organization. It was stated that the present duty of Adventists was to build up the household of God and to preach the gospel to every creature. However, a resolution was passed to abandon the use of camp meetings as a method of evangelization, because the original purpose of holding camp meetings--to awaken general interest--had been accomplished. Calls were also made "for the Advent congregations to unite under Apostolic order and discipline." In addition, two men were ordained to the gospel ministry and plans were made for future operations.[3] The statement on the organization of the movement reads as follows:

---

significant. Some sixty delegates met including Himes, Litch, Bliss, Hale, Galusha, and Lorenzo D. Fleming. On the actions of the Conference, see "Mutual Conference of Adventists at Albany," MW, May 8, 1845, pp. 149-152; VT, May 21, 1845, pp. 57-59; Damsteegt, Foundations, pp. 113-114; Arthur, "'Come Out of Babylon'" (1970), pp. 129-145.

[1]It is ironic that the proposed solution to the confusion among Adventists should be a statement of belief that, much like the despised creeds of the churches, only served to deepen the divisions among them.

[2]"Mutual Conference," VT, May 21, 1845, p. 58.

[3]Ibid., pp. 57-59.

Order is heaven's first law.   All things emanating from God, are
constituted on principles of perfect order.   The New Testament
rules for the government of the church, we regard as binding on
the whole brotherhood of Christ.   No circumstances can justify us
in departing from the usages established by Christ and his
Apostles.

We regard any congregation of believers who habitually
assemble for the worship of God, and the due observance of the
gospel ordinances, as a church of Christ.   As   such, it is an
independent body, accountable only to the great Head of the
Church.--To all such we recommend a careful examination of the
Scriptures, and the adoption of such principles of association
and order, as are in accordance therewith, that they may enjoy
the advantages of that church relation which Christ has
instituted.[1]

The system of church order proposed at Albany clearly

reflected the congregational method of organization, in that the Body

of Christ is fully represented in each local church and each

congregation is independent of any higher authority than Christ

Himself.[2]

One can recognize a development in attitude toward creeds or

statements of belief at the Albany Conference.   At the first Advent

Conference, held in Boston on October 14 and 15, 1840, all that was

required of the delegates was a declared belief in the soon return of

Christ.[3]   At Albany, some four and a half years later, issues such as

the restoration of the Jews and the nature of man and immortality

were included.   A major factor in this change of opinion was the

perceived danger of heresy and schism within the ranks which drove

delegates to a more precise definition of their beliefs than would

otherwise have been needed.[4]

---

[1]Ibid., p. 58.   [2]Cf. above, pp. 23-24.

[3]Cf. above, p. 40.

[4]Rowe, "Thunder and Trumpets" (1974),   p. 277, suggests that
the two major purposes of the Conference were (1) to formalize a

It is also clear that Millerites had been held together as a community by a single issue--their characteristic belief in the Second Coming. The Disappointment called this issue into question and thus removed the primary basis of their unity. The leaders, therefore, felt obliged to hold the group together by outlining other fundamental beliefs which were shared by the majority.

One should also consider that as long as the Millerites were members in good standing of the Methodist, Baptist, and other churches they affirmed their belief in the doctrines of those churches and felt no need of making a separate declaration of faith. Once they had left or been expelled from their churches, the Adventists were faced with the fact that there was no accepted norm of orthodoxy in their midst. Everyone was free to interpret or misinterpret the Bible on his own and to promote his ideas in the name of Adventism. The Albany Conference sought to correct this situation.

---

creed and (2) to condemn the radicals and their practices. It would seem that while these were the end results of the Conference, the first purpose, in particular, as stated by Rowe, was not consciously held by the leaders beforehand. Interpretations of the significance of the Albany Conference are varied. Most positive is Rowe's (pp. 284-285) which credits the Conference with enabling Adventists to avoid the total splintering of the movement and to survive until public prejudice against them waned and they could organize into a number of sects. Arthur ("'Come Out of Babylon'" [1970], pp. 116-122) is not so sure, but puts the blame for the failure of the Conference, or at least the delay in achieving its goals, on the radicals who refused to give up their fanatical practices. As some of the practices condemned included foot washing and the Sabbath, which were to become part of Sabbatarian Adventist doctrine, it is understandable that evaluations by Seventh-day Adventist authors of the Albany Conference have been generally negative. See Schwarz, Light Bearers, p. 56; Nichol, The Midnight Cry, p. 298; Froom, Prophetic Faith, 4:833-837; Damsteegt, Foundations, pp. 114-115.

Even so, the Conference did not end debate among the
Adventists. The chief objection to the proceedings of the meeting at
Albany came from Marsh, who had not been present but who criticized
the statement of beliefs as it appeared in the Millerite papers.
While he approved most of the actions at Albany, especially the move
toward church order, he disagreed with the designation of the
followers of Miller as "Adventists." Any name other than "Church of
God," he said, dishonors God because it is unscriptural and of human
origin. The statement of beliefs, he continued, amounted to a creed
which, as a human law, was an invasion of God's prerogatives, a
barrier to the unity of the churches, and imperfect, if not sinful,
in origin.[1]

Both Miller and Himes responded to Marsh's comments, defend-
ing vigorously the actions of the Albany Conference.[2] Miller
attempted to refute each of Marsh's main criticisms. The name
"Adventists," he said, was never intended as an appellation of
distinction, and in any case was no more exclusive than the name
"Church of God" (the title favored by Marsh), which was used as a
denominational name by other groups anyway. Furthermore, Miller
argued, the name "Adventist" did not imply that there were no others
who were Adventists, even though they had not attended or agreed to

---

[1][Joseph Marsh], "The Albany Conference," VT, May 21, 1845,
pp. 61-62. Cf. Joseph Marsh, "Existence of Creeds a Reason Why We
Should Not Go Back to the Church," VT, April 30, 1845, pp. 33-35.

[2]Letter, William Miller to Joshua V. Himes, MW, June 12,
1845, pp. 190-192. Himes responded to Miller's published letter with
similar comments in private correspondence addressed to Miller (see
Rowe, "Thunder and Trumpets" [1974], pp. 279-281).

everything done at Albany.[1] Responding to the expressed opinion
that Adventists should have no creed but the Bible, he wrote:

> The objector replies, we want nothing short of the entire
> Scriptures for our creed; they alone are sufficient. And they
> alone are sufficient for me. But while I receive the entire word
> of God according to my understanding of its teachings . . . have
> I no right to inform the world what I conceive to be the truths
> it inculcates?[2]

Clearly, the distinction in Miller's mind between a creed and a
statement of beliefs was that a creed was devised as a means of
separation between denominations, while a statement of beliefs was
intended to be a means of witness to the world.[3]

We find in this letter of Miller's what is probably the most
carefully stated definition of the church or, to be more precise, "a
church," to be found in his writings. It consists of "any
congregation of believers who habitually assemble for the worship of
God, and the due observance of the gospel ordinances as a church of
Christ."[4] Miller's definition and the statement of the Albany
Conference on organization demonstrate the inclination of the
Millerites toward a congregational structure and manifest the
influential role of Baptists and members of the Christian Church at
Albany.[5] Miller also found support for this way of designating and

---

[1]Letter, William Miller to Joshua V. Himes, MW, June 12,
1845, pp. 190-192.

[2]Ibid., p. 191.

[3]Cf. our discussion below (pp. 153-154) on the original
covenant signed by Seventh-day Adventists in October 1861.

[4]Letter, William Miller to Joshua V. Himes, MW, June 12,
1845, p. 190.

[5]Cf. above, pp. 28-32.

organizing a church in the New Testament. He noted that the church
in the New Testament was usually addressed by its local name, such as
"the church at Jerusalem."[1]

Miller concluded his arguments by presenting a clear choice
for his readers: "Shall we continue in the anarchy in which we have
been, or shall we take gospel measures to restore gospel order, that
at the Master's coming we may be approved of him?"[2]

A Need for Planning and Order

One of the main purposes of the Millerites as they sought to
hold together the movement after the Disappointment was to end the
confusion that had suddenly risen among them.[3] Having separated
from the established churches themselves, it was not easy for them to
forget the reasons for that separation, such as the ridicule they
faced, or the accusations of apostasy they had directed toward the
churches. When we remember, too, the antipathy they had expressed
toward divisive creeds, it is no wonder that they were reluctant to
organize themselves into a new denomination. Arthur suggests several

---

[1]Letter, William Miller to Joshua V. Himes, MW, June 12,
1845, p. 190. Others expressed the same ideas in correspondence
addressed to the Morning Watch. For example, one wrote, "Then let
us . . . come together in the order of the congregations at
Jerusalem, Samaria, Ephesus, Corinth, etc., etc." (Letter, "Z" to
Joshua V. Himes, MW, February 27, 1845, p. 70). On this point, Marsh
was also in agreement, supporting a congregational form of church
order ([Marsh], "The Albany Conference," pp. 61-62).

[2]Letter, Miller to Himes, MW, June 12, 1845, p. 192. It is
worth noting once again the similarity of Miller's language to
White's (see below, p. 130).

[3]Ibid., p. 190. Miller expresses this point explicitly,
that the end of confusion was the purpose of convening the Albany
Conference.

other reasons for their disinclination to unite as a church body,
including (1) the presence within the movement of several strong-
minded personalities, (2) the appearance of several new and divisive
doctrines, (3) conflict and competition among the various Millerite
periodicals, (4) fear of leadership and discipline, and (5) a rising
sectarian spirit.[1]

While Arthur's comments may be valid, it should be pointed
out that the Millerites in general were not anti-organizational in
their attitude. They did not wish initially to form another denomination, but were not averse to efficient planning and order for their
work. The heat of the controversies and struggles with the established churches in 1843 and 1844 led, for a short time, to extreme
positions' being expressed by some against organization, but even
then it was the existence of sectarian human creeds rather than
organization per se that the Millerites condemned.[2] From the

---

[1]Arthur, "'Come Out of Babylon'" (1970), p. v. We agree
that each of the points made by Arthur was an important factor at
Albany. We agree, too, that the Conference "made the division among
Adventists more permanent" (p. 139). However, his accusation that
the fanatical elements within the movement were responsible in large
part for its disintegration (pp. 116-122) is unwarranted. We have
observed above (pp. 84-85) that the formulation of a statement of
belief was a radical departure from earlier Millerite attitudes
toward "divisive creeds" and made the splintering of the Millerite
movement inevitable. It is hardly fair, either, to link together
under the same heading of "fanatical practices" such dissimilar
doctrines or activities as foot washing, the holy salutation, the
Sabbath, and spiritual wifery.

[2]See, e.g., Storrs's position, above, pp. 52-54. It should
be noted that Himes was the most influential leader in Adventism by
the time of the Albany Conference. Miller's poor health prevented
him from playing as important a role as before, and Himes's
background as a Christian Connection minister is reflected in the
congregational structure of Adventism and its desire to avoid
sectarian creeds.

perspective of church organization, the post-Disappointment Millerites arrived at a system of church government which was essential at the time for their survival.[1] This congregational form was chosen on the basis of its perceived fidelity to the New Testament pattern, and because it provided as much autonomy as possible while helping to allay fears that any organization would in time become "Babylon." It also reflected the denominational background of leaders such as Himes and Miller, who belonged to, or had belonged to, congregationally organized churches.

The Emergence of Sabbatarian Adventism

The Development of Seventh-day Adventism's Distinctive Doctrines

We turn our attention now to the beginnings of the movement which would develop into the Seventh-day Adventist Church. At the time of the Disappointment, none of those who were to become prominent leaders of Seventh-day Adventism had accepted the seventh-day Sabbath.[2] It is generally held that the Sabbath was first introduced to those who were to become Seventh-day Adventist pioneers at Washington, New Hampshire, by Rachel Oakes, a Seventh Day Baptist,

---

[1]One should not conclude that the Albany Conference solved Adventism's organizational problems. On the contrary, dissension, strife, additional date setting, and dwindling numbers plagued the movement throughout the rest of the decade and the 1850s as well (see Arthur, "'Come Out of Babylon'" [1970], pp. 280-371).

[2]Hereafter, we shall simply speak of the seventh day as "the Sabbath." We are aware that Frederick Wheeler, who accepted the Sabbath in March 1844, later served as a Seventh-day Adventist minister. However, his role in the formation of Seventh-day Adventist doctrine and the development of the organization of the Church was not as significant as, for example, the parts played by the Whites or Bates (see "Wheeler, Frederick," SDA Encyclopedia [1976], 10:1584, for a biographical sketch).

sometime in the winter of 1843-1844.[1] However, the Sabbath was regarded by virtually all Millerites before the Disappointment as an additional, unnecessary burden which would only divert attention from the one important issue, Christ's imminent return.[2] In the spring of 1845, Bates became convinced of the validity of the Sabbath after reading a tract by Thomas M. Preble and visiting Washington, New Hampshire, to study the subject with the small group of Sabbath-keepers there.[3] Still, Sabbatarian Adventists did not become identifiable as a distinct group until several closely-related themes were integrated with the Sabbath--the sanctuary doctrine, the third angel's message, and recognition of spiritual gifts--especially the gift of prophecy in the experience of Ellen G. White.

The Sabbath and sanctuary doctrines

The earliest insight into the Disappointment seems to have come to Hiram Edson. He said that on October 23, 1844, while on his way to encourage some fellow believers, he felt impressed that a mistake had been made in their understanding of the manner and

---

[1]See, e.g., accounts in Damsteegt, Foundations, pp. 136-146; "Sabbath," SDA Encyclopedia (1976), 10:1250-1253; Maxwell, Tell It to the World, pp. 67-94; Froom, Prophetic Faith, 4:941-962; Gordon O. Martinborough, "The Beginnings of a Theology of the Sabbath Among American Sabbatarian Adventists, 1842-1850," (M.A. thesis, Loma Linda University, 1976), pp. 29-49.

[2]See, e.g., Editorial, "'The Lord's Day,'" MC, September 5, 1844, pp. 68-69; September 12, 1844, pp. 76-77.

[3]Thomas M. Preble, A Tract, Showing That the Seventh Day Should Be Observed As the Sabbath, Instead of the First Day; "According to the Commandment" (Nashua, N.H.: Murray and Kimball, 1845). On the experience of Preble and Bates in discovering the Sabbath, see Maxwell, Tell It to the World, pp. 74-76.

location of Christ's coming as the Bridegroom, but not in the matter

of time. He remembered years later that

> Heaven seemed open to my view, and I saw distinctly, and clearly,
> that instead of our High Priest coming out of the Most Holy of
> the heavenly sanctuary to come to this earth on the tenth day of
> the seventh month, at the end of the 2300 days, that He for the
> first time entered on that day the second apartment of that
> sanctuary; and that He had a work to perform in the Most Holy
> before coming to this earth. That he came to the marriage at
> that time; in other words, to the Ancient of days to receive a
> kingdom, dominion, and glory; and we must wait for his return
> from the wedding.[1]

Edson claimed that orthodox Christianity had been wrong in

equating the coming of the Bridegroom to the marriage (Matt 25:10)

with the personal Second Advent of Christ. He connected the coming

of the Son of Man to the Ancient of Days (Dan 7:13-14) with the

coming of Christ as the High Priest to the Most Holy of the heavenly

sanctuary. Thus, according to Edson, Christ came to the "marriage,"

that is, to receive the kingdom on the tenth day of the seventh

month, 1844. It was the present duty of Adventists, he believed, to

wait for Christ's return from the marriage (cf. Luke 12:35-37).[2]

This exposition became the key to the Sabbatarian Adventists'

explanation of the Disappointment and, with minor differences and

---

[1]Hiram Edson, MS, "Experience in the Advent Movement," n.d.,
p. 9, Ellen G. White Estate Branch Office, Andrews University,
Berrien Springs, Mich. Recent questions have been raised about the
accuracy of Edson's autobiographical account written many years after
the event (see, e.g., Maxwell, Tell It to the World, pp. 51-52; and
Damsteegt, Foundations, p. 117). However, the overall theological
position of Edson's account coincides with the ideas published by
O. R. L. Crosier in "The Law of Moses," D-S, Extra, February 7, 1846,
pp. 37-44. This article was written as a result of the combined
study of Crosier, Edson, and Dr. F. B. Hahn.

[2]Edson, MS, "Experience in the Advent Movement," n.d., pp.
8-9. It is clear that Edson held the same interpretation as Hale and
Turner on this point (cf. above, pp. 80-81).

adjustments, has remained the basis of Seventh-day Adventist sanctuary theology. The principal themes of Edson, Crosier, and F. B. Hahn, as expressed in the February 7, 1846, Day-Star Extra article, also appeared in the writings of Ellen G. Harmon. She published accounts of her first two major visions, received in December 1844 and February 1845, respectively, based on the concept of a literal two-apartment sanctuary in heaven and expressed in terms of the coming of the Bridegroom to the marriage and of a transition of Christ's ministry from the Holy to the Most Holy Place.[1] Shortly after the publication of Crosier's article, Ellen G. Harmon (by this time Ellen G. White) received confirmation in vision that Crosier's understanding of the sanctuary doctrine was correct.[2]

Later, the doctrine of the Sabbath was incorporated into sanctuary theology through the writings of Bates and encouraged by visions of Ellen G. White.[3] On at least two separate occasions (March 6 and April 3, 1847), the latter saw a representation of the sanctuary in heaven with the ark in the Holy of Holies containing the ten commandments and a halo of light shining around the Sabbath commandment. This description confirmed and built on the works of

---

[1]Letters, Ellen G. Harmon to Enoch Jacobs, D-S, January 24, 1846, pp. 31-32; March 14, 1846, p. 7.

[2]Letter, Ellen G. White to Eli Curtis, A Word to the "Little Flock" (Brunswick, Me.: James White, May 1847; facsimile reproduction, Washington, D.C.: Review and Herald Pub. Assn, [1944]), pp. 11-14. The letter was written on April 21.

[3]Joseph Bates, The Seventh-day Sabbath, A Perpetual Sign, from the Beginning, to the Entering into the Gates of the Holy City, According to the Commandment, 2nd ed., rev. and enl. (New Bedford, Mass.: Benjamin Lindsey, 1847), p. iv. An account of Ellen G. White's visions may be found in Early Writings (Washington, D.C.: Review and Herald Pub. Assn, 5th ed., 1963), pp. 32-35. Bates also

Preble and Bates,[1] which stressed the perpetuity of the decalogue
and (especially in the case of Bates) suggested that the new interest
in the Sabbath after 1840 was a partial fulfillment of Daniel's
prophecy that knowledge would be increased in the time of the end
(Dan 12:4) and of the prophecy in Rev 11:19 of the opened temple in
heaven, in which was revealed the ark of the testament.[2]

The Sabbath and the third angel's message

Some Millerites had understood the three angels' messages
(Rev 14:6-11) to be the final warnings to be preached before the
return of Christ. The first angel's message (Rev 14:6-7) proclaimed
that the hour of God's judgment (in the Millerites' view an event
simultaneous to the Advent) was at hand. The second angel (vs. 8)
announced the fall of mystical Babylon, while the third (vss. 9-11)
pronounced divine wrath upon those who received "the mark of the
beast."[3] All three of these messages, Bates believed for a while,

---

published an account of the April 3 vision in his broadside,
A Vision (New Bedford, Mass.: Benjamin Lindsey, 1847).

[1]On Preble's role in the beginnings of Seventh-day Adventist
Sabbath theology, see Raymond F. Cottrell, "The Sabbath in the New
World," in The Sabbath in Scripture and History, ed. Kenneth A.
Strand (Washington, D.C.: Review and Herald Pub. Assn, 1982),
p. 248. On Bates's influential contributions to Sabbath doctrine,
see C. Mervyn Maxwell, "Joseph Bates and SDA Sabbath Theology," in
The Sabbath in Scripture and History, pp. 352-363.

[2]Bates, The Seventh-day Sabbath, A Perpetual Sign, 2nd ed.
(1847), pp. iii-iv. Cf. Maxwell, "Joseph Bates and SDA Sabbath
Theology," p. 356.

[3]For examples of Millerite interpretations of Rev 14:6-11,
see Henry Dana Ward, "To the Conference of Christians Expecting the
Lord's Appearing Convened in Boston 30th Nov., 1841," ST, January 1,
1842, pp. 145-147; Litch, The Probability of the Second Coming of
Christ, pp. 185-187; William Miller, "Miller's Lectures--No. 1," ST,
July 1, 1840, pp. 49-51.

were completed by the time of the Disappointment in 1844.[1]

After the Disappointment, Bates came to the conclusion in 1847 that those who worshipped "the beast and its image" were the ones who rejected the seventh-day Sabbath.[2] White was the first to suggest, in 1847, that the third angel's message was being proclaimed after "the 7th month 1844" and that those who kept "the commandments of God" were the ones who had paid heed to the warning of the third angel and had begun to observe the Sabbath.[3]

Another facet of Sabbatarian Adventist theology was added in the years 1848 and 1849, when the Sabbath was associated with "the seal of the living God." Bates, writing late in 1847, was the first to speak of the seal of God (Rev 7:1-3), identifying it with "character development."[4] As a result of a vision she received in November 1848, Ellen G. White identified "the seal of the living God"

---

[1]On the Millerite interpretation of the three angels' messages, see Damsteegt, Foundations, pp. 45-48.

[2]Bates, The Seventh-day Sabbath, A Perpetual Sign, 2nd ed. (1847), p. 59; A Vision. Cf. "Three Angels' Messages," SDA Encyclopedia (1976), 10:1483-1484.

[3]James White, "Thoughts on Revelation 14," in A Word to the "Little Flock" (Brunswick, Me.: James White, May 1847; facsimile reproduction, Washington, D.C.: Review and Herald Pub. Assn, [1944]), p. 11. Bates soon adopted White's point of view, probably in 1850. See, e.g., Joseph Bates, "The Laodicean Church," RH, November 1850, p. 8. Cf. C. Mervyn Maxwell, "Sanctuary and Atonement in SDA Theology: An Historical Survey," in The Sanctuary and the Atonement: Biblical, Historical, and Theological Studies, ed. Arnold V. Wallenkampf and W. Richard Lesher (Washington, D.C.: Review and Herald Pub. Assn, 1981), p. 527.

[4]Joseph Bates, A Vindication of the Seventh-day Sabbath, and the Commandments of God: With a Further History of God's Peculiar People, from 1847 to 1848 (New Bedford, Mass.: Benjamin Lindsey, 1848), p. 96.

with the Sabbath.[1] Bates acknowledged this contribution, modified his own views, and elaborated on her insight, identifying the Sabbath as a sign between God and His people (Exod 31:13, 17). He argued that by keeping the Sabbath and the other nine commandments, God's people would be ready to be sealed and only then could they be delivered by Him in the time of trouble.[2] Thus, the terms "sealing message," "third angel's message," "present truth," and "Sabbath truth" came to be closely associated, and were used virtually synonymously to describe the content of the message Sabbatarian Adventists were to proclaim to those who would listen.

The spirit of prophecy

It was in December 1844 that Ellen G. Harmon received her first vision, which she believed was given by God as a means of encouraging the "scattered flock."[3] At first, her visions were greeted with a great deal of skepticism by other Adventists, including Bates. In the two years after the Disappointment she made the acquaintance of White, and they often travelled together with other leaders to encourage the believers. This produced some gossip about their relationship and so, in spite of misgivings that marriage was an unwise step in view of the anticipated imminent return of

---

[1]Ellen G. White, MS 3, 1849; Ellen G. White, "To Those Who Are Receiving the Seal of the Living God" (Broadside), January 31, 1849.

[2]Joseph Bates, A Seal of the Living God (New Bedford, Mass.: By the Author, 1849), pp. 24-26.

[3]See Ellen G. White, Life Sketches, pp. 64-68, for an account of her first vision.

Christ, they were married in August 1846. The Whites had heard of the arguments in favor of the Sabbath from Bates, but it was not until the autumn of 1846, when they studied Bates's new pamphlet The Seventh-day Sabbath, A Perpetual Sign, that they were convinced that they should observe the Sabbath. Later that same year, Bates accepted Ellen G. White's prophetic gift as valid, persuaded by the knowledge of astronomy revealed in one of her visions.[1]

Toward theological consolidation

It is evident, therefore, that the coalescence of the unique and foremost doctrines of Seventh-day Adventism--the eschatalogical understanding of the Sabbath in the context of the three angels' messages, the sanctuary, and the role of Ellen G. White as a messenger of God--did not take place until 1846-1848.[2] Clearly, one cannot look for any form of ecclesiological self-understanding or organization until at least this time. Indeed, it was not until about the year 1848 that all the unique Seventh-day Adventist beliefs

---

[1]Ibid., pp. 95-103. Cf. Godfrey T. Anderson, Outrider of the Apocalypse: Life and Times of Joseph Bates (Mountain View, Calif.: Pacific Press Pub. Assn, 1972), p. 63.

[2]Ellen G. White was not the framer of any of the key doctrines of Sabbatarian Adventism. She furnished timely counsel and advice and, on some occasions, confirmation of the correctness of new doctrinal insights through her "testimonies." In only rare instances did she provide new theological perspectives, such as the relationship between the Sabbath and the sealing message. For further discussion on Ellen G. White's role in the development of Seventh-day Adventist doctrine see Arthur L. White, Ellen G. White: Messenger to the Remnant, rev. ed. (Washington, D.C.: Review and Herald Pub. Assn, 1969), pp. 34-37. Cf. also below, pp. 100-102.

mentioned above could be found in any one individual.[1]

The 1848 conferences

During the year 1848 a series of conferences was held which enabled those who had accepted the new teachings to develop a new unity and identity.[2] Almost without exception, Seventh-day Adventist writers have rightly identified these meetings as pivotal to the survival of the Sabbatarian Adventist movement.[3] At the first of these conferences the speakers included Bates, who spoke on the commandments, and James White, who spoke on the Sabbath.[4] The third conference (at Volney, New York) was also very significant. Apparently, there was considerable diversity of opinion as the meeting got under way. Ellen G. White was shown in vision the errors of those

---

[1]Maxwell, Tell It to the World, p. 86, mentions a few small groups led by individuals such as Otis Nichols and Stockbridge Howland who accepted some of the main features of Seventh-day Adventism by 1846. Of course, as other doctrinal elements were not consolidated until 1848, their understanding of Sabbatarian Adventism was at a rudimentary level at that time.

[2]The commonly used description "Sabbath" conference is somewhat misleading. They did not meet only on the Sabbath day, nor was the Sabbath doctrine the only subject for study. Apparently, the term was first used by A. L. White in Ellen G. White: Messenger to the Remnant (Washington, D.C.: Review and Herald Pub. Assn, 1954), pp. 38-40.

[3]See, e.g., Froom, Prophetic Faith, 4:1021-1048; Schwarz, Light Bearers, pp. 67-69; Maxwell, Tell It to the World, pp. 95-98; Loughborough, The Great Second Advent Movement, pp. 267-275; A. L. White, Messenger to the Remnant (1969), pp. 38-40. The seven conferences were held at Rocky Hill, Conn.; Bristol, Conn.; Volney, N.Y.; Port Gibson, N.Y.; Rocky Hill, Conn. (again); Topsham, Me.; and Dorchester, Mass. between April and November 1848. Maxwell ("Joseph Bates and SDA Sabbath Theology," p. 358) is the only writer who lists the seventh (at Bristol, Conn.).

[4]Letter, James White to Brother and Sister Hastings, April 27, 1848.

holding divergent opinions and urged those present to unite upon the fundamentals of Sabbatarian Adventist doctrine.[1] Further important developments took place at the Dorchester, Massachusetts, conference, held in November 1848. One of the main topics under discussion then was the Sabbath as the seal of God (cf. Rev 7:1-3), and a vision of Ellen G. White's broadened their understanding of the subject.[2] After the same vision, she said to White:

> I have a message for you. You must begin to print a little paper and send it out to the people. Let it be small at first: but as the people read they will send you means with which to print, and it will be a success from the first. From this small beginning it was shown to me to be like streams of light that went clear round the world.[3]

Ellen G. White's vision at Dorchester is frequently described as "the publishing vision" because, as a result of her instructions to her husband, the first Sabbatarian Adventist periodical (Present Truth) was launched, the first number appearing in July 1849.[4] This was the forerunner of the Review and Herald and an eventual world-wide multitude of Seventh-day Adventist periodicals.

Gordon O. Martinborough has challenged the theory that the 1848 conferences laid the foundation for Seventh-day Adventist doctrine.[5] He argues that the Sabbath and Sanctuary doctrines were

---

[1]Ellen G. White, Life Sketches, pp. 110-111.

[2]Cf. above, pp. 96-97.

[3]Ellen G. White, Life Sketches, p. 125.

[4]At the same time Ellen G. White told Bates to publish another book on the Sabbath and the sealing work, Bates, A Seal of the Living God, p. 26.

[5]Martinborough, "Beginnings of a Theology of the Sabbath" (1976), pp. 125-145.

being formulated _before_ 1848 and the 1848 meetings were regarded by the leaders of Sabbatarian Adventism as an opportunity to proclaim the newly discovered "present truth." The essence of this truth is described by the phrase "The Sabbath and Shut Door."[1] The present writer accepts this part of Martinborough's thesis, as we have already demonstrated that doctrinal discussions were well under way before 1848. It is also probably true that the meetings may better be described as "evangelistic seminars" (to use Martinborough's phrase) rather than "conferences," at which the listeners were instructed in the new theological insights rather than being engaged in a collective search for truth.

One might point to Bates's booklet, _A Vindication of the Seventh-day Sabbath_, which was written late in the autumn of 1847 and published in January 1848, as evidence that the main features of Sabbatarian Adventist doctrine were already well advanced before the 1848 conferences.[2] In this work Bates identified the sealing process of Rev 7 with the development of character in the lives of believers and asserted that it had been going on during the years 1840-1848--the time since the Millerite movement had first come to widespread attention. In the same booklet Bates linked Christ's work of cleansing the heavenly sanctuary with the purification of the

---

[1]See below, pp. 103-109.

[2]Estimates vary on the number of believers in 1848. Loughborough declares that there were less than one hundred (_The Great Second Advent Movement_, p. 275). Attendance at the first of the 1848 conferences was less than 30, and no more than 40 attended any one conference, according to White (_Life Incidents_, pp. 271-275). A number of people attended more than one of the conferences, of course.

lives of God's people on earth in preparation for the Second Advent. Acceptance of the Sabbath message, according to Bates, was an essential part of this preparation. As we have mentioned above,[1] Ellen G. White's Dorchester vision clarified their understanding of the seal, although its basic foundations were laid as much as a year earlier by Bates.

The foregoing does not mean, nor does Martinborough wish to imply, that the 1848 meetings were unimportant. We would suggest they were significant for reasons other than those generally recognized by some in the past. These reasons are: (1) the main doctrinal features of Sabbatarian Adventism had been settled and, as Martinborough points out, accepted for the first time by several nuclei of believers in New England and New York State;[2] (2) these nuclei provided the "basic ingredient" for eventual organization of the Seventh-day Adventist Church;[3] (3) the position of the Whites and Bates had been established as the recognized leaders of the movement; (4) the authority of Ellen G. White's prophetic gift was more widely accepted as a result of her part in resolving successfully doctrinal disputes at the Volney, New York, conference; and

---

[1]Bates, A Vindication of the Sabbath, p. 96. Cf. Maxwell, "Joseph Bates and SDA Sabbath Theology," pp. 357-358.

[2]Cf. above, p. 92.

[3]Martinborough, "Beginnings of a Theology of the Sabbath" (1976), p. 145. He is wide of the mark, however, when he adds in the same context, "it [the basic ingredient of nuclei or clusters of believers] represented most of what was done by way of organization for the next thirteen years"! As is demonstrated in chapter four, several fundamental developments took place in the intervening years which represented significant changes from the situation that obtained in 1848.

(5) provision was made for an expansion of the work of Sabbatarian Adventism, especially through the publishing of a new periodical.

The Shut Door in Sabbatarian Adventism, 1844-1848

It has been observed[1] that any thought of developing a form of church organization among Sabbatarian Adventists was initially out of the question until some measure of unanimity had been arrived at on key doctrines. An additional and important factor among these same people was the concept of the Shut Door. We have avoided discussion on this issue as it affected Sabbatarian Adventists until this point because it deserves separate treatment, and also because a sketch of the gradual blending of doctrinal ideas that occurred during the same time serves as a useful backdrop to the Shut Door question.

At first the Sabbath-keepers shared in common with many other Millerites the opinion that human probation had closed on October 22, 1844.[2] By the spring of 1845, as we noticed, Miller and other moderates had decided that they had been wrong on the date set for Christ's coming. They did not question their assumption that the close of probation coincided with the Second Coming. Thus, the shutting of the door must, by definition, still be in the future.

Sabbatarian Adventists, on the other hand, insisted from the beginning that they had indeed been correct on the matter of time. This conviction that October 22, 1844, had a particular significance

---

[1]See above, pp. 98-99.

[2]Cf. above, p. 73.

in biblical prophecy was never abandoned by Seventh-day Adventists.

These, the Seventh-day Adventist Encyclopedia reports,

> . . . refused to "deny their past experience," as most of the others seemed to them to have done. They sought another meaning in it and arrived at the conclusion that the cleansing of the sanctuary was not the return of Christ but involved another phase of His priestly ministry before His return to this earth. . . [1]

This meant that, for a time, Sabbatarian Adventists believed the door of mercy had closed on that date and that there was no further opportunity for repentance for those who had rejected the Midnight Cry message or for the rest of the wicked world. White acknowledged this quite clearly as he reflected on his past experience: "It is vain for any man to deny that it was the universal belief of Adventists, in the autumn of 1844, that their work for the world was forever done."[2]

Two questions concerning the Shut Door remain for us to answer, however: (1) How long did this "extreme"[3] Shut Door view persist among Sabbatarian Adventists? (2) After it was abandoned, did a "modified" Shut Door idea continue in their ranks for awhile?

---

[1]"Seventh-Month Movement," SDA Encyclopedia (1976), 10:1338. Cf. also the most recent Seventh-day Adventist Statement of Beliefs, voted at the 1980 General Conference Session, in "Session Actions: Fundamental Beliefs of Seventh-day Adventists--Church Manual Revision," RH, May 1, 1980, p. 27.

[2]White, Life Incidents, p. 190.

[3]Cf. above, pp. 73-75. While we label the position of White and other Sabbatarians at this point as "extreme," there was one basic difference between their understanding of the Shut Door and that of the non-Sabbatarian "extremists." The latter claimed that Christ's work of atonement had ended in October 1844, but the Sabbatarians believed that the Day of Atonement had just begun. At that time, White and a few others believed that Christ's new work of

James White's Shut Door Views, 1844-1848

As White was the main figure in the development of Seventh-
day Adventist church organization, his views on the Shut Door are
particularly significant. Soon after the Disappointment, he
predicted Christ would return on the tenth day of the seventh month,
1845.[1] Under the moderating influence of Ellen G. Harmon, who
advised him on the basis of a vision that if he held to this position
he would be disappointed again, he relinquished the new date set for
the Advent shortly before the day arrived.[2]

Having been convinced that October 22, 1844, was indeed the
correct date, White expressed his opinion in the Day-Star, January
1846, that "the midnight cry was finished" and "the exhortation to

---

atonement was only for those who had not rejected the Seventh Month
message, but it did leave open the possibility of a later softening
of their position.

[1]Letter, James White to Enoch Jacobs, D-S, September 20,
1845, pp. 25-26. Cf. Damsteegt, Foundations, p. 156.

[2]White, Ellen G. White, and Bates, A Word to the "Little
Flock," p. 22. The debate over Ellen G. White's teaching on the Shut
Door has had a particularly contentious history, which is not central
to our study. She admitted that at first she believed the door of
mercy was closed to the world, but claimed that she forsook this
position as a result of her first vision in December 1844 (Ellen G.
White, MS 4, 1883). The evidence suggests that her understanding of
the future work of Sabbatarian Adventism gradually broadened from
1844 to 1851, but that she never taught on the basis of her visions
that probation had closed for the entire world. It is also apparent
that Ellen G. White's thinking was ahead of her fellow leaders, White
and Bates, on the issue of the Shut Door. Of several recent works
which have discussed the question of Ellen G. White and the Shut
Door, the most significant is by Rolf J. Poehler ("'. . . and the
Door was Shut': Seventh-day Adventists and the Shut Door Doctrine in
the Decade after the Great Disappointment" [Research paper, Andrews
University, 1978]). His thoughtful work has proved particularly
helpful to the present writer. See also Damsteegt, Foundations,
pp. 149-164; Ingemar Lindén, The Last Trump: An Historico-genetical

contend for the faith [Jude 20] is to us alone."[1] It appears from this statement that White believed at this time the door was shut to all who had rejected Millerite preaching or who had denied the validity of the Seventh Month movement since the Disappointment.

Later in 1846, he conducted a funeral where he found himself preaching to "ugly Congregationalists and Methodists." Aware that it might seem inconsistent to proclaim the gospel to those who had rejected the Millerites' teaching, he said:

> Do not think Brother James is getting formal or is going to try to convert people to the advent faith. No, it's too [late]. But it's our duty on some occasions to give a reason of our hope, I think even to swine.[2]

White's language must be viewed in terms of Christ's counsel not to "cast your pearls before swine." Nevertheless, the tone of his language leads one to conclude that he placed those who rejected the Millerite message in the same category as the hypocrites condemned by Jesus in the Sermon on the Mount (Matt 7:6). In August 1848 in another personal letter he wrote:

> My Brother and Sister, here is the standard to rally around. Jesus has left his mediatorial throne. He is now claiming His new kingdom. . . . So the Shut Door and Sabbath is the present truth. These truths will form and keep up the same work of distinction between us and unbelievers as God made in 1844.[3]

Study of Some Important Chapters in the Making and Development of the Seventh-day Adventist Church (Frankfurt am Main: Peter Lang, 1978), pp. 92-100; Robert W. Olson, "The 'Shut Door' Documents," Ellen G. White Estate, Washington, D.C., April 11, 1982.

[1]Letter, James White to Enoch Jacobs, D-S, January 24, 1846, p. 30.

[2]Letter, James White to Brother Collins, August 26, 1846.

[3]Letter, James White to the Hastingses, August 26, 1848.

A comparison of these two quotations appears to indicate that White did not change his opinion in the years 1846-1848. The first was made in the same month as his marriage to Ellen G. Harmon. Had her ideas made any difference in his thinking since? The phrase "Jesus has left his mediatorial throne" appears conclusive enough, yet even this seemingly categorical statement needs to be carefully interpreted. Some three years later (1851), he still spoke of Jesus' closing His mediatorial work for the world in 1844, yet in the same breath he could speak of salvation being accepted even by members of the established churches.[1] The key question to be asked is "Was White working to convert anyone to the Sabbatarian Adventist faith during the period from 1846 to 1848?" As the August 1848 letter was written in the midst of the important 1848 conferences to which White and his companions travelled with the "new light" of the Sabbath and other related teachings, it is clear that some (even if only sincere Millerites who had not yet accepted the Sabbath) could yet be converted. Yet, his point of view on the Shut Door was still in 1848 more exclusive than his wife's, and he considered his task was primarily to care for "the scattered flock,"[2] which was made up only of those who had not rejected the Millerites' message or given up their faith after the Disappointment.

---

[1]James White, [Editorial Correspondence], RH, April 7, 1851, p. 64. Cf. also below, pp. 112-113.

[2]Such phrases as "the little flock," "the scattered saints," and "the little remnant" were among the most common descriptive terms used by Sabbatarian Adventists until the end of the 1840s. Cf., e.g., Letter, James White to Enoch Jacobs, D-S, September 6, 1845, p. 17; Letter, James White to Sister Hastings, August 22, 1847.

At the end of 1848, Sabbatarian Adventists stood with a newly found doctrinal unity and an expanding sense of mission[1] that gradually included those outside Sabbatarian Adventist circles. An important factor in this change of thinking was an Ellen G. White vision in March 1849. Paraphrasing Rev 3:7-8 she wrote "that Jesus had shut the door in the Holy Place, and no man can open it; and that he had opened the door in the Most Holy, and no man can shut it."[2] Ellen G. White and other Sabbatarian Adventists came to use the Shut Door in reference to those who had consciously repudiated the Millerite message. The Open Door referred to the door of mercy, or of access to the Most Holy Place in the heavenly sanctuary. In this second apartment Jesus stands by the ark containing the ten commandments, Ellen G. White wrote, from which the light of the decalogue (especially the Sabbath) was shining out.[3] Thus, the

---

[1]Cf. Damsteegt's analysis of the expanding sense of mission among Sabbatarian Adventists. He sees the period from 1844 to 1848 as a time of doctrinal consolidation during which the Whites and Bates believed their task was to care for the "scattered flock." Once theological unity had been achieved in 1848 and the Shut Door concept modified to include individuals from outside Adventist circles, Sabbatarian Adventist missionary work began to grow. Damsteegt identifies 1849 as the year in which these developments emerged, although "it was not until 1850 that the new mission efforts had success" (Foundations, pp. 161-164).

[2]Letter, Ellen G. White to Dear Brethren and Sisters, PT, August 1849, p. 21. The primary emphasis of this new concept was the presence of the ten commandments, including the Sabbath, in the Most Holy and that the Sabbath was indeed "present truth." As we have seen, the shut door of the Holy Place did not exclude all possibility of future repentance; rather, the Sabbath was to be the issue over which eternal decisions were to be made.

[3]Letter, Ellen G. White to Dear Brethren and Sisters, PT, August 1849, p. 21.

"Sabbath and Shut Door" came to be integrated with Sabbatarian Adventist Sanctuary doctrine.

Seventh-day Adventism has never entirely renounced the idea that those who rejected the Advent message in 1844 had, in turn, been rejected by God, and His Spirit had ceased to speak to them.[1] It is clear the Whites never changed their minds on this matter. For example, White wrote in 1863 that he did not doubt that "the salvation of the soul, or perdition, hung upon the manner in which those who heard treated that solemn message."[2] Perhaps the most emphatic statement in this context was made by Ellen G. White:

> I was shown in vision, and I still believe that there was a shut door in 1844. All who saw the light of the first and second angel's messages, and rejected that light, were left in darkness. And those who accepted it and received the Holy Spirit which attended the proclamation of the message from heaven, and who, afterward renounced their faith and pronounced their experience a delusion, thereby rejected the Spirit of God, and it no longer pleaded with them.[3]

"Towards an Open Door," 1848-1851[4]

The 1848 conferences, especially the vision of Ellen G. White at the final one, gave impetus to the task of proclaiming the Sabbath as the final test of God's people. Bates was the first to elaborate on this theme in A Seal of the Living God. Salvation was yet available (in Bates's opinion) to those who already believed in the

---

[1]Cf. Poehler, "'. . . and the Door Was Shut'" (1978), p. 102.

[2]White, Life Incidents, p. 185.

[3]Ellen G. White, MS 4, 1883.

[4]Using the date 1851 as the demarcation of this period is somewhat arbitrary. The year 1848 was undoubtedly a pivotal one, but it is not so easy to point to a specific event in 1851 that

Second Advent and now accepted the Sabbath readily, and to those who did not yet "so well understand the Advent doctrine," but would accept it and the Sabbath "as soon as they hear it explained."[1] In this way, "honest and candid enquirers after truth" were the proper targets of missionary endeavor.[2] For Bates the door of mercy was open primarily to those who had accepted and not given up later on the Millerite message, but apparently in his mind a few open-minded individuals, who had not consciously rejected Adventist preaching earlier, could still be saved.

A second factor which the three Sabbatarian Adventist leaders felt lent weight to their work was the occurrence of numerous revolutions and general unrest in Europe in 1848, events Ellen G. White referred to as "the shaking of the powers of Europe."[3] These developments, she said, indicated that the time for them to do their work was short. The interpretation of these events as "signs of the end" created a sense of urgency in Sabbatarian preaching and perhaps aroused renewed interest in eschatological events among the public.

A third occurrence, which in the end proved the most conclusive in broadening their thinking, was a rapid increase in the

---

marks it as a watershed in Sabbatarian Adventist thinking. Damsteegt (Foundations, pp. 162-163) attaches some importance to 1850 as a turning point in their missiological endeavors, while Poehler ("'. . . and the Door Was Shut'" [1978], p. 90) suggests that 1851 was the time when the Shut Door faded in importance as a facet of Sabbatarian Adventist preaching.

[1]Bates, A Seal of the Living God, pp. 61-62.

[2]Ibid., p. 27.

[3]Letter, Ellen G. White to Dear Brethren and Sisters, PT, August 1849, p. 24.

numbers joining their group. In March 1849, White wrote "the harvest indeed is great, and the laborers are few."[1] This was new language for him to be using and appears all the more remarkable when compared with a statement made just two years earlier, when he bemoaned the fact that "here [in Gorham, Maine] is not one soul that we can meet with or unite in serving the Lord."[2] In October 1849, he reported "quite a number" had recently accepted the Sabbath in Vermont, New Hampshire, Connecticut, New York, and Maine. In Western New York the number of Sabbath-keepers doubled in six months.[3]

It seems, then, that the new doctrinal unity achieved at the 1848 conferences, the momentous events taking place in the political world, and the broadening vision and missiological awakening that accompanied a gradual "opening" of the door of salvation all played an important part in the growth of the movement. Two other factors in the success of Sabbatarian Adventist work during this period were (1) the influence of the new periodical, Present Truth, first published in July 1849, and (2) a waning in the negative impact that the Disappointment had on the public mind, enabling Sabbatarian Adventists to proclaim the Sabbath without having to constantly defend the failure of their predictions in 1844.

---

[1]Letter, James White to the Hastingses, March 22, 1849.

[2]Letter, James White to Bro. Howland, March 14, 1847.

[3]Letter, James White to J. C. Bowles, October 17, 1849. Presumably most, if not all, of these converts were former Millerites. It was not until April 1851 that White expressed the view in print that those outside the Millerite movement might still be reached with the Sabbatarian Adventist message.

The following quotations from White, written in November 1849 and December 1850, respectively, reflect this new spirit among Sabbatarian Adventists:

> I believe the Sabbath truth is yet to ring through the land, as the Advent never has.[1]

> True, the "everlasting gospel" has not lost its power to affect the hearts of those who are still within the reach of mercy, and salvation; but that it has ceased to arouse and move men to repentance as in 1843, no sane man will deny.[2]

The latter statement reveals that by the end of 1850 in White's thinking the circle of those excluded from salvation had probably been narrowed to those who specifically rejected the Advent message before October 22, 1844. While the general lack of interest in the Sabbatarian Adventist message was seen by White to be evidence that their work was still a limited one, he had now passed the stage where his work was confined only to the ones who had not forsaken their former experience. By April 1851, White's beliefs had broadened sufficiently to include, though with some difficulty, some who had not responded to the Advent message earlier.

> We believe that God had reserved to himself a multitude of precious souls, some even in the churches. These he will manifest IN HIS OWN TIME. They were living up to the light they had when Jesus closed his mediation for the world, and when they hear the voice of the Shepherd in the message of the third angel they will gladly receive the whole truth. . . . We think we have no message to such now, still "He that hath an ear, let him hear." Our message is to the Laodiceans, yet some of these hidden souls are being manifested.[3]

---

[1] Letter, James White to J. C. Bowles, November 8, 1849.

[2] James White, "Our Present Position," RH, December 1850, p. 14.

[3] James White, [Editorial Correspondence], RH, April 7, 1851, p. 64. At this time White, Bates, and other Sabbatarian Adventists classified the Laodiceans as those Adventists who had

The development of White's thinking is clear. At first, all outside the "scattered flock" were considered to be lost. Later, room was made for those who had not consciously rejected the Advent message, and for children who were not yet at the age of accountability in 1844. By 1851, in White's opinion, even members of the established churches might be saved, if they had been "living up to the light they had" in 1844, though he was not ready to do much work for them yet. All that remained was for him to gain a wider concept of Sabbatarian Adventism's mission to the world.

Conclusion

It is difficult to draw parallels between the attitude toward organization among the Millerites who gathered at the Albany Conference and among the Sabbatarian Adventists. The former represented 30,000 to 50,000[1] who had shared a common experience, had been welded together by disappointment and fierce opposition, and who already had a rudimentary form of organization in their Advent associations. Sabbath-keepers only numbered about one hundred in 1848. Still, several observations relevant to church organization may be made about the Adventists in both camps.

1. All Adventists approached the question of organization and creedal statements with a great deal of suspicion. Establishment of

---

given up their belief in the Seventh Month movement. Thus, it was the task of Sabbath-keeping Adventists to convince them of the validity of their message then, and of the Sabbath in the present. By contrast, Sabbatarians were described as the Philadelphian church (cf. Rev 3:7-22).

[1]Cf. above, pp. 72, 78.

an organization and formation of a statement of beliefs appeared to many a reversion to the Babylonish state from which they had fled.

2. Pressure to organize at the Albany Conference came about as a result of the emergence of perceived heresy and schism.

3. The form of organization favored by the majority was intended to be identical to that found in the New Testament and interpreted to be a congregational type of structure.

4. The stronger one's belief in the Shut Door, the greater his antipathy to organization, as shown in the positions taken by such individuals as Marsh, Snow, and Pickands.

By 1851, Sabbatarian Adventism had reached the point where organizational developments had just begun to appear. Yet some of the events of the preceding years, 1844-1851, inevitably influenced these developments.

1. Insistence on the validity of their past experience provided Sabbatarian Adventists with strong feelings of alienation from those of the established churches which had rejected their message. When most Millerites refused to accept the doctrine of the seventh-day Sabbath, the rupture between the two groups of former Millerites similarly widened.

2. Consolidation of basic doctrinal beliefs had to be accomplished before any thought of organization could begin.

3. Sabbatarian Adventists' insistence on some form of the Shut Door theory meant that their antipathy to organization was as strong as among their counterparts, the non-Sabbatarian Millerites who criticized the organizational developments at the Albany Conference.

Thus, at the beginning of the 1850s, the pioneers of the Seventh-day Adventist Church were ready to grapple with the problems of a growing movement, and to seek ways of making their work more effective.

CHAPTER IV

JAMES WHITE AND THE DEVELOPMENT OF

SEVENTH-DAY ADVENTIST CHURCH ORDER

The years under study in this chapter fall naturally into two
main periods, 1849-1863 and 1863-1881. During the earlier era (1849-
1863), the main features of Seventh-day Adventist church order[1]
gradually took form, climaxing with the formation of the General
Conference in May 1863. This development will be presented in
three stages: (a) 1849-1854, the appearance of rudimentary organizational features, (b) 1854-1860, a time of discussion and controversy
over church order, and (c) 1860-1863, a period of rapid development
during which organization on local and general levels was accomplished.

The second part, the end of which is marked by the death of
White in 1881, saw some refinements in the basic pattern of
organization that had been adopted, but the center of interest
shifted to a new set of theological concerns on the nature and
organization of the church. One of the issues that arose between

---

[1]We use the phrases "church order" and "gospel order"
advisedly, as they were the terms appearing most frequently in the
earliest days of Sabbatarian Adventism. Cf., e.g., Letter, James
White to Leonard W. Hastings, March 18, 1850; Ellen G. White, MS 11,
1850; James White, "Our Visit to Vermont," RH, February 1851, p. 45;
[James White], "Publications," RH, March 1851, p. 54; "Our Tour
East," RH, November 25, 1851, p. 52.

1863 and 1881 was the nature and extent of the authority of the General Conference in relation to the rest of the church. We shall also seek to discover how the church, as it grew in numbers, came to understand the authority and jurisdiction of one level of church government over another, the significance of ordination, suitable qualifications for admission to the ministry, and what steps the church took to establish and administer church discipline.[1]

From a "Scattered Flock"[2] to an Organized Church, 1849-1863

Earliest References to Church Order Among Sabbatarian Adventists, 1849-1854

It has been shown in the previous chapter[3] that it was approximately 1851 when Sabbatarian Adventists began to grasp the fact that their mission was to a much wider audience than they had

---

[1]Numerous accounts have been written on the history of church organization in Seventh-day Adventism, notably, "Organization, Development of, in SDA Church," SDA Encyclopedia (1976), 10:1042-1054; A. W. Spalding, Origin and History of Seventh-day Adventists, 4 vols. (Washington, D.C.: Review and Herald Pub. Assn, 1961-1962), 1:29-311; Maxwell, Tell It to the World, pp. 125-146; Damsteegt, Foundations, pp. 254-259; Schwarz, Light Bearers, pp. 86-98; Froom, Movement of Destiny, pp. 135-141. However, as the pages cited are a small part of more general denominational histories or (as in the case of the encyclopedia article) a general introduction to the subject, no comprehensive account is available. In addition, none of these seeks to combine the historical description with a thorough examination of the theological and biblical foundation upon which Seventh-day Adventist pioneers built their church.

[2]The phrase "scattered flock," or others of a similar nature, is typical of the way the Advent movement's leaders addressed the believers in the early years. Cf., e.g., White, Ellen G. White, and Bates, A Word to the "Little Flock." Poehler ("'. . . and the Door Was Shut'" [1978], p. 100) points out that a change in terminology gradually appeared about 1852 as Sabbatarian Adventists described themselves more frequently as a "church."

[3]See above, pp. 112-115.

previously realized. The Shut Door theology, as Sabbatarian Adventists understood it, did provide them with a mission field, but it was one which expanded only gradually to include those who had accepted and remained true to the Millerite message and also those who had not consciously rejected that message. As the Sabbatarians' mission horizons broadened, the first published statements on the subject of church order began to appear. However, it should be remembered that the rejection by the established churches of the Millerite message prior to the Disappointment of 1844 had predisposed all Adventists, including those who came to observe the seventh-day Sabbath, to view with suspicion any organization that might take on the characteristics of the "Babylonish" churches they had left.[1] Some Millerites in the post-Disappointment years, including Sabbatarian Adventists, also feared the formation of human creeds which would lead to Babylonian sectarianism.[2]

The earliest statement by White on church order appeared in September 1849. He wrote:

> Now it does seem to me that those whom God has called to travel and labor in His cause should first be supported before those who have no calling from God are encouraged to go from place to place.[3]

---

[1]On the identity and characteristics of mystical Babylon, as the Millerites understood it before the Disappointment, see above, pp. 48-56.

[2]Cf., e.g., [Marsh], "The Albany Conference," pp. 61-62. Among Sabbatarian Adventists who objected to any creed but the Bible were J. N. Andrews ("Thoughts on Revelation XIII and XIV," RH, May 19, 1851, p. 84); J. N. Loughborough ("The Image of the Beast," RH, January 15, 1861, p. 69).

[3]Letter, James White to Bro. and Sister Collins, September 8, 1849.

Even though it was doubtless very rudimentary in form, the idea of financial support for travelling preachers had already formed in his mind. This idea may have been a carry over from his days in the Christian Church, which was based largely upon an itinerant ministry.[1] It should be noted, however, that the above statement appeared in the context of comments about a certain Sister Lawrence, who had been claiming support for her work, which White clearly felt lacked divine approval.[2]

We find another significant comment by White a few months later: "I hope that the church will soon get right when they can move in gospel order."[3] This statement also occurred in connection with White's remarks concerning an individual whom he believed God had never called to be a travelling preacher. It would seem, therefore, that White's earliest reflections on organization were in the context of minimizing or eliminating the influence of unauthorized preachers.

Ellen G. White's first comments on the subject of church order appeared in December 1850, based on a vision received earlier in the same year. She wrote:

> I saw how great and holy God was. Said the angel, "Walk carefully before Him, for He is high and lifted up, and the train of His glory fills the temple." I saw that everything in heaven was in perfect order. Said the angel, "Look ye, Christ is the head, move in order, move in order. Have a meaning to

---

[1]Cf. Morrill's claim, "Only heroic itinerancy has surpassed journalism in building the Christian denomination" (Morrill, A History of the Christian Denomination, p. 292).

[2]There is no further record of the nature of "Sister Lawrence's" work or its influence.

[3]Letter, James White to Leonard W. Hastings, March 18, 1850.

everything." Said the angel, "Behold ye and know how perfect, how beautiful, the order in heaven; follow it."[1]

The theme of the perfect order of heaven as the pattern upon which the church should build its organization occurs in the writings of Ellen G. White several times. She suggested that the nearer God's people come to the order of heaven the closer they will be to the state necessary for subjects of the kingdom of heaven.[2]

Ellen G. White's comments in December 1850 referred to individuals at Fairhaven, Massachusetts, who had been engaged in some ecstatic experiences in their worship meetings. Thus, the earliest remarks by both James and Ellen G. White spoke of the need to meet the divisive forces of fanaticism and unauthorized representatives within the scattered group.[3]

At this time, checking fanaticism and controlling the travelling preachers were apparently the main aims of the gospel order proposed by the Whites. An indication of White's position may be found in the editorial practices of the Review. In November 1850, he published an article by Bates which spoke approvingly of Marsh's stand against some of the decisions at the Albany Conference, held in

---

[1]Ellen G. White, MS 11, 1850. Cf. A. L. White, Messenger to the Remnant (1969), p. 45.

[2]Cf. Ellen G. White, Testimonies for the Church, 2:697-698; 1:191; 4:601-602.

[3]Cf. Loughborough's comment: "It seemed to require some adverse experiences to arouse them [Sabbatarian Adventists] fully to a sense of the necessity of the organization of conferences and churches and associations for the management of the temporalities of the cause" (Loughborough, The Great Second Advent Movement, p. 343).

April 1845.[1] Marsh had criticized three of the actions of the Albany Conference: adoption of the name "Adventist," the creation of a creed, and the formation of a new sect. He had not opposed the simple congregational organization proposed at Albany. White also considered it important to reprint a letter from the Millerite periodical, Harbinger and Advocate, supporting Marsh's position yet claiming even he had yielded too much. Referring to the attempts to bring order among the fanatical elements at Albany, E. P. Butler wrote: "I am glad that you stood aloof from, and protested against, its organization. But I fear even you have too much conformed to the powers that be."[2]

The Whites began the work of publishing the Review in Paris, Maine, in November 1850, moving to western New York State in June 1851. For the next several years, they visited the New England believers each autumn on their "Eastern Tour."[3] The situation they met with on these tours fixed more firmly in their minds the need for some form of order and discipline. Once again, fanaticism was a

---

[1]Bates, "The Laodicean Church," p. 7. On Marsh's critique of the Albany Conference, cf. above, p. 87.

[2]Letter, E. P. Butler to Joseph Marsh, RH, January 1851, pp. 38-39. White was not averse to printing articles on occasion that were contrary to his own way of thinking. We cannot be sure, therefore, that he agreed with the sentiments expressed in Butler's letter or in the article by Bates. However, the fact that he undertook to print a letter addressed to another periodical indicates that White considered the communication to contain something worth repeating.

[3]Places and dates for the publishing of the Review during White's lifetime are as follows: Paris, Me., November 1850-June 1851; Saratoga Springs, N.Y., August 1851-March 1852; Rochester, N.Y., May 1852-October 1855; Battle Creek, Mich., December 1855-1881. After the move to Battle Creek, western New York was included in the itinerary of their Eastern tour.

leading issue. For example, in February 1851, White wrote of the group at Waterbury, Vermont, that "A spirit of fanaticism, which has struggled hard in Vermont, was happily checked, and, we think a good step was taken to promote gospel order in the church."[1]

The concern about the threat of fanatical practices or unorthodox beliefs in the early days of Sabbatarian Adventism implies that the most prominent leaders at least, namely the Whites and Bates, had in their minds a clear conviction as to what constituted orthodox teaching and regarded the fledgling movement as a tangible entity to be protected by vigilant leaders. As has been mentioned in the previous chapter, the conferences held in 1848 played an important role in consolidating a new sense of identity.[2] The widely scattered membership was difficult to oversee effectively. Thus, one of the aims of the Whites on their travels was to instruct the believers more fully on the beliefs of Sabbatarian Adventism. One explanation White gave for the presence of false teaching was that some "had never heard our position fully explained."[3]

Several other significant actions were taken on the Whites' initial tour of New England. At Medford, Vermont, two individuals insisted on continuing to set new dates for the Second Coming in the face of advice from Ellen G. White. A vote was taken to withdraw fellowship from them.[4] Another person was disfellowshipped at

---

[1]White, "Our Visit to Vermont," p. 45.

[2]See above, pp. 99-103.

[3]White, "Our Visit to Vermont," p. 45.

[4]Letter, James White to Dear Brethren in Christ, November 11, 1851.

Washington, New Hampshire, on October 31, 1851, who had "fallen victim to the bewitching power of spiritualism."[1] At the same place, White reported that the "meeting closed, after choosing 7 men, (see Acts VI) to see to the wants of the church."[2] Following the precedent cited in Acts, he stopped short of calling them deacons.

Still other important elements of church order emerged on this tour. From Johnson, Vermont, White reported:

> Gospel order and perfect union among the brethren, especially those who preach the Word, were also dwelt upon, and all seemed to feel the importance of following our perfect guide, the Bible, on these subjects as well as all others.[3]

At Bethel, Vermont, White discussed the "importance of union, and the means God has used to unite his people. (Visions)."[4] These two statements reveal the continuing concern for maintaining unity of belief and action, especially among the travelling preachers, and the fact that for Sabbatarian Adventists the Bible was considered to be a perfect guide in matters of organization. The numerous actions taken while on this tour indicate that the Whites functioned as supervisors of the Sabbatarian believers and were regarded as such by most of

---

[1][White], "Our Tour East," p. 52.

[2]Letter, James White to Dear Brethren in Christ, November 11, 1851. Cf. Roy E. Graham, "Ellen G. White: An Examination of Her Position and Role in the Seventh-day Adventist Church" (Ph.D. thesis, University of Birmingham, 1977), p. 69. Graham describes this meeting at Washington, N.H., as "crucial" to the development of church order. The first recorded instance of individuals who were ordained to care for temporal needs being designated "deacons" was at Fairhaven (Bates's home church) and Dartmouth, Mass. (Letter, H. S. Gurney to James White, RH, December 27, 1853, p. 199).

[3][White], "Our Tour East," p. 52.

[4]Letter, James White to Dear Brethren in Christ, November 11, 1851.

those they visited. Ellen G. White's claim to the prophetic gift was the basis for the acceptance of her authority.[1] In the case of her husband, his publishing work probably was the main factor in the acceptance of his jurisdiction. The oversight of the work by the Whites may also have stemmed from the important role they played in the series of conferences that took place in 1848.

The early 1850s saw a continuation of the rapid growth rate and geographical expansion of Sabbatarian Adventism.[2] C. Mervyn Maxwell, for example, estimates that there were about two hundred adherents in 1850, and just two years later there were about two thousand.[3] To maintain unity at a time of such remarkable expansion required strong leadership on the part of the Whites and Bates, in particular.[4] One of the earliest methods used to consolidate the belief and practices of the group was to issue cards of identification for the "travelling brethren" in order to thwart imposters. These ministerial credentials were usually signed by White and Bates. This practice began in 1853, if not earlier.[5]

---

[1]Cf. above, pp. 97-98.   [2]Cf. above, pp. 110-111.

[3]Maxwell, Tell It to the World, p. 129. This estimate coincides with White's own account. In a review of the progress of the work, he said that in 1848 there were only twenty Sabbath-keepers in New York State, whereas in 1852 there were a thousand. In the western states (primarily Michigan and Ohio), there were no believers in 1848, but in 1852 there were several hundred. In the Canadas there were none in 1849, but in 1852 a goodly number ([James White], "A Brief Sketch of the Past," RH, May 6, 1852, p. 5). Circulation of the same issue of the Review was stated to be two thousand ([James White], "The Paper," RH, May 6, 1852, p. 8).

[4]Cf. Froom, Movement of Destiny, p. 136.

[5]According to Loughborough, in The Great Second Advent Movement, pp. 348-349, the first cards were issued in 1850. He received his first card, signed by White and Bates, in January 1853. The

The ordination of individuals to positions of leadership was also seen as an additional means of maintaining unity by the Whites and Bates. The first records of formal ordinations to the gospel ministry appear in 1853.[1] According to the Review, the seven men, ordained at three separate ceremonies, were [Horace W.] Lawrence, Andrews, A. S. Hutchins, C. W. Sperry, E. P. Butler, Elon Everts, and Josiah Hart.[2] On September 5, 1853, at the first of these three

---

credentials recommended him as an authorized representative "to the brethren where he may travel" (Adriel Chilson, ed., Miracles in My Life (Angwin, Calif.: Heritage Publications, n.d., p. 27). The latter work cited is a compilation of autobiographical statements by Loughborough. Cf. also, "Organization, Development of, in SDA Church," SDA Encyclopedia (1976), 10:1043; Spalding, Origin and History, 1:294-295; Froom, Movement of Destiny, p. 136. The problem of unauthorized representatives' visiting the scattered believers continued to concern White for some time. The following articles by him all refer to the unsettling influence of such individuals: James White, "The Faith of Jesus," RH, August 19, 1852, pp. 60-61; "Eastern Tour," RH, October 14, 1852, p. 96; "Dangers to Which the Remnant Are Exposed," RH, March 3, 1853, pp. 164-165; "Eastern Tour," RH, October 18, 1853, p. 117. White claimed that those travelling without approval lacked experience and were not called of God.

[1]The first recorded ordination was in 1851 when G. Washington Morse was ordained by George Holt. This took place in the summer and was simply reported in a letter to the Review. There seems to be some doubt as to whether the ordination of Morse was to the gospel ministry or to serve in a position equivalent to that of a local elder. The report reads that "Bro. Morse was set apart by the laying on of hands, to the administration of the ordinances of God's house" (Letter, Mrs. F. M. Shimper to James White, RH, August 19, 1851, p. 15). Morse recalled later that he was ordained to the ministry in 1852, but his memory may have been faulty (G. Washington Morse, "Items of Advent Experience During the Past Fifty Years.--No. 4," RH, October 16, 1888, pp. 642-643. Cf. "Ordination," SDA Encyclopedia [1976], 10:1037-1040). None of the prominent leaders of Sabbatarian Adventism seems to have been involved in Morse's ordination in 1851. One should keep in mind, however, that normal ministerial functions, such as baptisms, funerals, and the Lord's Supper, were continually administered among Sabbatarian Adventists from the earliest days by men such as White, John Byington, and H. G. Buck, who had been ordained to the ministry in other denominations.

[2]James White, "Eastern Tour," RH, September 20, 1853, p. 85; [James White], "Eastern Tour," RH, November 15, 1853, p. 148.

ceremonies, Lawrence was "set apart . . . to the work of the gospel ministry, to administer the ordinances of the church of Christ, by the laying on of hands."[1]

At the end of 1853, White wrote his first carefully considered exposition on the matter of church order, the first such study by a Sabbatarian Adventist.[2] The theme of the series was borrowed from 1 Cor 14:33, "For God is not a God of confusion but of peace." White argued that Sabbatarian Adventists must avoid, on the one hand, the extreme of confusion and lack of order that characterized other sects which were "a perfect Babel of confusion";[3] and, on the other hand, the inflexibility of human creeds.

Proper church order, White continued, should be based on the New Testament evidence which provides for order and strict discipline in the church of Christ. It is especially vital that religious teachers should be perfectly united in sentiment and action.[4] The specific suggestions that he drew from the New Testament were as follows: (1) Jesus' appointment of the apostles is a perfect example of the mission of Christ's ministers today (Matt 28:16-20; Eph 4:11-16); (2) it is God who calls the minister to preach the gospel, and

---

[1]White, "Eastern Tour," RH, September 20, 1853, p. 85. Cf. Maxwell, Tell It to the World, pp. 130-131.

[2][James White], "Gospel Order," RH, December 6, 1853, p. 173; December 13, 1853, p. 180; December 20, 1853, pp. 188-190; December 27, 1853, pp. 196-197.

[3][White], "Gospel Order," RH, December 6, 1853, p. 173.

[4]Ibid., December 13, 1853, p. 180.

the church will recognize that fact; (3) baptism should be administered upon an individual's acceptance of the faith, not after a six-month period of waiting to see if he backslides (Acts 2:28, 41; 8:12, 26-40; 16:13-15); (4) only those who are called to preach may administer baptism;[1] (5) the terms "elder" and "bishop" are interchangeable in the New Testament (Titus 1:5-7); (6) those who are called by God to preach and baptize should be set apart for the ministry by the laying on of hands, an act on behalf of the church (2 Tim 1:6); (7) the purpose of ordination is to qualify one to preach the Word, to secure the union of the church, and to shut the door against Satan--that is, to protect the church against false teachers.[2]

It will be noted that the main thrust of the above is related to the authority of the minister and his role as the one to maintain discipline in the church. White's solution to the challenges presented by false teachers and fanatics[3] is to be found in what he perceived to be the "divine" and "sufficient" order in the New

---

[1]Interestingly, White drew this conclusion from the experience of Philip, one of the seven set apart by the apostles to care for the administrative matters of the church, and who is later called an "evangelist" (Acts 6:1-6; 21:8).

[2][White], "Gospel Order," RH, December 20, 1853, pp. 188-190.

[3]One of the earliest splinter groups causing trouble for Sabbath-keeping Adventists was the Messenger Party, led by A. S. Case and C. P. Russell at Jackson, Michigan ("Messenger Party," SDA Encyclopedia [1976], 10:870-871). Several of White's statements on church order are in the context of this case. Case and Russell defected because they resented Ellen G. White's reproof of them for their harsh spirit toward other members. The name of the offshoot was derived from its magazine, Messenger of Truth.

Testament.[1] In view of what we shall notice later concerning
White's approach to the New Testament as a model for church
organization,[2] it is significant that at this point he built his
case expressly on biblical precedent, presupposing that the actions
taken by Christ and the apostles provided a valid basis for church
order among Sabbatarians.

At this stage, there was no significant opposition to
White's ideas. Responses in the Review were positive.[3] Only the
"imposters," presumably, were unhappy, but their reactions are not
recorded. White was able to look upon the situation in 1854 with
some satisfaction. There is, he wrote, "union of sentiment, feeling
and action," especially in Michigan, that was not present before the
subject of church order was introduced.[4]

From what we have seen, White from the beginning was at the
forefront of the discussion on church order. He and his wife were
agreed on the need for organization, although it is not possible to
say whether or not Ellen G. White's visions initiated interest in the
subject. There is evidence that White was reflecting on it even
before his wife's vision in December 1850. In addition, Ellen G.
White did not provide specific suggestions for the form that

---

[1][White], "Gospel Order," RH, December 6, 1853, p. 173.

[2]See below, pp. 130-131, 144-145, 189-190.

[3]Letter, H. S. Gurney to James White, RH, December 27, 1853, p. 199; Letter, John P. Kellogg to James White, RH, January 24, 1854, p. 7; Letter, G. W. Holt to James White, RH, January 31, 1854, p. 15.

[4][James White], "Western Tour," RH, July 4, 1854, p. 172.

organization should take. The actual methods and principles of church order were derived by White from Scripture.[1]

At this time, White's voice was virtually the only one being heard on the subject. This is not surprising, in view of his extensive travels with his wife and his involvement in the publishing work of the movement. Both of these activities made more apparent to him than to anyone else the need for some form of order and discipline. Once he had overcome the limitations to his thinking imposed by Shut Door ideas, his plans for the future and the energy with which he promoted them were crucial to the growth of Sabbatarian Adventism.

An Era of Discussion and Controversy
Over Church Order, 1854-1860

The period 1854-1860 may be described as one of transition. White had by 1854 established in his own mind the practical need and biblical basis for the ordination, authorization, and financial support of the ministry; and also the appointment of deacons,

---

[1]Ellen G. White's views on church order, based on her visions in 1850 and 1851, were published in Ellen G. White, Supplement to the Christian Experience and Views of Ellen G. White (Rochester, N.Y.: James White, 1854). See also Ellen G. White, Early Writings (1963), pp. 97-104. It should also be mentioned that during the initial development of church order (1851-1855), White refrained from any reference to his wife's visions in the Review because some claimed Ellen G. White's prophetic gift had been made a test of fellowship. "The Review for five years has not published one of them. Its motto has been, 'The Bible and the Bible alone, the only rule of faith and duty,'" White declared (James White, "A Test," RH, October 16, 1855, p. 61). Ellen G. White's opinions on church order, as expressed in 1854, were simply that Sabbatarian Adventism should emulate the order of heaven and the New Testament church. Apart from warnings against sending inexperienced men into the field and condemnation of other "self-sent" teachers (Early Writings [1963], p. 98), at no time did Ellen G. White express herself before 1863 on the precise form of organization to be adopted.

centrally organized assignments for ministers, and regular conferences to make plans for the work.

Inasmuch as White had come to firm conclusions on church
order by the middle of 1854, little on the subject appeared from his
pen until the spring of 1860. What he did say during this time may
be summarized in three points. First, he wished to avoid the
extremes of "popery" on the one hand and of "anarchy" on the other.
Between these extremes, he believed, lies the true Bible position of
order and discipline which is in accordance with the gospel. "A
church united without a human creed, built on Bible discipline and
Bible union, will be a glorious edifice indeed."[1]

Second, he was aware that the idea of gospel order would be
opposed by some, such as "Brother Over-cautious" and "Brother
Confusion."[2] Writing in July 1859, White declared that the fact
that some had fallen into the trap of relying on human creeds was no
reason to err in the other direction--disorder. The aim of this
particular article was to advocate yearly conferences to be held in
each state to accomplish "systematic action of the entire body."[3]
In particular, this would mean the assignment of ministers on an
equitable basis to their fields of work.[4] In this regard, White

---

[1]James White, "Extremes," RH, March 24, 1859, pp. 140-141.

[2]James White, "Yearly Meetings," RH, July 21, 1859, p. 68.

[3]Ibid.

[4]Complaints arose from areas which had no resident ministers
over the fact that Battle Creek had five ministers in residence. In
response White agreed, "System in labor, or, in locating preachers'
families near their fields of labor, may be called for . . ." (James
White, "A Complaint," RH, June 16, 1859, p. 28).

wrote: "We lack system. And we should not be afraid of that system which is not opposed by the Bible, and is approved by sound sense."[1] Had his viewpoint changed since he wrote, in 1847, that the Bible was the only rule of faith and practice?[2] It seems he had moved away, perhaps unconsciously, from the idea that the only valid principles of organization were those specifically indicated in the Bible, to a less restricted view that any method of organization was acceptable if effective, provided that it was not specifically opposed by Scripture. We observe, also, that the importance of "sound sense" fitted in with his pragmatic nature and echoed the common-sense approach of the Millerites who believed that the Bible and sanctified human reason were in total harmony.[3]

The third theme found in White's writings between 1854 and 1860 is the role of the spirit of prophecy and the work of Ellen G. White in the church. At two conferences held in Battle Creek on November 6, 1857, and June 3-6, 1859, the study of this subject was

---

[1]Ibid. Other articles by White on church order, expressing similar ideas during this period (1854-1860), include [James White], "Church Order," RH, January 23, 1855, p. 164; James White, "The Cause," RH, August 13, 1857, p. 116; James White, "Unity and Gifts of the Church, No. 2," RH, December 10, 1857, p. 37.

[2]White, Ellen G. White, and Bates, A Word to the "Little Flock," p. 13.

[3]The outlook of the religious world in 19th-century America was, in the words of Ahlstrom, "characterized by an immense confidence in the workings of the human mind and a determination to make the Christian message as simple and acceptable as possible" (Ahlstrom, "Theology in America," p. 244). White linked the ideas of church order and common sense on more than one occasion. After the organization of the Seventh-day Adventist General Conference in 1863 he wrote, "Now we are happy to see so many rally around the standard of order and common sense" ([James White], "Organization," RH, April 19, 1864, p. 164).

one of two important items on the agenda.[1] Discussion of the role
and authority of Ellen G. White marked a shift from the earlier
(1850-1855) editorial policy of her husband in the Review, which had
been to refrain from mentioning her visions in print.[2] Out of the
first of these conferences grew a four-part Review series by White in
which he sought to demonstrate from Scripture the perpetuity of the
prophetic gift beyond the time of the New Testament, and that the
remnant church of the last days, in particular, would possess this
gift.[3]

White did not mention his wife by name in his exposition on
the unity and gifts of the Spirit. In fact, he was mindful of the
need to show that the doctrine of the gift of prophecy in the
remnant[4] church is a biblical one. In the first of the four-part

---

[1]At both conferences attention was also given to "the duty
of the church in making a proper use of their possessions to advance
the cause" (James White, "Conference," RH, November 12, 1857, p. 4).
This system of stewardship became known as "Systematic Benevolence"
and was adopted officially at the Battle Creek Conference held June
3-6, 1859 (see below, pp. 141-142, for a discussion on the decisions
made at the conference).

[2]White, "A Test," pp. 61-62.

[3]White, "Unity and Gifts," RH, December 3, 1857, p. 29;
December 10, 1857, p. 37; December 31, 1857, pp. 60-61; January 7,
1858, pp. 68-69. On the June 3-6, 1858, conference see Editorial,
"The Conference," RH, June 9, 1859, p. 20. At this conference, a
testimony from Ellen G. White was read to the 250 people present and
later published in the Review (Ellen G. White, "'He Went Away
Sorrowful, For He Had Great Possessions,'" RH, November 26, 1857, pp.
18-19). The main thrust of her message was the need to support the
work of the church through frugal living and sacrificial giving.

[4]On the remnant motif as understood within Seventh-day
Adventism, see "Remnant Church," SDA Encyclopedia (1976), 10:1200-
1201; Gerhard F. Hasel, The History and Theology of the Remnant
Idea from Genesis to Isaiah, 3rd ed. (Berrien Springs, Mich.:
Andrews University Press, 1980); Ellen G. White, The Remnant Church
(Mountain View, Calif.: Pacific Press Pub. Assn, 1950).

series, he argued that the unity and gifts of the church are one and the same subject.[1] He reiterated a point that he had made earlier, namely, that in breaking away from the bondage of human creeds there was a danger of going to the opposite extreme of anarchy.[2] The freedom of the gospel, he added, is not contrary to perfect order in the church.[3]

White based the second article of the series on Eph 4:11-16; Rom 15:5-6; Phil 2:1-2; and 1 Cor 1:4-10.[4] The thrust of his argument was drawn from the latter passage in particular. All members of Christ's church, he said, should speak the same thing, be perfectly joined together, and be of the same mind and the same judgment (see especially vs. 10).

In the third and fourth articles he sought to set forth the biblical evidence that the Sabbath-keeping remnant would possess the spirit of prophecy.[5] He concluded his remarks by drawing four points from the prophecy of Joel 2:28-32: (1) the Spirit is to be poured out in His fullness, (2) females are not excluded from the promises of the prophetic gift, (3) the manifestations of the Spirit

---

[1]White, "Unity and Gifts," RH, December 3, 1857, p. 29.

[2]See above, p. 130.

[3]The theme of the perfection of church order in the New Testament church and among Sabbatarian Adventists is one to which White returned later. See below, pp. 171-175, for a discussion on White's intent in describing church order as "perfect."

[4]White, "Unity and Gifts," RH, December 10, 1857, p. 37.

[5]Ibid., December 31, 1857, pp. 60-61; January 7, 1858, pp. 68-69.

are connected with the signs of the return of Christ, and (4) the remnant would be delivered when it called on the name of the Lord.

While White's mind was settled on the subject of church order as he understood it, others carried on a lively debate about it in the Review. Bates added his opinions, which were invariably supportive of White on the major issues. Writing in August 1854, Bates asserted that the New Testament church represented a system of perfect order which had been "deranged" by the papacy and must be restored before the Second Coming. The process of restoration, he believed, was then in progress among Sabbath-keepers.[1] This idea of restoration of proper church order appeared here for the first time in Sabbatarian Adventist writings. It reflects a theological concern that the church should not only be organized to deal with the practical necessities of administration, but that it also return to the New Testament ideal of simple, effective gospel order introduced by Christ and His apostles.

Bates recognized that within the perfect system found in the New Testament there had been a development in methods of church order, witnessed by differences between the system described by Acts and the one found in Paul's writings. He also realized that the duties of the officers of the church (elder and deacon) sometimes overlapped, as in the cases of Stephen and Philip who, while deacons, also preached the Word. In addition, Bates made a distinction

---

[1]Joseph Bates, "Church Order," RH, August 29, 1854, p. 22. It is noteworthy that the motif of restoration was also prominent in Bates's Sabbath theology (cf. Maxwell, "Joseph Bates and SDA Sabbath Theology," p. 360).

between two classes of elders--those who "rule" and those who "labor in the word and doctrine."[1]

The two other individuals who expressed themselves on the issues of church order during this period were J. B. Frisbie[2] and R. F. Cottrell.[3] Both of these men confined their comments at this time to matters concerning order in the local church. By contrast, as has been shown, White was already speaking of yearly conferences to coordinate work, to impose discipline, and to achieve unity of belief on a wider basis. Frisbie claimed that only those actions by the church that were specifically approved in Scripture were acceptable.[4]

---

[1]Ibid. Cf. "Church Elder," SDA Encyclopedia (1976), 10:299-300. Bates agreed with White that the terms "bishop" and "elder" were used interchangeably in the New Testament.

[2]See especially J. B. Frisbie's four-part series, "Church Order," RH, June 19, 1856, pp. 62-63; June 26, 1856, pp. 70-71; July 3, 1856, pp. 78-79; July 10, 1856, p. 86. See also idem, "Church Order," RH, December 26, 1854, pp. 147-148; "Gospel Order," RH, January 9, 1855, pp. 153-155; "Deacons," RH, July 31, 1856, p. 102; "Church Order," RH, October 23, 1856, p. 198; Order in the Church of God (Battle Creek, Mich.: Review and Herald Pub. Assn, 1859). Frisbie (1816-1882) was granted a ministerial license by the Methodists in 1843 and ordained in 1846. At first he strongly opposed Sabbatarian Adventism, but joined its ranks in 1853. He later left the ministry and gave up observance of the Sabbath for a time, although he returned to his ministerial work later. Cf. "Frisbie, Joseph Birchard," SDA Encyclopedia (1976),10:484.

[3]R. F. Cottrell, "What Are the Duties of Church Officers?" RH, October 2, 1856, p. 173. Cottrell's voice became much more prominent after 1860 (see below, pp. 143-149). Cottrell (1814-1892) was brought up as a Seventh Day Baptist, joining Sabbatarian Adventism in 1851. A poet, writer, and minister, he served on the editorial committee of the Review, contributed frequently to Seventh-day Adventist publications, and served in evangelistic work in New York and Pennsylvania. For further biographical information see, "Cottrell, Roswell F.," SDA Encyclopedia (1976), 10:354.

[4]Frisbie, "Church Order" (1854), p. 147.

As has been noted, there seems to have been little, if any, opposition to White's proposals concerning the organization of local churches. However, his suggestions concerning the general supervision of the work under a centralized form of government aroused opposition. Cottrell's objections are easier to understand as he, as a former Seventh Day Baptist, would have been familiar with a congregational system.[1] Frisbie, on the other hand, would have found White's proposals to be similar to the system to be found in Methodism, which combined a strong hierarchical structure with itinerant ministers' visiting their scattered members.[2] Perhaps Frisbie's opposition arose from this very similarity. Having rejected Methodism upon joining the Sabbath-keepers, he may have viewed the suggestion of wider supervision to be a return to the Methodist economy which he had left.

This distinction between congregational and centralized organization may well have lain at the base of disagreements between Frisbie and Cottrell on the one hand, and White on the other, which continued for several years. Another fundamental difference between Frisbie and White lay in their approach to the interpretation of Scripture. While Frisbie retained his insistence that each detail of

---

[1]Seventh Day Baptists in North America adopted the same system of government as the Baptist churches from which they had separated. In fact, the Sabbath-keepers who first formed corporate congregations in the 17th century were regarded for a time as part of the Association of Baptist Churches (William L. Burdick, "The Eastern Association," in Seventh Day Baptists in Europe and America, comp. Seventh Day Baptist General Conference, 2 vols. [Plainfield, N.J.: Seventh Day Baptist General Conference, 1910], 2:594-600). On Baptist organization, see below, pp. 249-252.

[2]Cf. below, pp. 252-257.

church government have its support in the Word of God, White, as has been noted,[1] believed by this time that only the general principles of organization might be found in the New Testament church.

Frisbie was the first to raise the issue of the name of the church. As far as he was concerned, the only acceptable name was "Church of God," because that was the form used in the New Testament to address "The Church of God in Galatia," and so on.[2] Frisbie also opposed the keeping of church lists on the basis that it was sufficient to have one's name written in the heavenly books.[3] In view of the fact that he agreed that it might sometimes be necessary to disfellowship a member, the inevitable question was asked: If members may be voted out, why can they not be voted in?[4] Frisbie's opinions in these matters seem quite similar to those expressed by Marsh after the Albany Conference.[5]

We would suggest that White's leadership of the publishing work of the movement had a marked effect on his thinking and was probably one of the primary reasons why his ideas were well in

---

[1]See above, pp. 130-131.

[2]Frisbie, "Church Order" (1854), p. 147.

[3]Ibid., pp. 147-148.

[4]Letter, A. S. Hutchins to Uriah Smith, RH, September 18, 1856, p. 158. Hutchins also raised the question of problems that might be caused by members' moving to another area and wishing to transfer their membership. Such a happening would require some understanding of the relationship among congregations. Frisbie responded without answering the questions satisfactorily in "Church Order," RH, October 23, 1856, p. 198.

[5]Cf. above, p. 87.

advance of colleagues such as Frisbie and Cottrell.[1] In 1855, the press was moved to Battle Creek, Michigan. The pressure of work and the responsibility of owning everything in his own name led him to resign as editor of the Review.[2]

White also expressed concern about difficulties encountered in supporting the paper financially.[3] As a result, he suggested for the first time that the "office" (i.e., the publishing house and its assets) be owned by the church.[4] In 1855, he was not ready to advocate legal incorporation.[5] Instead, he recommended that a committee of three or more own the property on behalf of the church. In this way, the practical business problems of the church led White to reflect on the biblical rationale for a central administrative authority to oversee its needs. Similar discussions arose around 1857 over the need to build and own meeting houses.[6] It is

---

[1]See above, pp. 128-129.

[2]Uriah Smith, "To the Friends of the Review," RH, December 4, 1855, p. 76.

[3]See, e.g., J. N. Andrews, R. F. Cottrell, and Uriah Smith, "The Office," RH, December 5, 1854, pp. 124-125.

[4]Letter, James White to Brother Dodge, August 20, 1855.

[5]At first, legal incorporation was considered by some to be a dangerous step which would lead back to Babylon by allying the church with the civil power. For a later discussion on this see below, pp. 143-149.

[6]According to Loughborough, the first meeting house was built in Battle Creek in 1855 (The Great Second Advent Movement, p. 288). In 1857, it was decided to replace it with a larger building, seating 300-400, suitable for conferences (Joseph Bates and Uriah Smith, "Business Proceedings of the Battle Creek Conference," RH, April 16, 1857, p. 188).

noteworthy that there is no record of any dissent against the building of a larger meeting house at Battle Creek. The account of the proceedings records the action in favor of the plan to build in a matter-of-fact way, with no indication of tension between the construction of a larger church and belief in the near approach of Christ.[1]

The move to Battle Creek and the building of larger meeting houses demonstrate the continued growth and geographical expansion of the Sabbatarian Adventist movement. The development of Battle Creek as the headquarters of the church led to the concentration of several leading ministers in Battle Creek and the corresponding neglect of the areas that they had left. Complaints were received from outlying churches which were, on occasion, without a preacher on the Sabbath for as long as three months, while Battle Creek had five ministers who were members of the congregation.[2] White felt that the move from the East to the West was justified, as New England was "gospel hardened" and workers could see far more results from their labors in the West where, he said, the same efforts would convert twenty

---

[1]Ibid. Construction of the Millerite tabernacle in Boston (dedicated May 4, 1843), which seated over 3,000 people, aroused questions from non-Millerites concerning its appropriateness in view of Christ's imminent return. The Millerites themselves had no qualms, regarding it as a necessary center for the preaching of Adventism. Its construction was defended on the basis of its "simplicity, comfort and frugality" (Christian Herald, quoted in "The Boston Tabernacle," ST, June 14, 1843, p. 119). The nine-member tabernacle committee argued further: "We are commended to occupy till Christ comes" (Prescott Dickinson et al., "To the Public," ST, May 10, 1843, p. 75). Apparently, those who built the Battle Creek tabernacle had similar views.

[2]White, "A Complaint," p. 28.

instead of one.[1] Still, it made him aware of the need to engage the work force more systematically.[2]

Unfortunately, numerical growth, though much slower in the mid 1850s than the extremely rapid expansion from 1850 to 1852, was also accompanied by waning zeal and spirituality among the members. This apathy led White to suggest that Sabbatarian Adventists, as well as non-Sabbatarian as had been previously believed, were represented by the lukewarm Laodicean Church of Rev 3.[3] The modification in the thinking of Sabbatarians that this new application of the Laodicean message required is all the more striking when compared with earlier statements. Bates, in particular, had decried the "downward progress" of the Laodiceans (non-Sabbatarian Adventists) from 1844 to 1850.[4] He had accused the Adventists who had accepted the decisions of the April 1845 Albany Conference of falling into the Laodicean state of the church. More than anything else, it was the denial of the October 22, 1844, date as the end of prophetic chronology that convinced Bates that many Adventists were "'wretched, and miserable, and poor, and blind, and naked'."[5]

White's new interpretation caused quite a stir in the church,

---

[1]James White, "Moving West," RH, May 7, 1857, p. 5.

[2]James White, "New Fields," RH, October 6, 1859, p. 156.

[3]James White, "The Seven Churches," RH, October 16, 1856, pp. 188-189, 192.

[4]Bates, "The Laodicean Church," pp. 7-8; cf. above, pp. 112-113.

[5]Ibid., p. 8.

but apparently it was accepted by virtually all without question.[1]
Diminished spirituality, along with continued problems with offshoot
movements,[2] again served to underline the need for better organization and discipline.

Another step toward organization that occurred during this
era was the maturation of the concept of "Systematic Benevolence."
As has been shown, arguments had been put forward by White for the
support of the ministry since 1849,[3] but it was not until ten years
later that a thorough plan was established. In April 1858 a group of
ministers met at Battle Creek under the leadership of Andrews to
study the scriptural basis for the support of the ministry.[4] Their
recommendations were adopted by the church at large at a conference
in 1859.[5] In reporting the discussion in the Review, White put
forward three arguments in favor of systematic benevolence: (1) it

---

[1]Cf. Maxwell, Tell It to the World, pp. 147-151. Numerous
letters were addressed to the editor of the Review, accepting White's
interpretation and confessing the Laodicean state of the church.
See, e.g., J. H. Waggoner to Uriah Smith, RH, November 20, 1856,
p. 24; J. F. Case to [Uriah Smith], RH, December 4, 1856, pp 38-39.

[2]D. P. Hall and J. M. Stephenson led an offshoot movement in
Wisconsin (1854-1855) known as the "age-to-come" party. They later
allied with the Messenger Party of Case and Russell.

[3]See above, pp. 118-119.

[4]J. N. Loughborough, Rise and Progress of the Seventh-day
Adventists (Battle Creek, Mich.:   General Conference Association of
the Seventh-day Adventists, 1892), p. 215.

[5]The general meeting of the church was held June 3-6, 1859.
Members, including twelve ministers, attended the session from all
areas where Sabbatarian Adventists were working. However, they did
not attend as delegates. All church members were free to participate
in the meetings, including the business sessions (Editorial, "The
Conference," RH, June 9, 1859, p. 20; Joseph Bates and Uriah Smith,
"Business Proceedings of the General Conference of June 3-6, 1859,"
RH, June 9, 1859, pp. 20-21).

is scriptural, (2) it is reasonable, in that all can afford to participate, (3) it is necessary, as all ministers need to be free of financial embarrassment in order to work effectively.[1]

The details of the plan adopted at the conference were as follows: (1) each "brother" was asked to "lay by him in store on the first day of each week" (cf. 1 Cor 16:2) from two to twenty-five cents, (2) each "sister" should lay aside one to ten cents a week, and (3) both men and women should set aside one to five cents extra a week on each $100 of property owned.[2]

The arguments of White presented in support of the plan show that the imminent expectation of Christ's return pervaded this part of the life of the church as well. Christians, he argued, were to separate themselves from the world, and systematic, sacrificial giving to support the Sabbatarian Adventist movement would help them to forsake the distractions that riches bring. Their particular situation at the end of time, he continued, called for even greater sacrifices than Christians were asked to make in earlier generations. Sabbatarians believed that time was short and there was a great work to be done. For this reason, White said, the church had no settled pastors, only travelling missionaries. Once more the anticipation of the Second Coming influenced the nature of the movement's

---

[1]James White, "Conference Address," RH, June 9, 1859, pp. 21-23. At this time, the tithing principle as now understood by Seventh-day Adventists was not explicitly proposed. Ellen G. White followed the usual pattern by endorsing the principle of systematic benevolence after the church had studied its biblical basis (Ellen G. White, "Testimony for the Church No. 5," RH, June 16, 1859, p. 32).

[2]White, "Conference Address" (1859), p. 22.

organization.[1] The argument was, essentially, that in view of the shortness of time the situation "called for activity, means, sacrifices and persevering efforts."[2]

General Conference Organization
Established, 1860-1863

Between 1860 and 1863, events happened rapidly, and controversy over church order continued even more vigorously.

Early in 1860, White raised the question of legal organization and adopting a name for the denomination.[3] The two issues were closely related, as it was necessary to provide a name for the organization if it was to be recognized as an incorporated body by the State of Michigan, legally empowered to own the Review printing office and the Battle Creek meeting house. The strongest opposition came from Cottrell, who raised the familiar theme of "Babylon" as an argument against both a name and legal organization.[4] He reasoned that the steps necessary for legal incorporation would require the church to enter into an alliance with the state. By definition, in his view, such an alliance constituted "Babylon." Instead, Cottrell suggested that individuals could own the property, as White and Stephen T. Belden were presently doing in owning the printing office and meeting house, respectively. This brought a spirited reply from

---

[1]Cf. above, pp. 114-115.

[2]White, "Conference Address" (1859), p. 21.

[3]James White, "Borrowed Money," RH, February 23, 1860, p. 108.

[4]R. F. Cottrell, "Making Us a Name," RH, March 23, 1860, pp. 140-141.

White, who was "not a little surprised" that Cottrell should take
such a stand. He asked what would happen if the individual owner
should apostatize, and cited instances where such defections in the
Millerite movement had taken place.[1] Cottrell soon responded with a
conciliatory letter stating that he was willing to follow the Lord's
leading in the matter.[2] After White had a few more weeks' time to
compose his arguments, he made a much more detailed response to
Cottrell's views, in which he gave several reasons for his present
stand. He said, "We have hesitated six months" for fear of prejudice
and opposition. On their Eastern tour of 1859, however, the Whites
found less resistance to their ideas than expected, which encouraged
White to propose legal incorporation so that individuals might give
their property to the cause, particularly through wills.[3] He also
mentioned "a testimony"[4] from his wife, which advocated the same and
influenced him to propose a legal organization.

On another of his suggestions, insurance of church property,
he was willing to bow to the wishes of the brethren, some of whom
felt that carrying insurance was a sign of lack of faith in God's
protection. However, he reiterated his belief that there was no
biblical objection to holding property legally or insuring it. He
stated a rule on which it seems he built much of his doctrine of

---

[1]James White, "Making Us a Name," RH, March 29, 1860,
p. 152.

[2]R. F. Cottrell, "A Response," RH, May 3, 1860, p. 188.

[3]James White, "Making Us a Name," RH, April 26, 1860, pp.
180-182.

[4]Ellen G. White, Testimonies for the Church, 1:191.

church order: "All means which, according to sound judgment, will advance the cause of truth, and are not forbidden by plain scripture declarations, should be employed."[1]

White's arguments had the desired   effect on some. M. E. Cornell wrote   that his mind had been changed in the past week. "I wish to admit the necessity of complete organization," he said.[2] Cottrell, however, was not finished yet. In two additional letters he admitted the necessity of holding property legally and approved the idea of local church organization. However, he opposed insurance on the   basis   that   one's trust should be in God   rather   than man (Ps 37:39-40; 146:3) and because he felt that   acquiring   insurance represented   an   alliance   with the world.   Cottrell objected   to   a distinctive name for the church, as he was not willing to acknowledge an unscriptural title, and because such appellations were already used of "sects or factions." He also implicitly opposed the idea of a General Conference, arguing that the necessary legal requirements for holding property could be met by the organization of local churches.[3]

Thus the matter stood as the Battle Creek Conference, held September 28-October 1, 1860, approached. Before   describing the proceedings, it is necessary to present briefly the developments

---

[1]White, "Making Us a Name," RH, April 26, 1860, p. 180.

[2]M. E. Cornell, "Making Us a Name," RH, May 29, 1860, pp. 8-9.   Cornell declared that objections to a name and legal incorporation had come about because of false applications of Scripture.

[3]Letter, R. F. Cottrell to Uriah Smith, RH, June 5, 1860, p. 20; Letter, R. F. Cottrell to James White, RH, June 19, 1860, p. 36.

leading to the choice of a name at that conference. White had come
out strongly for the name "Church of God" in the Review.[1] He was
perhaps influenced by his earlier membership in the "Christian
Church," which adopted that name because it was perceived as biblical
and God-given, rather than of human devising; and because it made no
presumptive claims.[2] White put forward the same arguments in favor
of the name "Church of God."[3]

References to the name "Seventh-day Adventist" are scanty
before the 1860 conference.[4] At first the name seems to have been
used by the opponents of Sabbatarian Adventism and had a somewhat
derogatory connotation.[5] Another early reference was a letter from
J. C. Rogers, a Seventh Day Baptist, who wrote to White in 1853
saying that he had been "instructed to correspond with the Seventh-
day Advent people and learn of their faith."[6] Loughborough recorded
the fact that in advertizing a meeting in Hillsdale, Michigan, to be

[1]James White, "Organization," RH, June 19, 1860, p. 36.

[2]See above, pp. 29-32.

[3]White, "Organization" (1860), p. 36.

[4]For a fuller--though not completely accurate--account of the
choice of name, see Godfrey T. Anderson, "Make Us a Name," Adventist
Heritage, July 1974, p. 30.

[5]See, e.g., an editorial, "The Advent Question," AH, November
27, 1847, p. 133, which decried the growing divisions in Adventism as
follows: ". . . are there not 'Albany Conference' Adventists,
'Hartford Convention' Adventists, and Anti-conference Adventists?
Seventh day, first day, and every day Adventists? Workers and no
workers? Shut-door, open-door, feetwashers? 'Whole truth' and
'apostate' Adventists? Baptist, Methodist, Calvinist, Episcopal,
Congregational and Presbyterian Adventists?"

[6]Letter, J. C. Rogers to James White, RH, August 11, 1853,
p. 52.

held October 17-20, 1856, the name "Seventh-day Advent people" was used on the handbills.[1] The first person to use the exact form "Seventh-day Adventist" in the Review was a certain Sister P. P. Lewis in August 1859.[2] Opposition to the name "Church of God" came from R. Miles, who would only accept the name "Remnant";[3] and, after the selection of the name "Seventh-day Adventist," from W. Phelps who withdrew his membership over the matter.[4] Ultimately, "Seventh-day Adventist" won the day, because "Church of God" was a name already used by some denominations and was, it was decided, a "presumptive" title after all. By contrast, "Seventh-day Adventist" was "simple" and "expressive of our faith and position."[5]

The selection of a name was one of five objectives White had in mind for the conference held September 28-October 1, 1860. The other four were (1) the legal incorporation of the publishing association, (2) the organization of churches on a local level to own

---

[1]J. N. Loughborough, "Eastern Tour," RH, November 13, 1860, p. 205.

[2]Letter, P. P. Lewis to Uriah Smith, RH, August 18, 1859, p. 103. "Sister" Lewis spoke of Seventh-day Adventists in the context of her decision to join the church. One might imply from the natural way in which she used the name that it was quite familiar to her.

[3]James White, "'I Want the Review [sic] Discontinued,'" RH, September 25, 1860, p. 148.

[4][James White], "Organization," RH, July 16, 1861, pp. 52-53. Phelps also objected to the enrollment of members' names in a church book.

[5]"Business Proceedings of the B.C. Conference," RH, October 23, 1860, p. 179. Ellen G. White commented on the appropriateness of the name thus: It is "a standing rebuke to the Protestant world" and "carries the true features of our faith in front and will convict the enquiring mind" (Testimonies for the Church, 1:223-224).

church properties, (3) insurance of the publishing association and church buildings, and (4) a General Conference organization.

The strongest opposition at the conference came in the form of a letter read to the delegates on behalf of Cottrell. He repeated his claim that any organization must be on New Testament lines--that is, in order to conduct worship and administer the ordinances. That, and no more. It is unscriptural, he held, to reorganize in any other way, such as to own church property legally. An account of the protracted discussion--in which White was prominent and, in the end, swayed almost all to his point of view--appeared in the Review.[1] A reading of the proceedings of the conference reveals that White's rhetorical ability was an important factor in persuading the delegates to accept his suggestions. He took Cottrell to task for frequently changing his position on organizational matters and spoke of his own heavy responsibilities that came from holding the property of the publishing association in his own name. In the end, he argued that legal incorporation and a simple form of organization were required by "the necessities of the case."[2] His response to Cottrell's letter reveals the different hermeneutical approaches of the two men. Whereas Cottrell wrote, "We should fear organization as a church which has no warrant from the Scriptures,"[3] White said,

---

[1]"Business Proceedings of the B.C. Conference," RH, October 9, 1860, pp. 161-163; October 16, 1860, pp. 169-171; October 23, 1860, pp. 177-179.

[2]Ibid., p. 162.

[3]Ibid., p. 163.

"The Scriptures do not tell us how the church built upon the foundation of prophets and apostles, can hold power presses, offices, etc."[1]

At the time of the conference, White did not succeed in obtaining approval for insurance and a General Conference, but his reaction to the proceedings was one of satisfaction. "The action upon securing church property legally is all that we have ever suggested, and more than we ever expected would be so unanimously adopted."[2] Perhaps he was a little too sanguine in this opinion, for while much had been accomplished, it was still short of what he wanted.

From this time on, further developments in church organization came more rapidly than prior to the September 28-October 1, 1860, conference. The next spring "a more complete organization of the church" was proposed by Loughborough at another conference at Battle Creek.[3] At that meeting, held April 26-29, 1861, the legal incorporation of the Publishing Association, agreed to in principle earlier, was accomplished. Also, the former name--Advent Review Publishing Association--was changed to Seventh-day Adventist Publishing Association.

A committee of nine, which included White, was appointed to study the question of organization in its entirety and give a full

---

[1]Ibid., p. 169.

[2]James White, "Western Tour," RH, October 30, 1860, p. 188.

[3]"Business Proceedings of the B.C. Conference," RH, April 30, 1861, p. 189.

presentation of the subject in the Review.[1] The report of the committee shows evidence of a full exchange of views among its members and resulted, for the first time, in a fully developed plan of organization. The committee surveyed the past, outlining the reasons for fear of organization--the belief that salvation was not open to those not in the 1844 movement and fear that even the simplest form of organization might lead to "tyranny over the minds of Christians."[2] It strongly advocated both state conferences and a General Conference. For the first time the idea of delegates chosen on a numerically proportionate basis was mentioned. The purpose of such an organization was to make the evangelistic outreach of the church more efficient, to handle the rapid increase in membership, to conduct the business matters of the church, to own property, and to administer church order and discipline. For the first time, letters of transfer were advocated.

Reaction to this article was strong. While on his annual Eastern tour, White reported that New York and Pennsylvania had "voted down organization" and that Ohio had been "dreadfully shaken." He attributed the opposition in the East to Cottrell's negative attitude and the silence of several influential ministers. He mentioned by name those who were reluctant to state their position-- William S. Ingraham, Andrews, and Frederick Wheeler. In addition, the Battle Creek meeting house was still owned by Belden, because White and his associates were waiting for the whole church to be with

---

[1]J. H. Waggoner et al., "Conference Address. Organization," RH, June 11, 1861, pp. 21-22.

[2]Ibid., p. 21.

them before moving ahead. He concluded by saying that the church had regressed on the subject of unity in the three years since he wrote on the subject.[1] In the same issue, Ellen G. White echoed her husband's words. The churches they had visited in central New York were "perfect Babylon," and the blame rested largely on the "cowardly" ministers who believed in organization but did not speak out in favor of it. She accused them of waiting to see what the popular position was before taking a stand, although she did not mention specific names.[2] White's discouragement over the confusion of the work[3] (especially in New York) was in complete contrast to his optimistic tone at the close of the conference in the fall of 1860.

White's comments produced a flood of replies, all supporting him. Andrews wrote in an apologetic tone, followed by J. H. Waggoner, B. F. Snook, Ingraham, Rufus Baker, Hutchins, and Cottrell.[4] White appears to have been somewhat harsh with the brethren he named and accused of failure to support him. Ingraham and Andrews had merely refrained from voting on the name "Seventh-day Adventist," and Wheeler had supposedly failed to stand when a vote in favor of organization was taken at Roosevelt, New York, in August

---

[1]James White, "Organization," RH, August 27, 1861, p. 100.

[2]Ellen G. White, "Communication from Sister White," RH, August 27, 1861, pp. 100-102.

[3][James White], "Eastern Tour," RH, September 3, 1861, p. 108.

[4]See letters published in RH, September 17, 1861, p. 124; September 24, 1861, pp. 132, 135; October 1, 1861, p. 142; October 8, 1861, p. 151.

1861.[1] Actually, White's memory was faulty. No vote was taken.[2]

Andrews had, in fact, generally supported church organization in the past. When the question of legal incorporation first arose, he had cautiously suggested that a general meeting be held on the subject before a decision was made. White himself stated that Andrews had been "all right" on the organization question as early as January 1860. This he knew from a private conversation with Andrews.[3] This demonstrates how involved White was in the question of organization. Having borne the brunt of the responsibility of the publishing work and of unifying a scattered people, he apparently found it difficult to understand why others were not as eager to move on as he.

The intensity of White's feelings about the conflicts during the period 1858-1861 is shown by the following comment, written in October 1861:

> The past two years have been especially perilous to the cause. . . . The cause has stood in fearful peril from want of union among those to whom the flock should look for example. . . . The differences among us have been in consequence of blind prejudices, resulting from lack of consecration, and also opposition to the plain testimony. . . . We look back upon near two years as a blank. . . . A gloom has been increasing over us, injurious to the mind and to the health, until the world seemed mantled with the pall of death, our love for the word of God and spiritual things was waning, and the grave presented a welcome resting place.[4]

---

[1][James White], "Remarks," RH, September 24, 1861, pp. 134-135.

[2][James White], "Correction," RH, October 14, 1862, p. 160.

[3]J. N. Andrews, "The Review Office," RH, August 21, 1860, p. 108; [White], "Remarks," pp. 134-135.

[4][James White], "The Cause," RH, October 29, 1861, p. 172.

In the same year, Ellen G. White published "a testimony" which supported the concept of legal ownership of property.[1] She stated that Cottrell's opposition to church order had brought about a "scattering influence" in the church. Clearly referring to her husband's experience, she wrote: "Those who do not feel the weight of the cause upon them, do not feel the necessity of anything being done to establish church order."[2] Still writing in the context of church order, she added: "I saw that the living pointed testimony had been crushed in the church."[3] Evidently, the Whites had both experienced considerable opposition to the idea of the proposed organization. Most likely, their visits East were a primary cause of their dissatisfaction with the church's support on church order.

However, the influential leaders of the church now lined up behind White,[4] and at a conference held from October 4 to 6, 1861, the churches of Michigan joined together to form the first state conference. Bates was appointed as chairman,[5] Smith as clerk and Loughborough, Moses Hull, and Cornell as members of the conference

---

[1]Ellen G. White, Testimony for the Church. No. 6 (Battle Creek, Mich.: Review and Herald Pub. Assn, 1861).

[2]Ibid., p. 5.   [3]Ibid., p. 8.

[4]Communications supporting White's proposals were received from J. N. Andrews, "Organization," RH, September 17, 1861, p. 124; J. H. Waggoner, "To All the Brethren," RH, September 24, 1861, p. 132; Letter, R. F. Cottrell to James White, RH, September 24, 1861, p. 132; B. F. Snook, "Organization," RH, September 24, 1861, p. 132; Letter, William S. Ingraham to James White, RH, September 24, 1861, p. 134; Rufus Baker, "Necessity of Church Order," RH, October 1, 1861, p. 142; Letter, A. S. Hutchins to James White, RH, October 8, 1861, p. 151.

[5]Bates served as chairman of the conference session and as its chief officer during the ensuing year.

committee. A procedure was established for providing credentials to ministers in the conference and a vote was taken to study and publish in the Review instructions on organizing churches. The Michigan churches adopted a covenant which stated: "We, the undersigned, hereby associate ourselves together as a church, taking the name Seventh-day Adventists, convenanting to keep the commandments of God and the faith of Jesus Christ."[1]

The influence of the covenantal or federal theology of Puritanism on this covenant is apparent.[2] The Puritan covenant was a voluntary agreement among the "visible saints" in a community to establish a congregation with Christ as its ruler, to call and ordain its ministry to rule, admonish, and discipline its membership.[3] The covenant was also, of course, predicated upon and patterned after the covenants God had made with His people in Scripture. Adoption of a covenant was likewise a custom of congregationally organized churches.[4] The Seventh-day Adventist covenant was not intended to

---

[1]Joseph Bates and Uriah Smith, "Doings of the Battle Creek Conference, October 5 and 6, 1861," RH, October 8, 1861, pp. 148-149. It is worth noting the simplicity of the original Seventh-day Adventist statement of faith.

[2]On Puritan covenant theology see Ahlstrom, "Theology in America," pp. 240-242; A Religious History, pp. 130-133; Simpson, Puritanism in Old and New England, pp. 19-38; William Haller, The Rise of Puritanism (New York: Harper & Row, 1938), p. 180; Perry Miller, ed., The American Puritans: Their Prose and Poetry (Garden City, N.Y.: Doubleday Anchor Books, 1956), pp. 143-149.

[3]Cf. Ahlstrom, A Religious History, p. 133.

[4]According to Haller, the covenant, or solemn pledge with one another and God, became "the normal feature . . . of all the separatist groups," i.e., those who broke away from the Church of England (The Rise of Puritanism, p. 180). Cf. above, p. 23.

be, nor should it be regarded as, even a rudimentary creedal
statement.

Discussion at the organizational conference of Michigan
Seventh-day Adventists revolved around the very question of creeds.
When the covenant statement was put to a vote it passed, but not
unanimously. Desiring unity among the members, White proposed a
further interchange of ideas on the subject. Three reasons were then
put forward in favor of the covenant. First, it was suggested by
White that it would "tend to unity in the church."[1] Second, Cornell
cited biblical precedents for the people of God entering into a
covenant (2 Chron 15:12). In the third place, Moses Hull added that
it was according to apostolic custom. It was decided that "making a
creed is setting the stakes and barring the way to all future
advancement" and might prevent the acceptance of new light. The
simplicity and the perceived biblical character of the proposed
covenant resulted in its unanimous adoption when the vote was
retaken.[2]

The committee appointed to provide guidelines for organizing
churches reported ten days later.[3] In its report was a detailed
discussion on the New Testament basis of organization along with
procedures on the election and ordination of officers, reception of

---

[1]Bates and Smith, "Doings of the Battle Creek Conference,"
p. 148.

[2]Ibid.

[3]J. N. Loughborough, Moses Hull, and M. E. Cornell,
"Conference Address. Organization," RH, October 15, 1861, pp. 156-
157.

new members into fellowship, and letters of commendation for trans-
ferring members.

Six New Testament offices were named and discussed in the
report. The office of apostle was identified with, but not confined
to, the twelve. The list of spiritual gifts presented in Eph 4:11-13
was cited as evidence that the apostolic function might continue. In
addition, it was pointed out that several who were not among the
twelve, including Christ Himself, Paul, Barnabas, Titus, and
Epaphroditus, were all called apostles in the New Testament (Heb
3:1; Acts 14:4, 14; 2 Cor 8:22-23; Phil 2:25). Therefore, any who
were sent out, especially those who taught new truth or advocated
reform (such as Luther, Wesley, and Miller), might properly be
regarded as apostles.

The title "evangelist" was applied to those who travelled
from place to place as missionaries. The offices of elder, bishop,
pastor, and deacon, on the other hand, were confined to the local
church. Also, the terms of elder, bishop, and pastor were interchangeable, describing the same work of overseeing the congregation
(Titus 1:5, 7). An additional distinction was made between apostles
and evangelists on the one hand, and local officers on the other.
The former received their call from God, while elders, pastors,
bishops, and deacons were chosen by the local church. It is not
likely that the intent of this demarcation was to deny God's blessing
on the "lower" offices. It does indicate, however, that a three-
level hierarchical structure of ministers, elders, and deacons
existed within Seventh-day Adventism by 1861.

According to Loughborough and his colleagues, apostles and

evangelists operated in a wider sphere and therefore had wider authority. The Seventh-day Adventist "travelling brethren" were regarded as the equivalent of these "higher" offices. Only they, therefore, could organize churches. The elder, however, was qualified to administer baptism and the Lord's Supper, though only in the case of the unavoidable absence of a "higher" officer.

It is from this same report, apparently, that Seventh-day Adventists adopted their present position that one ordained to a higher office is automatically qualified to fill "any of the lower."[1] A New Testament precedent given for this practice was the fact that Peter and Paul spoke of themselves as both elder and deacon (1 Pet 5:1; Acts 11:30; 2 Cor 8:4).

The conference report confined the work of the deacon "exclusively to the temporal matters of the church."[2] Reception into membership was to be by unanimous vote of the church, and a person who transferred membership from one Seventh-day Adventist church to another was to provide a letter of commendation from the former church, signed by the church clerk. It was stated that this practice was to serve the same purpose as cards of recommendation for travelling preachers--to thwart "false brethren."

Within a year of the organization of the Michigan Conference, seven other state conferences were organized and White returned to a

---

[1]The rule was stated thus: "That no person by virtue of a lower office can fill a higher one; but any one filling a higher office, can by virtue of that office, act in any of the lower" (ibid, p. 157). Cf. Seventh-day Adventist Church Manual ([Washington, D.C.]: General Conference of Seventh-day Adventists, 1981), p. 83.

[2]Loughborough, Hull, and Cornell, "Conference Address. Organization," p. 157.

more optimistic frame of mind. In October 1861 he could write: "We are glad to see our people awake to this subject. To us it is a sign of better days."[1] Two weeks later he was even more cheerful: "All now rejoice in the triumphant success of the organization question."[2]

White could now look back on the recent struggle and say:

> Then we stood nearly alone. The battle went hard, and we needed help; but many of our very prudent men saved their ammunition to fire away upon the subject of organization now when the battle is fought and the victory won. Almost every day we receive a communication from some good brother upon the subject of organization. A few only of these have found place in the Review.[3]

Actually, the battle was not quite won yet--the General Conference organization lay ahead, and with it a few more discouraging moments for White. Before that, the first annual session of the newly formed Michigan Conference met on October 4, 1862, at Monterey, Michigan. The highlights of the meeting were as follows: seventeen churches were admitted to membership, ministers were assigned areas of responsibility, the question of the status of divorced individuals who remarried before joining the church was referred to the conference committee, and other states were invited to send delegates to the first General Conference the next year.[4] Possibly out of concern on the part of the leaders to maintain proper

---

[1][James White], "Organization," RH, October 22, 1861, p. 164.

[2][James White], "The Battle Creek Church," RH, November 5, 1861, p. 180.

[3][James White], "Organization," RH, January 7, 1862, p. 44.

[4]Joseph Bates and Uriah Smith, "Business Proceedings of the Michigan State Conference," RH, October 14, 1862, pp. 156-157.

discipline and unity in the church in the face of schismatics and false teachers, it was also decided that ministers of other denominations who joined the Adventist ministry must be reordained. This provision appears somewhat inconsistent, since White himself and several other ministers had come out of other churches and not been reordained. Another action, seemingly designed to maintain order, was taken that ministers not yet ordained could not baptize even though, just one year previously, Loughborough and his committee had declared that local elders might perform baptisms.[1]

Both of these decisions, to require reordination and allow only ordained ministers to baptize, were part of a trend to concentrate authority in the ministers who administered the work at state conference or General Conference level. It was not, perhaps, simply a matter of ordination that qualified one to maintain discipline and unity, but, as White remarked on other occasions, a question of experience. He believed that only when one had struggled through challenging circumstances, such as Sabbatarian Adventist pioneers had done in the years immediately after the Disappointment, could an individual be prepared to direct the work of the church on a wider scale.[2] In addition, refusal to recognize the validity of ordinations performed in other denominations was justified on the basis that other churches held doctrines and creeds that were

---

[1]See above, p. 157.

[2]Cf. James White, "Things in Maine," RH, November 26, 1867, p. 378; [James White], "Order in the Church of God," RH, December 12, 1871, p. 204; James White, "Tract and Missionary Work," November 5, 1872, p. 164.

contrary to Bible truth. Any minister ordained by them was therefore "ordained in error."[1]

This October 1862 Michigan Conference session chose William S. Higley, Jr., a layman, as chairman of the conference for the coming year.[2] The selection of someone from outside the ministerial ranks should not be considered at variance with attempts at the same session to maintain discipline in the church by stressing the importance of ordination to the gospel ministry. Even though Seventh-day Adventists were moving toward a centralized structure, the appointment of Higley may indicate the continuing influence of a congregational form of organization. Congregationalists tradition- ally assigned the task of administration to a lay officer (i.e., local elder).[3]

The autumn of 1862 found the Whites on their usual Eastern tour on which they met the familiar problem of disorder in the churches. This led White to present another argument for a General Conference. He complained that travelling ministers had to come under the jurisdiction of less experienced colleagues, and this would not be the case if there were a general organization.[4] He experi- enced opposition in New York, Pennsylvania, Ohio, Iowa, and New

---

[1]James White, "Re-Ordination," RH, August 6, 1867, p. 120.

[2]Bates and Smith, "Business Proceedings of the Michigan State Conference," p. 157.

[3]Cf. above, pp. 23-24.

[4][James White], "General Conferences," RH, July 1, 1862, p. 37. The strength of White's feelings on the matter is reflected in his declared intention not to leave Michigan again until the situation was changed.

England. The details of the opposition are not available because he refused to publish the proceedings of meetings where organization was voted down.[1]

Wishing to avoid further controversy and perhaps convinced by White's arguments concerning organization, Andrews,[2] Snook,[3] and Cottrell[4] wrote in, expressing their approval of White's statements concerning the need for a General Conference. Cottrell, happily forgetful of past disagreements, claimed, "I have never opposed . . . church organization." He also urged the organization of the New York Conference, but it is doubtful that he had much influence, as the conference had already been called and met just five days later.

The First General Conference Session

The first General Conference meeting had originally been set for October 1863 but was moved forward, at White's suggestion, to May. All the leaders hurriedly wrote in, expressing their approval.[5] Just prior to the conference, White wrote twice in the Review presenting the purpose of a General Conference organization.

---

[1][James White], "Organization," RH, September 30, 1862, p. 140.

[2]J. N. Andrews, "General Conferences," RH, July 15, 1862, p. 52.

[3]B. F. Snook, "General Conferences," RH, July 29, 1862, p. 72.

[4]R. F. Cottrell, "System--Order," RH, October 21, 1862, pp. 165-166.

[5]Letters to James White from B. F. Snook, A. S. Hutchins, I. Sanborn, J. N. Andrews, J. H. Waggoner, and Moses Hull appeared in the Review, March 24, 1863, p. 132.

Speaking of an equitable assignment of ministers to their work, he asked, ". . . must not the General Conference be the great regulator?" At the present time, he said, Vermont and Michigan had more than their share of ministers, while all other areas were "almost destitute." He argued further that to avoid these inequalities the General Conference must have jurisdiction over state conferences, and over the ministers, and must also be responsible for their support, not the local congregation.[1]

Finally, the conference convened on May 20, 1863, with Michigan, Wisconsin, Iowa, Minnesota, New York, and Ohio represented, though not yet on a numerically proportionate basis. A constitution was adopted and one also recommended for state conferences. White was elected unanimously as president, but because of his role in urging organization he declined to serve. John Byington took his place.

---

[1][James White], "General Conference," RH, April 28, 1863, p. 172. Before the conference convened, a committee appointed to vindicate the character of White met, because there were "certain reports prejudicial to the character of Eld. White . . . being extensively circulated through the country" (Uriah Smith, "Business Meeting of the Church in Battle Creek," RH, March 31, 1863, p. 141). White's success in his business ventures, especially his management of the Publishing Association, had resulted in some gossip concerning his integrity. In order to put these rumors to rest Smith, as chairman, called for people with evidence on both sides of the question to send in their testimonies (cf. Robinson, James White, pp. 207-209). To White's gratification, his personal character was vindicated with seventy-four letters received in his favor, none against (John Byington and Uriah Smith, "Report of General Conference of Seventh-day Adventists," RH, May 26, 1863, pp. 204-206). Cf. [Uriah Smith, G. W. Amadon, and E. S. Walker], A Vindication of the Business Career of Elder James White (Battle Creek, Mich.: Seventh-day Adventist Pub. Assn, 1863).

Reflections on Church Order, 1863-1881

Growth of Seventh-day Adventism

During the period 1863-1881, the Seventh-day Adventist Church grew steadily from approximately 3,500 members in 1863 to about 7,500 in 1874, and 15,570 at the time of the 1880 General Conference session, the last one in White's lifetime. At the same time, the number of conferences grew from five in 1863 to thirteen in 1874 and twenty-four in 1880, one of which was Denmark, the first outside the United States. By 1880, the church was also operating eight mission territories, five of them in North America and three in Europe.[1] The years from 1863 to 1881 may be described, therefore, as a time of consolidation and expansion, as the church built upon the organizational platform established in 1863.

New institutions and societies added to the increasing complexity of the work of the leading administrators. These included the Health Reform Institute, Battle Creek College, and the Tract and Missionary Society. Concentration of these organizations in Battle Creek,[2] along with the General Conference itself and the already

---

[1]See Uriah Smith, "The Seventh-day Adventists: A Brief Sketch of Their Origin, Progress, and Principles," RH, November 10, 1874, p. 156; "General Conference Statistics, 1880," RH, October 28, 1880, p. 280. For an account of the development of Seventh-day Adventists' sense of world-wide mission, see Damsteegt, Foundations, pp. 285-293.

[2]For several years White encouraged people to move away from the "gospel hardened" East to the West, and to Battle Creek in particular (White, "Moving West," p. 5). References to problems connected with over-centralization appear in the 1870s. White wrote, "I think Brother Butler makes a mistake in making Battle Creek the hub, and making all the rest of the world whirl about it" (Letter, James White to William C. White, July 5, 1874). For Ellen G. White's

established Publishing Association, led to a relatively large influx
of members to live in the area and placed considerable strain on the
human and financial resources of the small and young movement.[1]

As the developments described above did not bring about any
major changes in the system of church order during this time,[2] a
detailed historical account of such matters is not essential as a
background to the discussions which took place on authority and
leadership.[3] Before turning to the organizational issues, however,
we will provide additional information to that given in chapter one
on White's personal experience during these years, so that we may
determine the role played by him in church organization between 1863
and 1881.

---

views on concentration of members and institutions, see Letter,
Ellen G. White to the Managers of the Battle Creek Sanitarium,
October 16, 1890. Cf. also Spalding, Origin and History, 1:265-278.

[1]Short historical sketches of these organizations may be
found in "Battle Creek Sanitarium," SDA Encyclopedia (1976), 10:135-
140; "Andrews University," 10:45-52; "Tract and Missionary Societies," 10:1495-1497.

[2]In fact, no major change was made until 1901, when
continued growth demanded reorganization. Though significant, the
changes made in that year may be described as modifications of an
already existing system. They did not change the basic structure of
the church, which remains essentially the same today as in 1863.
Apart from a brief description and analysis in the conclusion (see
below, pp. 272-278), the events of 1901 fall outside the scope of
this dissertation, but accounts of them may be found in Schwarz,
Light Bearers, pp. 267-281; Spalding, Origin and History, 3:19-46;
A. V. Olson, Through Crisis to Victory, 1888-1901 (Washington, D.C.:
Review and Herald Pub. Assn, 1966), pp. 175-199. Cf. also Anderson,
"The History and Evolution of Seventh-day Adventist Church Organiza-
tion" (1960), pp. 205-234.

[3]Good historical studies of this period of Seventh-day
Adventist history are limited. The reader may wish to consult
Schwarz, Light Bearers, pp. 151-165; Spalding, Origin and History,
2:7-89.

James White's Physical and Emotional Health

Growth and expansion were not without problems. On White, in particular, the additional strain of administration fell. For example, in 1871, he was re-elected president of the General Conference, even though he was already president of the Publishing Association, the Benevolent Association, and the Tract and Missionary Society, and was also serving as editor of the Review and of the Health Reformer.[1] In 1874, he was serving as president of the General Conference, the Publishing Association, the Health Reform Institute, the Tract and Missionary Society, and the Education Society;[2] all of this, in spite of the fact that he had suffered a severe stroke in 1865, followed by several partial ones in 1871 and 1873.[3] It is probably true that he never fully recovered from the first setback.[4] Virgil Robinson, whose biography of White is generally sympathetic, admits that "in his later years, James White found it increasingly difficult to accept opposition. Weakened by disease, he at times was irrational."[5] Yet Robinson could also state that about 1876 "James was at the height of his powers spiritually and mentally."[6] This point of view, that his spiritual and mental abilities were not permanently impaired even if his

---

[1]Robinson, James White, p. 230.

[2]Smith, "Seventh-day Adventists," p. 148.

[3]For an account of White's health and its effect upon his work, see Robinson, James White, pp. 207-293.

[4]Schwarz, Light Bearers, p. 164.

[5]Robinson, James White, p. 290.

[6]Ibid., p. 259.

physical powers were, is echoed by Richard W. Schwarz who writes: "The dedication, imagination, and concern of earlier years remained; the physical abilities did not."[1]

The validity of the above analyses is best evaluated by an examination of the content and logic of White's articles on such issues as authority and leadership. This should help to determine whether or not his mental powers diminished after 1865 and will be undertaken later in the chapter, but the opinions of his contemporaries and his own statements concerning his mental state in his published works and private letters will be considered first.

Butler (1834-1918),[2] who served as General Conference president during 1871-1874 and 1880-1888, part of the time because of White's incapacity, wrote after the latter's death:

> It has been my fortune to labor in connection with him in this cause when our views were in harmony in reference to measures; also when they were not in harmony. Such things occur in every cause. Yet I feel sure he labored for what he thought was right, and honestly felt he must make efforts to carry out his convictions. With such force of character, such aggressive instincts and tenacity of purpose as he possessed, it was

---

[1]Schwarz, Light Bearers, p. 164.

[2]Butler's family had joined the Millerite movement in 1843. Disillusioned by the Disappointment in 1844, young Butler rejected the Christian faith and remained a skeptic for twelve years. His parents, however, became Sabbatarian Adventists a few years after the Disappointment and were well acquainted with the Whites. Upon conversion, Butler joined the Sabbath-keeping Adventist church in Waukon, Iowa, and was soon ordained, first as deacon and then elder. He became president of the Iowa Conference of Seventh-day Adventists in 1865 and was ordained to the gospel ministry two years later. He served as president of the General Conference from 1871 to 1874, and from 1880 to 1888. He showed particular interest in the development of Seventh-day Adventist institutions and in questions of authority and leadership in the church (see below, pp. 175-178). For a biographical study of Butler, see Emmet K. Vande Vere, Rugged Heart: The Story of George I. Butler (Nashville, Tenn.: Southern Pub. Assn, 1979).

inevitable that he should come into conflicts with the men he found in his way in the carrying out of his plans. This is always so with men of earnest purpose who attempt the work of a reformer.[1]

Later, Butler wrote in a personal letter and perhaps, therefore, more openly, "Our dear Brother White thought we were his enemies because we did not see things as he did. . . . I attributed it all to disease and infirmity."[2]

Ellen G. White also commented on her husband's actions and emotional state. In 1872 she attributed the fact that he sometimes had spoken "without due consideration and with apparent severity" to the pressure of excessive responsibilities at Battle Creek.[3] In the same year, she faulted him for "talking out his discouragements and dwelling upon the unpleasant features of his experience," but also placed some of the blame on his ministering brethren who dropped responsibilities upon him which they should have borne themselves.[4]

White's tendency to be critical of others and to give way to discouragement was reflected in his writing. He complained that "Eld. White and his wife are reproached from Maine to California,"[5] and reported that "for more than a year past we have been sinking in health, faith, hope, and courage, under the many cares and labors

---

[1]G. I. Butler, "The Death of Elder White," RH, August 16, 1881, pp. 120-121.

[2]Letter, G. I. Butler to J. N. Andrews, May 25, 1883.

[3]Ellen G. White, Testimonies for the Church, 3:86.

[4]Ibid., p. 96. Cf. also ibid., p. 508 (written in 1875).

[5]James White, "Permanency of the Cause," RH, July 8, 1873, p. 28.

placed upon us."[1] During another time of discouragement he exclaimed, "My brethren are all crazy. . . . I am the only sane man in the crowd."[2] He did recognize, however, that some of the blame for his troubles rested on his own head. Several statements may be found by him similar to the following: "I have tried to do too much. At present I shall leave the planning to wiser heads, and the work to men of firmer nerves."[3]

It would seem that White, apart from his health problems, at times had difficulty in adjusting to the changing situation brought about by the growth of the church. He was used to being intimately involved in every aspect of the work of the church, to approaching problems aggressively, speaking directly, and rebuking his associates openly if they failed to measure up. In the early days, the church needed his vigorous and charismatic leadership, but times changed and it became no longer possible for one man to directly supervise everything. White admitted this himself:

> The time was when it was my place to lead off, and where necessary to storm it through. Times changed, and organization came in. Then I had to hold the important offices from necessity. But the work became too large for any one man to stand at the head of all branches. And now the time has come for me to retire, and let younger men come to the front. I had a

---

[1][James White], "Eastern Tour," RH, November 14, 1871, p. 172.

[2]Letter, James White to Dear Children, May 3, 1879.

[3]Letter, James White to Dear Children, May 11, 1879. See also White, "Permanency of the Cause," pp. 28-29; Letter, James White to G. I. Butler, July 13, 1874; Letter, James White to Ellen G. White, April 16, 1880; Letter, James White to William C. White, May 4, 1880; Letter, James White to Ellen G. White, February 7, 1881.

work to do, a place to fill. Now the work is too large for one of my age and temperament to preside over.[1]

We would suggest that White's evaluation of his own temperament and abilities was, in this case at least, quite accurate.

As a result of his style of leadership and his tendency to censure those whom he thought were not pulling their weight, there was an inclination on their part to let White do it all himself. This tendency he realized in later years.[2] Perhaps his desire to control every detail of administration contributed to the decision of the General Conference annual session, in 1865, that it was "highly important for the well-being of the cause that the president of the General Conference should attend the session of each of the State conferences."[3] A year later the delegates to the General Conference agreed that two other members of the General Conference committee should share the responsibility of attending state conference sessions,[4] but after a time, as the number of conferences increased, even this became impracticable.

It is perhaps significant that the record in the Review of the decision that a General Conference committee member should attend each conference session is followed immediately by a resolution to disfellowship Elders Snook and W. A. Brinkerhoff from membership of

---

[1]Letter, James White to Dear Children, May 11, 1879.

[2]James White, "Leadership," RH, May 23, 1878, p. 164. Cf. Robinson, James White, p. 290.

[3]"Report of the Third Annual Session of the General Conference of S. D. Adventists," RH, May 23, 1865, p. 197.

[4]"Fourth Annual Session of General Conference," RH, May 22, 1866, pp. 196-197.

the Iowa Conference. They had been president and secretary,
respectively, of the Conference until 1865, when they broke away,
partly because of their opposition to centralized authority in the
Seventh-day Adventist Church. One of the aims in appointing representatives from the General Conference to state conferences was,
therefore, to maintain doctrinal unity and effective discipline
within the church.[1] The disaffection of Snook and Brinkerhoff served
as an early test for the General Conference in its relationship with
a local conference. In view of the prominent positions of their
former leaders, the constituency of the Iowa Conference found it
helpful to turn to the General Conference as an independent body to
act in an advisory capacity.[2]

From what has been said above, we would gather that White's
overwork probably contributed to his stroke, which left his physical

---

[1]Cf., e.g., a comment by Ellen G. White which, though written
in 1907, reflects the same view of the purpose of organization:
"Thorough organization is essential and will be the greatest power to
keep out spurious uprisings and to refute claims not endorsed by the
word of God" [emphasis mine], (Ellen G. White, Testimonies to
Ministers [Mountain View, Calif.: Pacific Press Pub. Assn, 1962],
p. 489).

[2]See, Loughborough, Rise and Progress of SDAs, pp. 267-269;
"Marion Party," SDA Encyclopedia (1976), 10:853-854. In "confes-
sions" in the Review, Snook and W. H. Brinkerhoff gave other reasons
for their disaffection: (1) unwillingness to accept Ellen G. White's
visions, (2) belief that the church had become too conformed to the
world, (3) personal conflicts with the Whites, and (4) the General
Conference had become (in their opinion) too domineering (Letter,
B. F. Snook, to James White, RH, July 25, 1865, pp. 63-64; Letter,
W. H. Brinkerhoff to James White, RH, July 25, 1965, p. 64). Snook's
and Brinkerhoff's repentance did not last long. In May 1866, the
General Conference session recommended that the Iowa Conference
committee drop the two Iowa men from church membership (John Byington
and Uriah Smith, "Fourth Annual Session of General Conference," RH,
May 22, 1866, pp. 196-197). For Ellen G. White's assessment of the
reasons for Snook's "rebellion," see MS 1, 1865.

abilities permanently weakened and made him susceptible to recurring bouts of discouragement and depression. Whether or not his condition permanently lessened his mental powers will become clear as we discuss the theological debates of this period.

The "Perfect Success"[1] of Organization

Ever pragmatic, White believed that the organization which had been achieved was a success because it worked. "Our people are well organized," he wrote. "Our Church Organization, State Conferences, General Conference, Systematic Benevolence, and Publishing organizations can hardly be improved. To say the least, the machinery works well."[2] In 1871 he attributed "the perfection and efficiency of our organization"[3] to the fact that Seventh-day Adventists tried to incorporate, as far as possible, "the efficiency of expression and form in the New Testament. The more of the spirit of the gospel manifested, and the more simple, the more efficient the system."[4]

It may seem curious that a "perfect" organization might be

---

[1]Thus, White described the situation on several occasions. See, e.g., [James White], "An Appeal to the General Conference Committee on Behalf of New England," RH, October 6, 1863, p. 148; "Organization," (1864), p. 164.

[2][James White], "Mutual Obligation," RH, October 17, 1871, p. 140.

[3][White], "Conference Address" (1873), p. 184.

[4]James White, "Organization and Discipline," RH, January 4, 1881, p. 8. Cf. other references by White to the simplicity of the system: [White], "Mutual Obligation," RH, June 20, 1871, p. 4; [James White], "Organization," RH, August 22, 1871, p. 76; White, "Permanency of the Cause," pp. 28-29.

modified or improved upon. The need to reorganize did arise later
(notably in 1901),[1] but the addition of another level of administration[2] did not substantially change the way in which the church
worked. In other words, perfect church order must be viewed as that
which meets the present needs of the church as simply and efficiently
as possible.

The theme of the perfect order of heaven, which served as a
pattern for Israel in the wilderness and should serve as a similar
example in the present, is also prominent in Ellen G. White's
writing.[3] "Perfect order" characterizes the work of the angels, she
wrote in 1868. If ministers failed to follow the example of the
angelic host, "who are thoroughly organized and more in perfect
order," she continued, the angels would be unable to "work for us

---

[1]An edited record of the proceedings at the time of
reorganization is available in the General Conference Daily Bulletin
for the 1897, 1899, 1901, and 1903 sessions. For historical accounts
of later organizational developments, especially in 1901, see,
Schwarz, Light Bearers, pp. 267-281, 373-392; Anderson, "The History
and Evolution of Seventh-day Adventist Church Organization" (1960);
G. Jorgensen, "An Investigation of the Administrative Reorganization
of the General Conference of Seventh-day Adventists as Planned and
Carried Out in the General Conference of 1901 and 1903" (M.A. thesis,
SDA Theological Seminary, 1949).

[2]Union conferences were introduced in N. America in 1901.
They are "a unit of church organization formed by a group of local
conferences or missions" ("Union," SDA Encyclopedia [1976], 10:1514).
Unions were designed originally to distribute power from General
Conference headquarters and stood between the conference and General
Conference administrative levels. In 1913 "divisions" of the General
Conference were created in an effort to bring decision-making powers
even closer to the constituency. However, divisions are units of the
General Conference, not an additional administrative level (see
"Division," SDA Encyclopedia [1976], 10:393-394).

[3]See Ellen G. White, Testimonies for the Church, 1:179, 650-
651; 4:199, 429; Testimonies to Ministers, p. 29.

successfully."[1] The context of this statement indicates that she did not so much have in mind the precise method of order, as its spirit. Harmony, intelligence, faithfulness, and exactness are attributes required of a perfect worker and a perfect organization.

Several benefits derived from the efficiency of the work were mentioned by White, such as the end of "secession" from the church,[2] numerous conversions to the faith,[3] and "unity of feeling" which was attributable largely to the General Conference itself--"a powerful means of union and strength."[4] As Butler noted, structural unity had also ensured doctrinal unity. Not only did everyone believe the same thing "from ocean to ocean," but "not a single theological position have our people, as a whole, ever accepted that they have been obliged to give up," he declared.[5]

It is doubtful that Butler intended to imply that the thorough organization of Seventh-day Adventism was the sole or even the main cause of theological accord. There were other factors that should be considered, such as a common hermeneutical approach to the Scriptures, a sense of shared experience in the Disappointment (still

---

[1]Ellen G. White, Testimonies for the Church, 1:649. Cf. Ellen G. White, The Story of Patriarchs and Prophets (Mountain View, Calif.: Pacific Press Pub. Assn, 1958), p. 376.

[2][James White], "The Association," RH, June 2, 1863, p. 4.

[3][James White], "Eastern Tour," RH, November 24, 1863, p. 204.

[4]White, "Tract and Missionary Work," p. 164. Cf. "Business Proceedings of the Twelfth Annual Meeting of the S.D.A. General Conference," RH, November 25, 1873, p. 190.

[5]G. I. Butler, "Stability a Characteristic of Our Work," RH, April 15, 1873, p. 140.

present thirty years later), the unifying influence that acceptance
of Ellen G. White's prophetic role created, and her husband's leadership qualities. Nevertheless, it seems Butler believed that it
was not possible for a church to be theologically unified under a
non-centralized form of government. The conviction that Seventh-day
Adventism had been entrusted with God's final message of salvation
to the world implied that possible distortion of the message by
leaving theological interpretation to the inclinations of local
congregations could not be risked.

White was in no doubt as to the reason for the unity of
Seventh-day Adventism:

> The Guiding Hand was with them, which is the reason why the lapse
> of more than ten years has not revealed defects which have
> demanded changes. We unhesitatingly express our firm conviction
> that organization with us was by the direct providence of God.
> And to disregard our organization is an insult to God's
> providential dealings with us, and a sin of no small
> magnitude.[1]

The observations on the success of organization by White and
Butler expressed above indicate that, to their way of thinking, one
justification for the Seventh-day Adventist system of church order
lay in its achievements. The church was growing, defections were
minimal, and harmony prevailed in doctrine as well as in personal
relationships. In reality, their statements offered in proof of
God's direction differed little from the arguments given by White
when the subject of organization was first aired.[2] The regulation of
travelling preachers and quelling fanaticism were the problems in the

---

[1] James White, "Organization," RH, August 5, 1873, p. 60.

[2] Cf. above, p. 128.

early 1850s. The measures taken then were designed to promote "union of sentiment, feeling and action."[1] In the 1870s, White spoke in terms of the "unity of feeling" among Seventh-day Adventists. His pragmatic approach to both situations, to rudimentary organization and General Conference supervision, was the same.

Leadership

One of the most significant issues that arose during the years 1863 to 1881 was the role and authority of the leaders of the church. It was raised by Butler in an address to the General Conference session on November 14, 1873, when he argued that every great movement in history, from Noah to Miller, had a leader in a position of authority who, because of God's gifts, could see clearer than the rest.[2] In response to this address, the General Conference session resolved:

> That we fully indorse [sic] the position taken in the paper read by Eld. Butler on Leadership. And we express our firm convic-tion, that our failure to appreciate the guiding hand of God in the selection of his instruments to lead out in this work has resulted in serious injury to the prosperity of the cause, and in spiritual loss to ourselves. And we hereby express our full purpose of heart faithfully to regard these principles, and we invite all our brethren to unite with us in this action.[3]

Butler elaborated on his original article in an eight-part Review series, between July 28 and October 13, 1874. He built his

---

[1][White], "Western Tour" (1854), p. 172.

[2]A transcript of Butler's address appeared in a pamphlet (G. I. Butler, Leadership [Battle Creek, Mich.: General Conference of Seventh-day Adventists, 1873]), and an edited version was published in the Review (G. I. Butler, "Leadership," RH, November 18, 1873, pp 180-181).

[3]"Business Proceedings of the Twelfth General Conference," p. 190.

case upon the creatorship of God. All authority and government, of nations, families, and the church, is derived from God's government and authority as Creator, he argued.[1] The true church, which takes the Scriptures as its only rule of faith and practice, is the human agent by which God educates and saves man, he said. Butler likened the role of the church in disciplining its members to that of a school or an army.[2] He saw the church as the home of the regenerate only, although he admitted that all are more or less unworthy to be called followers of Christ.

Butler's model for church organization was the New Testament church. He perceived a parallel between the various levels of church government in the New Testament and the structure of the Seventh-day Adventist Church. Thus, the Jerusalem Council (c. A.D. 49) corresponded to the General Conference, the geographical subdivisions of the church—such as Judea, Galatia, and Asia Minor—comported with state conferences, all of which were built on the basic unit, the local church. In both the apostolic and the Seventh-day Adventist Church, he continued, they followed the same rule: "The simplest means . . . would be the one to choose."[3]

The officers of the New Testament church also corresponded, Butler felt, to the system within Seventh-day Adventism. Building his exposition on Eph 4:11, he suggested that the evangelist's work was analogous to the minister's in the Seventh-day Adventist Church.

---

[1]Butler, "Thoughts on Church Government," RH, July 28, 1874, pp. 52-53.

[2]Ibid., August 4, 1874, p. 60; August 18, 1874, p. 68.

[3]Ibid., August 18, 1874, p. 69.

The term "elder" he applied to both ministers and teachers on the one hand (those who carried a wider responsibility than the local church), and to local elders whose duties were restricted to a particular congregation on the other. He felt that deacons' responsibilities should be confined to temporal affairs in harmony with New Testament practice.[1]

Butler was president of the General Conference when he expressed his ideas on leadership. Yet he did not have himself in mind when he wrote. Rather, he was referring to the Whites, in particular to James, as the ones to whom respect and submission were due as founders of the movement. Butler argued that there are occasions when God "designs to accomplish a special work" through specially chosen leaders upon whom he has placed gifts of leadership.[2] He continued by comparing White's role in the emergence of the Sabbatarian Adventist movement with Moses' work in leading the children of Israel through the wilderness.[3] In view of White's twenty-five years of successful management, Butler wrote, "in all matters of expediency with the cause," it was right "to give his [White's] judgment the preference."[4]

White's reply appeared soon after Butler's series on church government.[5] His theme was that there is only one leader of the

---

[1]Ibid., August 18, 1874, p. 69; September 1, 1874, p. 85; September 8, 1874, pp. 92-93.

[2]Butler, Leadership, p. 7.   [3]Ibid., p. 12.

[4]Ibid., p. 13.

[5]James White, "Leadership," RH, December 1, 1874, pp. 180-181.

church, namely Christ. In the time of the apostles, he argued, "the mark and office of leadership has not been laid on any one person." Instead, Christ taught that "he that is greatest among you will be your servant." White spoke of "mutual submission," which is demanded of all. "Christ's ministers are shepherds of the flock and leaders of the people in a subordinate sense," he said.[1]

In Life Sketches, the Whites wrote of Butler: "Some, taking extreme positions upon the subject of leadership, have been ready to acknowledge us as the leader of this people."[2] Seeking to counteract this tendency toward one-man rule, they pointed out that "organization was designed to secure unity of action, and as a protection from imposture." It was never intended, they added, "as a scourge to compel obedience."[3] The purpose of local, state, and General Conference organization, in their view, then, was to harness power, not create or enhance it.

The moderation of this position was clear and resulted in the rescinding by the General Conference session, in August 1875, of its earlier resolution to recognize the preeminent authority of the Whites.[4]

---

[1] Ibid.

[2] James White and Ellen G. White, Life Sketches, Ancestry, Early Life, Christian Experience, and Extensive Labors of Elder James White and His Wife, Ellen G. White (Battle Creek, Mich.: Seventh-day Adventist Pub. Assn, 1888), p. 408.

[3] Ibid.

[4] "Proceedings of the Fourteenth Annual Session of the S.D. Adventist General Conference," RH, August 26, 1875, p. 59. Ellen G. White also wrote in 1875 of the danger of one man's mind controlling another's, and asserted that administrative responsibilities should be more widely spread (Testimonies for the Church, 3:492-493).

Authority of the General Conference

The position and authority of leaders in the church naturally gave rise to the question of the role and area of jurisdiction of the General Conference. White may have argued against one individual's having too much authority, but he did underline the importance of the role of the General Conference committee's supervision of the work. An enlightening insight may be found in a private letter from White to Loughborough in 1878.[1] The latter had been working in California for the previous ten years since pioneering Seventh-day Adventist work in that state, but the General Conference had voted that he should be transferred to England to lead out in the recently started work there. Judging by the remarks in White's letter, Loughborough had indicated that he was not inclined to accept the invitation to move. White admitted that it was not within the province of the General Conference committee to direct, but advise, but then proceeded to exert as much pressure as possible to persuade Loughborough to accept the committee's "advice."[2] White's arguments were effective. Loughborough went to England that same year.[3]

---

[1]Letter, James White to J. N. Loughborough, July 19, 1878.

[2]Ibid. Some of White's arguments hardly seem designed to induce cooperation. One of the reasons given for the proposed transfer was "the best of your days for labor are behind you." Other more positive arguments were that change would be beneficial to the preacher and the congregation for which he had been working, the Seventh-day Adventist Church in England would benefit by his services, the younger ministers in California would develop more rapidly without him to rely on, and people on both sides of the Atlantic would be disappointed if he did not go, as his appointment had already been announced!

[3]On Loughborough's work in Britain, see "A Century of Adventism in the British Isles," British Advent Messenger, Centennial

White's persuasion of Loughborough was not the only time he suggested that the General Conference must have authority to administer the field and to send ministers from place to place.[1] The attempt to control unauthorized travelling preachers as early as 1850 had presaged more systematic distribution of the work force in later years.[2] In 1871 he argued that because of the experience of the men at the General Conference they must have the right to send ministers from place to place. It was the duty of young ministers to raise up new churches and the responsibility of the veteran workers to visit from church to church to oversee the work, he said.[3]

White reiterated on several occasions his position on the authority of the General Conference. "Our General Conference is the highest earthly authority with our people," he declared in 1873.[4] Again, the reason given for the need to respect the General Conference committee was that their experience made them the "safest counselors."[5] He also made the point that members of the committee were in a better position, as overseers of the world-wide work, to

---

Historical Special, 1974, pp. 5-6; "Great Britain and Northern Ireland, Development of SDA Work," SDA Encyclopedia (1976), 10:528-531; "Loughborough, John Norton," SDA Encyclopedia (1976), 10:815-816.

[1]Cf. above, pp. 161-162.

[2][White], "Order in the Church of God," p. 204.

[3]White, "Organization" (1873), p. 60. Cf. also [White], "Conference Address" (1873), p. 180; James White, "Organization," RH, June 24, 1880, p. 8; "Organization and Discipline," pp. 8-9.

[4]White, "Organization" (1873), p. 60.

[5]Ibid.

understand the needs of the Seventh-day Adventist Church than those with responsibilities at a state or local level.[1]

The success of the church's organizational structure led White to claim that "the S.D. Adventists are said to be the most thoroughly organized Christian people known."[2] In view of the numerous well-established denominations in the United States at the time, it was quite a declaration.[3] However, such complete order was not a total blessing, in his opinion. In the same context he remarked that the large number of institutions and duties placed too great a burden on such a comparatively small church.

White's views on the authority of the General Conference were shared by his wife. In the context of a discussion on the need to avoid dissension within the church, she wrote in 1880: "Let individual judgment submit to the authority of the church."[4] In the same article, she recognized that leaders may have their faults and make the wrong decisions at times, yet, "notwithstanding this, the church of Christ on earth has given them an authority that cannot be lightly esteemed."[5] The elders of the Battle Creek church drew up a

---

[1]Ibid.

[2]White, "Organization" (1880), p. 8.

[3]We have already remarked on the dim view Seventh-day Adventists took of the "confusion" within other churches (see above, pp. 118, 126) and on Butler's claim that Seventh-day Adventism's system of organization had helped to avoid doctrinal differences (see above, p. 173).

[4]Ellen G. White, "Unity of the Church," RH, February 19, 1880, p. 113.

[5]Ibid.

pledge in 1880 which echoed the regard for the authority of the church expressed by the Whites. They affirmed that

> the General Conference, aided by the counsel of those whom we believe the Lord has chosen to lead out in this work from its very commencement, and by the spirit of prophecy graciously manifested among us, is the highest authority ordained by the Lord in his church, and that the action and advice of this authority, in all matters of expedience and discipline, should be received and respected by all this people.[1]

The statement by the elders of the Battle Creek Church provides some nuances that may not be apparent from the discussion of White's views on authority. The power of the General Conference was not absolute, in their view. The counsels of Ellen G. White (regarded by the elders and the General Conference committee members as a messenger of God), and of other experienced leaders who had been prominent from the earliest days of Sabbatarian Adventism (presumably they had in mind White, Loughborough, S. N. Haskell, and maybe a few others), were to be taken into account by the General Conference before their decisions were to be regarded as worthy of acceptance.

Other Organizational Developments, 1863-1881

In addition to the authority of its leadership, attention was also given to other matters relating to church organization. As with all emerging religious movements, the qualifications for, and nature of, the work of the ministry soon became an issue.

Within seven years of the organization of the General Conference, the idea of a ministerial training institute was first

---

[1]"Battle Creek," RH, February 5, 1880, p. 89.

proposed--by White.[1] It may be that the need for such an institution became apparent to him as he viewed what he considered to be numerous unproductive ministers in the field.[2] At any rate, a Ministers' Lecture Association was formed and a course of study outlined, including a list of subjects to be covered, prescribed reading, even the careful practice of penmanship. It was further stated that "all will be expected to bear examination on these points."[3] This may be regarded as the starting point for the present ministerial training program of the Seventh-day Adventist Church.

Seventh-day Adventist writers also began to reflect on the nature of the minister's work and his spiritual qualifications. Andrews wrote that, above all else, a minister must be deeply spiritual and sure of his call to the ministry by the Holy Spirit. In addition, he needed to be a diligent student of the Scriptures and have good common sense.[4] In White's opinion, a minister was first

---

[1]See, "Business Proceedings of the Eighth Annual Session of the General Conference of S. D. Adventists," RH, March 22, 1870, pp. 109-110.

[2]White expressed concern several times about the "ease" of the contemporary ministry, compared to the dedication and sacrifice required in earlier days (cf., c.g., James White, "Present Truth, and Present Conflicts," RH, November 8, 1870, pp. 164-165; November 15, 1870, pp. 172-173; November 22, 1870, pp. 180-182; November 29, 1870, pp. 188-189; [White], "Mutual Obligation," June 6, 1871, p. 196; June 13, 1871, p. 204; June 20, 1871, p. 4; October 17, 1871, p. 140).

[3]See James White and Uriah Smith, "Ministers' Lecture Association," RH, April 12, 1870, pp. 132-133, on the formation of the Association. See James White et al., "Course of Study for Ministers," RH, May 10, 1870, p. 164, for the list of requirements. No immediate reaction to the Association, either positive or negative, is recorded in the Review.

[4]J. N. Andrews, "The Call to the Christian Ministry," RH, June 29, 1869, p. 4.

of all an ambassador for Christ. "He speaks to the people in Christ's stead. He is, if he is what he should be, Christ's representative in an eminent sense."[1] Because of the holiness and dignity of his work and position, it was imperative that he be a man of God, a man of prayer, and a student of the Word of God, White continued.

Butler wrote the one article that appeared in the Review during this period on the significance of ordination.[2] He began with a definition: "Ordination is the formal act by which a person is set apart by the laying on of hands, and prayer."[3] He continued with a discussion on the validity of apostolic succession as held by the Roman Catholic, Greek, and Episcopalian Churches. His conclusion was that an unbroken succession could not be established from history, and that one ordained under such a system could not be certain of the validity of the ceremony.[4]

According to Butler, a person who had been ordained was separated from the ranks of the laity. Ordination to the ministry (in contrast to ordination as an elder or deacon) was to be carried out by authority of the local conference, he added. It was not the local congregation that designated a person to serve as minister. This is, of course, not surprising, as at that time ministers were not associated with a local Seventh-day Adventist church, but instead

---

[1]James White, "The Cause of God," RH, December 2, 1880, p. 360.

[2]G. I. Butler, "Ordination," RH, February 13, 1879, pp. 50-51.

[3]Ibid., p. 50.

[4]Ibid.

worked in much the same way as the Methodist circuit-rider. The local elders carried out many of the functions that the church pastor does today. Thus, Butler said, "they may baptize and administer the ordinances, and may do any of the duties proper to be done by those in offices lower than themselves."[1]

Frequent mention was made of the role of the minister as a servant. Christ was given as the example, and His ministers were encouraged to emulate Him. As White wrote shortly before his death:

> Christ is Lord and Master of all, and yet he is servant of all. He is the Chief Shepherd of the flock, and, in a subordinate sense, his ministers are shepherds, guides and guardians of the sheep of his fold. Was Christ servant of all! Much more should his chosen servants willingly and faithfully serve the church.[2]

In bringing to an end these reflections on authority and leadership, we return to the question raised earlier concerning the mental abilities of White during this era.[3] On more than one occasion, especially when writing on the authority of the church and its leaders, his voice was often more moderate than those of his contemporaries. He was no doubt susceptible to discouragement and inclined to be censorious and critical; but the content of his articles on church organization during this time reveals no circumscription of his mental abilities.

---

[1]Butler, "Thoughts on Church Government," RH, September 1, 1874, p. 85. On the qualification of elders to perform duties of "lower" officers (i.e. deacons), see above, pp. 156-157.

[2]James White, "Christ and His Ministers," RH, April 19, 1881, p. 248. See also, White, "Organization" (1873), pp. 60-61; S. N. Haskell, "Responsibility of Christ's Ministers," RH, June 17, 1880, p. 395; [J. N. Andrews], "The Wants of the Cause of Christ," RH, July 6, 1869, p. 12.

[3]Cf. above, pp. 165-166.

Conclusion

It has been suggested that organizational developments in Seventh-day Adventism came about very slowly.[1] However, one wonders if the fifteen years between the emergence of distinctive Sabbatarian Adventism and the organization of the General Conference (1848-1863) cannot rightly be considered an unusually short time for a community of believers to grow from a small handful of scattered individuals to a centrally administered church of approximately 3,500 members,[2] with three levels (local congregation, conference, and General Conference) of administration.

When one remembers the theological and missiological outlook of those believers in 1848, it is, in fact, a remarkably rapid development. First, they remembered the arbitrary treatment and expulsion of the Millerites from "Babylon" prior to the Disappointment. "They were thus instinctively set against organizing another church, or formulating any restrictive creed-- or even a specified Statement of Faith."[3] Sabbatarian Adventists had found their anti-organizational fears confirmed when the Millerites organized at the 1845 Albany Conference and immediately emulated the Babylonish churches they had left by formulating a statement of beliefs and rejecting fellowship with those who engaged in "fanatical" practices such as observance of the Jewish

---

[1]Froom, Movement of Destiny, p. 134.

[2]See, e.g., Schwarz, Light Bearers, p. 97.

[3]Froom, Movement of Destiny, p. 134.

Sabbath[1] and footwashing, or who continued to propose the Shut Door.[2]

Second, the most prominent leaders of Sabbatarian Adventism (White and Bates) had both been members of the Christian Connection. More than any other denomination, the "Christians" had shown in their history an antipathy to creeds, to a distinctive sectarian name, and to anything but the most rudimentary form of church structure.[3] Both Himes and Marsh, editors of important Millerite papers, had been prominent in the Christian Connection, and the ideas and publishing work of both men extended their influence to Sabbatarian Adventists.[4] Himes's publishing activities had a profound effect on White's later literary endeavors, although the former's vigorous leadership at Albany greatly diminished his standing with White and associates. Marsh's anti-organizational ideas expressed in the Voice of Truth were repeated in Present Truth and the early issues of the Review.[5]

In the third place, as has already been discussed,[6] Shut Door

---

[1]The Albany Conference resolved "that we have no fellowship for Jewish fables and commandments of men." While the Sabbath is not mentioned specifically, it is probable that the delegates had it in mind as they passed the resolution ("Mutual Conference," VT, May 21, 1845, p. 59). Cf. above, p. 86.

[2]Cf. Damsteegt, Foundations, pp. 121-122; Froom, Prophetic Faith, 4:833-842.

[3]See above, pp. 29-32. Cf. also Anderson, Outrider of the Apocalypse, p. 75, who describes the acrimony in the 1850s between Bates and Albany Conference Adventists, whom Bates described as "Laodicean" because of their rejection of Sabbatarian Adventist teachings.

[4]See above, p. 40. Cf. also Froom, Prophetic Faith, 4:634-635.

[5]See above, pp. 120-121.

[6]See above, pp. 103-109.

ideas limited the missiological vision of Sabbatarian Adventists until about 1850 or 1851. As their views on the Shut Door were allied to the expected imminent return of Christ, we would suggest that the establishment of a centralized ecclesiastical administrative structure and the evangelization of the world by a group of one to two hundred people implied a longer delay of the Second Coming than they could imagine.[1]

What factors, then, brought about the radical change of attitude toward organization? Three seem most significant.

1. A careful reading of the Review indicates that the foundation on which Seventh-day Adventist church organization was based was a desire to be true to the biblical (and especially New Testament) pattern. At first, it was considered that every detail of church order must have the specific backing of a New Testament precedent,[2] but later, almost entirely through White's strong leadership, a broader approach was adopted. Gradually, Seventh-day Adventist leaders came to recognize that there was development and modification of church organization within the New Testament itself, and that only the principles of church order were stated in Scripture. Thus White, and later the other leaders, came to the conclusion that any practice that would increase the effectiveness of the church's work was appropriate, as long as it was not directly opposed in Scripture.[3]

---

[1]Cf. above, pp. 117-118.

[2]See, e.g., White, "Our Tour East," p. 52. Cf. also [White], "Church Order," p. 164, where he advocated the "perfect system of order set forth in the New Testament."

[3]The choice of a name for the church is one instance when White claimed that the New Testament did not provide specific

At virtually every conference up to 1863, therefore, where important decisions were taken to establish new structural forms or administrative practices, a committee was established to study the biblical basis for innovation, or review of scriptural support for their actions took place on the floor of the conference itself.[1]

The final exposition on the subject of church order by White, which appeared in January 1881,[2] furnishes an instance of his mature reflection on the subject and reinforces the importance of the hermeneutical methods of Seventh-day Adventism in the emergence of church organization. As White wrote, "The testimony of the Bible, therefore, especially of the New Testament, must be allowed to decide these subjects [of order and discipline] of vast importance to the prosperity of the church."[3] Still, at the same time, White maintained that the system of Christian organization is not given fully in the New Testament.[4] As has been mentioned above,[5] this opinion of his may well have lain at the foundation of some of the disagreements with others, especially Cottrell. The number of occasions this different hermeneutical method appeared indicates that

---

guidance. Selection of a name, he said, "is left as a matter of propriety and convenience" ([James White], "Organization," RH, October 1, 1861, p. 140). On at least three occasions White reiterated this pragmatic approach to scriptural authority for church order (see above, pp. 130-131, 144-145; below, pp. 189-190).

[1]Conferences where time was given to the study of biblical church organization, and described earlier in this chapter, include: November 6, 1857, and June 3-6, 1859; the April 1858 study group on Systematic Benevolence led by Andrews; September 28-October 1, 1860; April 26-29, 1861; October 5-6, 1861.

[2]White, "Organization and Discipline," pp. 8-9.

[3]Ibid., p. 8.   [4]Ibid.   [5]Cf. above, pp. 136-137.

it was a decisive factor in the development of Seventh-day Adventist organization. We would also conclude that White's more flexible approach was eventually accepted and provided Seventh-day Adventism with the freedom to adapt its system and institutions to meet the needs of the present. Thus, whatever the situation, whether "thwarting imposters" in 1850[1] or appraising the jurisdiction of the General Conference over the church in North America and Europe in 1881, Seventh-day Adventists claimed that they were true to scriptural principles.

2. The strong leadership qualities and practical approach of White were also major forces in the development of Seventh-day Adventist organization. Despite his earlier experiences as a Millerite that inclined him against the established churches, he overcame his bias against organized religion to become known as "the father of church order among Sabbatarians."[2] We have already indicated that his publishing activities and travels among the scattered believers reinforced what was probably a natural inclination to conduct matters in an orderly, down-to-earth manner.[3] Thus, numerous statements may be found by White that organization came about through the "sheer necessity of the case."[4]

---

[1]See above, pp. 119-120.

[2]Froom, Prophetic Faith, 4:1059.

[3]See above, pp. 137-138.

[4]White, Life Incidents, p. 299. Cf. also his statement, "We first suggested organization as a matter of pure necessity" ([White], "Organization," RH, July 16, 1861, p. 52). Loughborough, who participated in the organizational debate, echoed the same idea. He argued that New Testament church order was established as necessity appeared, and that it was therefore appropriate for Seventh-day

Another principle advocated by White was that organization should be "the simplest form possible."[1] He was aware that there was potential danger in increasing the size and scope of the church's structure and authority, but this danger was far preferable to its alternative--anarchy.[2] The aim of White and the other supporters of organization in Seventh-day Adventism is well expressed by Loughborough:

> Those who drafted the form of organization adopted by Seventh-day Adventists labored to incorporate into it, as far as possible, the simplicity of expression and form found in the New Testament. The more of the spirit of the gospel manifested, and the more simple, the more efficient the system.[3]

3. Finally, the role of Ellen G. White cannot be ignored in this summary. Her influence has been described as crucial and in opposition to the general trend of Adventist thinking at the time,[4] but the weight of the evidence cited in this chapter demonstrates that, in

---

Adventists "to supply the lack as far and as fast as a necessity for system in working should appear" (Loughborough, The Church: Its Organization, Order and Discipline, p. 66). Contemporary Seventh-day Adventist writers have recognized the pragmatic nature of early church order. George W. Reid, for example, suggests that early Seventh-day Adventists "moved under the pressure of practical necessity toward organizing, rather than from theological constraint" (Reid, "Time to Reorder the Church?" p. 14). Cf. also Veltman, "The Role of Church Administrators and Theologians" (1980), p. 2.

[1]White, "'I Want the Review [sic] Discontinued,'" p. 148. White expressed exactly the same words at the September 28-October 1, 1860, Battle Creek Conference ("Business Proceedings of the B.C. Conference," RH, October 9, 1860, p. 162).

[2]See, e.g., White, "Extremes," pp. 140-141.

[3]Loughborough, The Great Second Advent Movement, p. 346.

[4]See, e.g., Graham, "Ellen G. White: An Examination of Her Position and Role in the Seventh-day Adventist Church" (1977), p. 72; Spalding, Origin and History, 1:293-295. Graybill in "The Power of Prophecy" (1983), pp. 140-144, claims that Ellen G. White's endorsement was essential to the success of White's "innovations" on church

this specific area at least, it was her husband who prosecuted the battle on the front line. Her writing on the subject was always supportive of White's aims; but, as far as church order was concerned, her comments were mainly in general terms. She remained in the background in comparison to her husband's prominence. In view of the general acceptance of her prophetic gift by Seventh-day Adventists, her opinions were no doubt valued and her influence must have contributed to the eventual accomplishment of an effective system, but the substantive decisions made grew out of vigorous and open discussion and careful examination of the biblical model.[1]

---

order. However, he fails to substantiate his point, especially in view of the fact that he admits that Ellen G. White's views were less influential on doctrinal developments in the church before 1865 (ibid., p. 27).

[1]Cf. Ellen G. White's own account of her role in the development of church order in Testimonies to Ministers, pp. 24-32. She wrote: "We had a hard struggle in establishing organization. Notwithstanding that the Lord gave testimony after testimony upon this point, the opposition was strong, and it had to be met again and again" (p. 26).

CHAPTER V

THEOLOGICAL REFLECTIONS AND CONCLUSIONS

From the historical account and analysis undertaken in the previous chapters several important factors have emerged. These may be grouped under four main headings: (1) theological concerns which undergirded the practical organizational developments, (2) the biblical foundation of Seventh-day Adventist organization, (3) the influence of the prevailing organizational philosophies and practices of other denominations in 19th-century America on early Seventh-day Adventist thought, and (4) personal and pragmatic factors. While it may be necessary to make such distinctions for the sake of clarity, it is recognized that each of the issues listed above is closely bound up with the others.

Three theological motifs of Seventh-day Adventism emerge as vital foundational elements in the development of church order. They are: (1) the awareness of a task or mission which must be accomplished in the context of Christ's imminent return,[1] (2) the belief that purity and unity of doctrine must be achieved and maintained among those who are preparing to meet the soon coming

---

[1]The development of the Seventh-day Adventist sense of mission has been described above, pp. 103-113.

Christal,[1] and (3) the authority of the leadership of the church which
is needed to provide efficient organization to pursue the church's
perceived mission and to maintain doctrinal unity.[2]

Our purpose in examining the biblical foundation for church
organization is to determine as far as possible the faithfulness of
those who formulated the Seventh-day Adventist doctrine of church
order to the biblical (especially the New Testament) pattern as they
perceived it. In other words, were Seventh-day Adventist leaders
faithful to their presuppositions and to their claim that the
biblical norm is of the utmost priority? It should also be asked how
developments and innovations in church order were justified in terms
of their fidelity to the biblical model.

The survey of the systems of church polity of the more
prominent denominations of that day is to depict the religious
setting out of which Seventh-day Adventist church order emerged. We
seek here to discover the characteristics of the major Protestant
organizations and determine the extent to which these systems
influenced the framers of Seventh-day Adventist church government.

In considering the personal factors behind the emergence of
Seventh-day Adventist church order, the personality of White has been
shown to be a crucial factor. In this evaluation we also seek to
express the impact of his religious experience as a participant in
the Millerite movement and the Disappointment of 1844, and as a

---

[1]On the developments that led to doctrinal agreement, see
above, pp. 91-103.

[2]The extent of the leaders' jurisdiction became an issue in
the 1870s. See above, pp. 175-178.

pioneer in the early days of Sabbatarian Adventism, upon his beliefs in the area of church organization. Of course, White did not stand alone. The effect of interaction with other independent and strong-minded leaders also needs to be taken into account.

In conclusion, we shall attempt to identify the implications of this study for some contemporary issues that have arisen in Seventh-day Adventism in the area of church order. In so doing we shall seek to discover to what extent principles established and policies adopted during the era under consideration (1844-1881) provided the foundation for later expansion and efficiency--or lack of it--of Seventh-day Adventist endeavors on the one hand, and gave rise to possible problems and conflicts on the other.

Theological Grounds for
Seventh-day Adventist Organization

The continued dialogue among early Seventh-day Adventists, described in the previous chapter, indicates that the form church order took was not a matter of indifference. Bates's call for restoration of proper church order, for example, reflected a belief that correct organization as well as doctrinal purity were required of a church living in expectancy of the imminent Second Advent.[1] Early Seventh-day Adventists appear to have been convinced that effective order was an essential prerequisite for efficient witness. In fact, we would suggest that church order, built in harmony with

---

[1] See, e.g., above, p. 134.

the principles of the New Testament, was considered to be a part of the proclamation of the church.[1]

The Seventh-day Adventist Sense of Mission

In contrast to the Millerites,[2] who believed that their work in proclaiming Christ's return would be completed by the time of the expected Advent in 1844, Sabbatarian Adventists gradually came to the view that their work of warning the world of Christ's imminent return had just begun.

At the heart of their new sense of mission was the conviction of Sabbatarian Adventists that they constituted a prophetic movement--the "remnant church" of Rev 12:17--which was called by God in the last days to proclaim the Second Coming of Christ.[3] The message to be preached by the "remnant" was summed up in the three angels' messages of Rev 14:6-11. White, Bates, and Andrews each wrote extensively on these verses.[4]

---

[1]Cf. above, pp. 173-174. Harmony in doctrine and church order were regarded as evidence of the validity of the Seventh-day Adventist message. Eduard Schweizer, commenting on the order of the New Testament church, writes: "The New Testament's pronouncements on Church order are to be read as a gospel--that is, Church order is to be regarded as a part of the proclamation in which the Church's witness is expressed" (Church Order in the New Testament [London: SCM Press, 1961], p. 14).

[2]See above, pp. 95-96.

[3]See, e.g., James White, "The Third Angel's Message," PT, April 1850, p. 66.

[4]See Bates, A Seal of the Living God; Andrews, "Thoughts on Revelation XIII and XIV," pp. 81-86; "The Three Angels of Rev XIV, 6-12," RH, February 6-May 1, 1855; J. N. Andrews, The Three Messages of Revelation XIV, 6-12 (Battle Creek, Mich.: Seventh-day Adventist Pub. Assn., 1877); [James White], "The Angels of Rev. XIV," Nos. 1-4, RH, August 19, 1851, p. 12; September 2, 1851, p. 20; December 9, 1851, pp. 63-64; December 23, 1851, pp. 69-72.

The proclamation of the first angel (Rev 14:6-7) was an announcement of the judgment at hand "that has been given to the present generation."[1] Sabbatarian Adventists at first understood the work of the first angel to have taken place prior to the Disappointment, from about 1840 to 1844.[2] The second angel (vs. 8) announced the fall of Babylon. Sabbatarian Adventists, in keeping with their Millerite heritage, interpreted the fall of Babylon as the moral fall of the "nominal churches."[3] The third angel's warning against receiving the "mark of the beast" and worshipping "the beast and his image" was understood by White and his colleagues to be directed toward those who "observe the first day of the week, instead of the fourth commandment."[4] A contrast was drawn between "the saints" who kept God's commandments (see vs. 12), including the Sabbath, and those who followed the practice established by Rome of observing the first day of the week.[5]

---

[1][White], "The Angels of Rev. XIV.--No. 3," RH, December 9, 1851, p. 63.

[2]Ibid. Cf. Andrews, "The Three Angels of Rev XIV, 6-12," RH, February 6, 1855, p. 169.

[3][White], "The Angels of Rev. XIV.--No. 3," p. 64; Andrews, "The Three Angels of Rev XIV, 6-12," RH, February 20, 1855, pp. 177-178.

[4][White], "The Angels of Rev. XIV.--No. 4," p. 71; Andrews, "The Three Angels of Rev. XIV, 6-12," RH, April 3, 1855, pp. 203-204. Bates's contribution to Seventh-day Adventist understanding of the message of the third angel and its relationship to the Sabbath was particularly important. See above, pp. 95-97. Cf. Maxwell, "Joseph Bates and SDA Sabbath Theology"; Damsteegt, Foundations, pp. 140-146.

[5][White], "The Angels of Rev. XIV.--No. 4," pp. 70-71; Andrews, "The Three Angels of Rev. XIV, 6-12," RH, April 3, 1855, p. 204. Cf. Bates, A Seal of the Living God, pp. 24-26, 54-56.

The messages of the three angels of Rev 14 were more than urgent warnings of impending judgment in the view of Sabbatarian Adventists. They were also needed by the true worshippers of God (cf. Rev 14:7) "to bring out, and perfect the church of Christ preparatory to his Second Coming."[1] Thus, the angels of Rev 14 represented at least a twofold work to be done. On the one hand their messages were seen as announcements of judgment upon those who received the mark of the beast and on the other hand "the patience of the saints" stood in contrast, representing those who, according to White, endured beyond the Disappointment by keeping "the commandments of God and the faith of Jesus" (Rev 14:12).[2] While White did not specifically refer to the establishment of church order as an essential part of this perfecting and preparatory process prior to the Second Coming, such an application was made by Bates, who viewed the restoration of the Sabbath and proper church organization as necessary prerequisites for readiness to meet the Lord.[3] Bates declared: "This unity of the faith, and perfect church order, never has existed since the days of the apostles. It is very clear that it must exist prior to the second advent of Jesus."[4]

---

[1] [White], "The Angels of Rev. XIV.--No. 2," RH, September 2, 1851, p. 20.

[2] Ibid., No. 4, December 23, 1851, p. 71.

[3] On the restoration of the Sabbath, see Bates, The Seventh-day Sabbath, A Perpetual Sign, 2nd ed. (1847), p. 60. On the restoration of church order, see Bates, "Church Order," p. 22. See also above, p. 134.

[4] Bates, "Church Order," p. 23. Cf. two comments by White: "The whole church should be taught to feel that a portion of the responsibility of good order, and the salvation of souls rests upon her individual members" ([White], "Gospel Order," RH, December 27,

One should also bear in mind that, partly because of the influence of their Millerite heritage, early Sabbatarian Adventists continued to regard the creedal differences and denominational divisions of the churches as evidence of the fallen condition of the established denominations. Andrews, for example, believed the moral fall of Babylon (nominal Christianity) announced by the second angel (Rev 14:8) was illustrated by the false doctrines taught by the creedal churches.[1]

The interpretation of the three angels' messages provided a biblical rationale for the contrast Sabbatarian Adventists drew between the confused doctrines of Babylon and the doctrinal unity of the "remnant," a term used by Seventh-day Adventists to describe themselves based upon Rev 12:17 and 14:12.[2]

The significance of the remnant motif for early Sabbatarian Adventists was expressed by White. He stated that they "must be the last end of the church; those who live in the last generation before Christ comes. Sabbath-keepers will understand it, when they are

---

1853, p. 196). God "is waiting for his people to get right, and in gospel order . . . before he adds many more to our numbers" ([James White], "Gospel Order," RH, March 28, 1854, p. 76).

[1]The false doctrines named by Andrews were: the idea of a temporal millennium or a thousand years of peace, infant baptism, Sunday observance, the immortality of the soul, the doctrine of the Trinity, belief in a spiritual Second Advent, and slavery (Andrews, "The Three Angels of Rev. XIV, 6-12," RH, March 6, 1855, pp. 185-186).

[2]Rev 12:17 depicts the remnant which remained after the 1260 days of persecution in the wilderness as those "who keep the commandments of God and have the testimony of Jesus." For a valuable summary of the development of Seventh-day Adventist understanding of the three angels' messages, see Damsteegt, Foundations, pp. 165-242.

reviled, and called Jews, fools, fanatics, etc."[1] In another context White indicated that the remnant are characterized by their observance of the ten commandments, "the revival of the gifts, and acknowledge the gift of prophecy among them."[2]

In view of the perceived unique mission of the remnant and the shortness of time before Christ's expected return, the leaders of the church expressed the need for efficiency and simplicity.[3] White voiced the opinion in 1859, when discussion on the organization of conferences was at its highest, that because there was "a great work to do in a short time" Sabbatarian Adventists must work as perseveringly, efficiently, and sacrificially as possible.[4] Two years later a conference address, which represented the views agreed upon by the General Conference delegates in session, was published in the Review. Reflecting on the reasons for past opposition to organization, which included the belief that their work of preaching to the world was finished, the address stated: "According to our views of

---

[1]James White, "Signs of the Times," RH, September 13, 1853, p. 75.

[2]White, Life Incidents, p. 326. In commenting on White's exposition, Damsteegt concludes (somewhat surprisingly, in our opinion) that "the Remnant motif does not appear to have directly contributed to the growth of SDA missionary consciousness." In view of the fact that he admits that the remnant concept provided "a positive argument for their uniqueness in history" it would seem to follow that Seventh-day Adventists would be convinced of the urgent need to proclaim a message which in their view was not being given by any other Christians and must be preached before Christ's return (Damsteegt, Foundations, p. 244).

[3]Cf. above, p. 191.

[4]White, "Conference Address" (1859), p. 21.

the work was our method of labor."[1] The same address pointed out that as the awareness of the church's mission to the world developed, the need for organization became essential because "the world is going down to ruin and must be warned."[2]

It is apparent that Seventh-day Adventist convictions concerning the urgency and uniqueness of the message to be proclaimed had an impact upon church order. However, while one would conclude that the unique eschatological emphasis of Seventh-day Adventist beliefs was the primary theological influence in the formation of church organization, other theological concerns, as well as some practical considerations, emerged as time passed which were in tension with the prophetic message of Christ's imminent return. In short, Seventh-day Adventists became aware that there might be a "delay" before the Second Advent.[3]

The Delay of the Second Coming

Immediately after the Disappointment of 1844 Adventists believed their work of warning the world had been completed. Early Sabbatarian Adventists in particular clung to the conviction that the

---

[1]Waggoner et al., "Conference Address. Organization," pp. 21-22.

[2]Ibid., p. 22. Numerous other statements by early Seventh-day Adventist leaders expressed the belief that proper gospel order is essential to the church's mission to the world. We cite just a few: [White], "Gospel Order" (1854), pp. 76-77; White, "Yearly Meetings," p. 68; White, "Making Us a Name," RH, April 26, 1860, pp. 180-182; [White], "Conference Address" (1873), pp. 180-181; J. N. Andrews, "Duty Toward Those That Have the Rule," RH, September 16, 1873, p. 108; Butler, "Leadership," pp. 180-181.

[3]In speaking of a "delay" of the Second Advent it is recognized that we articulate human attitudes, not God's point of view. There is no delay in the fulfillment of God's purposes.

eternal destiny of all had been decided on October 22, 1844.[1]
Recognition of a still to be accomplished mission dawned slowly.
Nevertheless, such an understanding of a future task did take shape
(especially after Seventh-day Adventist doctrinal tenets had been
consolidated by the end of the 1848 conferences); but belief that the
Sabbath must be preached, proper church order restored, and a people
perfected before the Second Coming implied an extension of time.[2]

The dilemma among Seventh-day Adventists as they preached an
imminent Second Coming while also establishing "permanent"
educational, health, and publishing institutions first became
manifest in the 1860s. It was no accident that legal incorporation
of the Battle Creek publishing house was at the center of early
debates over organization. Such a step not only brought the church
into unwanted involvement with the state but also implied that the
institution was expected to last for some length of time.[3]

The sending of Andrews to Europe in 1874 as the first
official overseas missionary of the Seventh-day Adventist Church
represented an important step in the realization that a world-wide
mission lay ahead.[4] Thus, Seventh-day Adventists increasingly found

---

[1]Cf. above, pp. 103-113.

[2]On the question of "delay" and imminence of the Second
Advent, see also above, pp. 187-188.

[3]On the debate over legal incorporation, see above, pp. 143-
152.

[4]On the development of Seventh-day Adventist mission theory
between 1844 and 1890, see Borge Schantz, "The Development of
Seventh-day Adventist Missionary Thought: Contemporary Appraisal,"
2 vols. (Ph.D. dissertation, Fuller Theological Seminary, 1983), pp.
199-278. Cf. also Damsteegt, Foundations, pp. 103-298.

themselves in the situation of praying, "Come quickly, Lord Jesus," and at the same time entreating God for time and peace in order that the church might continue its work.

The continuing growth of the Seventh-day Adventist Church, and the increase in number and size of its institutions and administrative structure, placed the church in a potential quandary with which it had to come to grips. How could Seventh-day Adventists keep in creative tension the expectancy of Christ's Second Coming and at the same time build for a seemingly overwhelming task of preaching the gospel "to every nation, and kindred, and tongue, and people" (Rev 14:6)?

It would seem that Seventh-day Adventists found themselves in a similar position to Christ's first followers, who also expected His imminent return while faced with the task of fulfilling the gospel commission (Matt 28:19, 20). Christ's parable of the nobleman who went to a distant country to receive a kingdom before returning to his waiting servants (Luke 19:12-27) expresses the appropriate attitude with which Christians should look forward to the Second Coming. The instruction to "occupy till I come" (vs. 13)[1] concisely voices the right viewpoint. It maintains a fine balance between the imperative to carry on the work of the gospel and anticipation of the Master's return. Christ's commendation to the faithful servants who increased the amount with which they were entrusted (vss. 17-18) reinforces the point that the nearness of His return requires increased vigilance and faithfulness. Surely the church of Christ,

---

[1] "πραγματεύσασθε ἐν ᾧ ἔρχομαι." Cf. the NEB paraphrase: "Trade with this while I am away."

acting as a faithful steward, can only be true to its commission by using the most effective means possible to organize for service.

Lewis S. Fiorelli has asked if there is in the New Testament a directly inverse relationship between expectancy of an imminent Parousia and concern with church order.[1] His method is twofold. On the one hand he examines the earliest New Testament writings, when the expectancy of the Second Advent was most acute, to determine if there is evidence of any concern for church order. On the other hand he studies the later New Testament writings for references to the Second Coming.[2] Given that the return of Christ and church order are mentioned side by side in Paul's earlier writings, such as the epistles to the Thessalonians, Fiorelli concludes that expectancy of the Parousia does not preclude concern for church order.[3] Paul's later writings, the pastoral epistles, deal for the most part with church order, according to Fiorelli; but they also express hope in "the appearing of the glory of our great God and Savior Jesus Christ" (Titus 2:13).[4] Fiorelli's conclusion is obvious. Belief in the imminent Second Advent and interest in church order are not mutually exclusive.[5]

The most significant work by a Seventh-day Adventist writer

---

[1]Lewis S. Fiorelli, "Expectancy of an Imminent Parousia and Concern with Church Order: An Inverse Relationship?" The Thomist 39 (January 1975):1-23.

[2]Ibid., pp. 2-3.   [3]Ibid., pp. 10-12.

[4]Ibid., pp. 12-13.

[5]See, e.g., ibid., p. 17. The validity of Fiorelli's attempt to interpret parallel references to the Parousia and church order in terms of "cultic order" within the early church (p. 23) is beyond the immediate concern of the present study.

on the Christian hope of the Advent is by Jonathan Gallagher.[1] He recognizes that the church's eschatological expectation has implications for its ecclesiological self-understanding. A community that awaits the last events will seek to keep itself holy and without blemish. The foundation of its message and mission will be belief in a near advent.[2]

While Gallagher examines the implications of a delay in Christ's return for the Seventh-day Adventist doctrine of the nature of the church, the question of its impact on church order falls outside the limitations of his study. He does cite examples, however, of instances where an overemphasis on the nearness of the Second Advent has produced some misguided actions on the part of the church. Imminence of the Advent was given as a reason for building, in 1901, the new college at Berrien Springs (the forerunner of Andrews University) of wood rather than brick. Leasing of land for church buildings instead of purchasing is mentioned as another commonly used cost-saving device, defended by Seventh-day Adventists on the basis of Christ's soon return.[3]

The above examples represent occasions when the Seventh-day Adventist Church planned in the short term because of overemphasis on the imminence of the Second Coming. A sign of the opposite view-point, that "my Lord delayeth his coming" (Matt 24:48), would be

---

[1]Jonathan Gallagher, "Believing Christ's Return: An Inter-pretative Analysis of the Dynamics of Christian Hope" (Ph.D. dissertation, University of St. Andrews, 1982). Cf. also the same author's "The Delay of the Advent," Ministry, June 1978, pp. 4-6.

[2]Gallagher, "Believing Christ's Return" (1982), p. 277.

[3]Ibid., p. 280.

increased and unwarranted institutionalization. It would seem that the oft-repeated principle of simplicity[1] is still a vital rule to be followed. It is clear that the increase in membership accompanied by inevitable expansion of the church's organizational fabric has intensified for present-day Seventh-day Adventists the dilemma of maintaining the proper balance between permanence and expectancy.

The Importance of Doctrinal Unity

In His prayer for the unity of the church (John 17:22-23), Jesus expressed the importance of Christian harmony and fellowship if the world were to believe in Him. Sabbatarian Adventists attached similar importance in the post-Disappointment years to the doctrinal unity achieved by the end of the 1848 conferences. The integration of the Sabbath doctrine with a new understanding of Christ's work in the heavenly sanctuary afforded them the rationale for understanding the Disappointment and provided a foundation on which to build a theology of mission.[2]

It is, of course, difficult to conceive that Seventh-day Adventists could have developed a sense of mission without doctrinal consensus. Sabbatarian Adventists were well aware of the perceived divisiveness of the creeds of the established churches and the failure of the Millerites to come to agreement at Albany in April 1845. Unity of doctrine became crucially important so that Sabbath-keepers might stand in happy contrast to the confused sects around

---

[1]See, e.g., above, p. 191.

[2]On the consolidation of Seventh-day Adventist doctrines, see above, pp. 91-103. Cf. Damsteegt, Foundations, pp. 103-164.

them. The experience of Sabbatarian Adventists at the Volney, New York, conference in the summer of 1848 serves as an appropriate illustration of the importance of the doctrinal unity achieved there and at the other conferences held that year.[1] It was at these pivotal meetings that Sabbatarian Adventists began to develop a sense of mission. Thus, doctrinal consensus not only provided the platform on which to build the eschatological message of the three angels, but actually became an integral part of the message itself. As we have indicated earlier,[2] the remnant church which keeps "the commandments of God, and the faith of Jesus" (Rev 14:12) stood in contrast to the fallen and confused churches. In the view of early Seventh-day Adventists, the unity of those who had accepted Sabbatarian Adventist interpretation of the three angels' messages was seen to be in itself an important evidence of the truth of their position.

In the succeeding years Seventh-day Adventist writers returned frequently to the theme of doctrinal unity and identified church order as the most important instrument in maintaining that unity. Bates associated "unity of the faith and perfect church order" (both essential prerequisites for readiness for the Second Advent) under his characteristic motif of restoration.[3]

White linked the two themes of church order and doctrinal

---

[1]Cf. above, pp. 99-103. At the Volney Conference Ellen G. White urged the contending factions to unite upon the fundamentals of Sabbatarian Adventist doctrine (Ellen G. White, Life Sketches, p. 111). In the words of Froom, "The conference closed in a triumph of unity" (Prophetic Faith, 4:1022).

[2]See above, pp. 199-201.

[3]Bates, "Church Order," p. 22. Cf. above, pp. 134, 198.

unity on several occasions. As early as 1851 he wrote, "There can be no permanent and scriptural union, without an agreement in views of bible truth."[1] In his opinion, submission to the authority of church organization and agreement in doctrine were especially vital for "those who preach the Word."[2] He also contrasted the harmony of Sabbatarian Adventists with the "miserably confused condition of those who reject organization."[3] White was in no doubt as to what lay at the foundation of the agreement, doctrinal unity, and prosperity of the church: "Organization has saved the cause, secession among us is dead."[4]

Not surprisingly, in view of his penchant for authoritative leadership, the most decisive statement associating doctrinal unity and organization comes from the pen of Butler:

> We are a thoroughly organized people, and our organization is not based on mere appearance, but upon a solid foundation. Having struggled against all kinds of influences, within and without, and being now a unit, speaking the same thing from ocean to ocean, it is not an easy thing to shake us to pieces. It has been tried many times and failed.[5]

It is at this point perhaps that Ellen G. White's influence on Seventh-day Adventist theology of organization is best raised, since the predominant theme in her writings on church order was that of unity. Her first comments on the subject emerged from a vision

---

[1][James White], "Gospel Union," RH, November 25, 1851, p. 56.

[2][White], "Our Tour East," p. 52. Cf. White, "The Cause" (1857), p. 116.

[3][White], "Organization" (1864), p. 164.

[4][White], "The Association," p. 4.

[5]Butler, "Stability," p. 140. Cf. above, pp. 175-178.

received in December 1850.[1] Writing in the context of the need to thwart unqualified preachers' travelling in the name of the fledgling Sabbatarian Adventist movement, she said: "The church must flee to God's word, and become established upon gospel order which has been overlooked and neglected. This is indispensably necessary to bring the church into the unity of the faith."[2]

Ellen G. White based her appeal for unity upon the order to be found in heaven. The same perfect organization, she wrote, was established by Moses under God's guidance in the wilderness and in the church by Christ when He was on earth.[3] In her view, times of crisis, such as Israel's wilderness experience and the early development of the Christian Church established by Christ, especially required harmony and union among God's people. Living in such a time of crisis, "these last days," she wrote, "while God is bringing his children into the unity of the faith, there is more real need of order than ever before."[4]

---

[1] Ellen G. White, MS 11, 1850. She elaborated upon her original comments in Ellen G. White, Supplement to Experience and Views, pp. 15-23. See also Ellen G. White, Early Writings (1963), pp. 97-104.

[2] Ellen G. White, Supplement to Experience and Views, pp. 18, 19. Cf. above, pp. 119-120.

[3] Ibid., p. 15. Cf. also Ellen G. White, The Acts of the Apostles (Mountain View, Calif.: Pacific Press Pub. Assn, 1911), pp. 91-92; Ellen G. White, Testimonies for the Church, 1:649-653.

[4] Ellen G. White, Supplement to Experience and Views, p. 12. The theme of unity "as we near the close of time" appears several times in Ellen G. White's writings. See, e.g., Ellen G. White, Testimonies for the Church, 1:210; Letter B-32a, to Brethren of the General Conference, December 19, 1892; Letter W-27a, to Ellet J. Waggoner, December 27, 1892; MS 177, 1899; Fundamentals of Christian Education (Nashville, Tenn.: Southern Pub. Assn, 1923), p. 529.

Another reason given by Ellen G. White for efficient church
order and unity in the church was "the perversity of human nature."[1]
Both Ellen G. White and her husband expressed concern about the
Laodicean condition of the church, which characterized by the
perceived decline in spirituality among Sabbatarian Adventists.
Order and discipline in the church of Christ were required, in their
view, as a partial means of restoring the movement to its earlier
piety.[2]

Perhaps even more importantly, Ellen G. White regarded unity
and love within the church as a "powerful evidence" to the world "in
favor of the Christian religion."[3] Such unity and love, she wrote,
created by and manifested in proper organization, are "the divine
credentials which the Christian bears to the world."[4] On the other
hand, dissension and differences among the people of God would bring
dishonor to Jesus Christ.[5] Possibly Ellen G. White's clearest statement linking the concepts of church organization and its mission to
the world was expressed in 1900, during a critical time in Seventh-
day Adventist history, which led to important developments and
changes in church order a year later.[6] She wrote: "God's people

---

[1]Ellen G. White, "Order in the Church," RH, April 15, 1880,
p. 241.

[2]See above, pp. 140-141.

[3]Ellen G. White, "Unity of the Church," p. 113.

[4]Ellen G. White, "Unity and Love," RH, August 12, 1884,
p. 513.

[5]Ellen G. White, "Unity of the Church," p. 113.

[6]Cf. below, pp. 272-278.

have a great work to do. Seeds must be planted which will produce the right kind of harvest. The world must see in the church of God true order, true discipline, true organization."[1]

Ellen G. White's position on church order, as expressed above, indicates that she was strongly supportive of her husband's stance from the beginning of organizational developments in Sabbatarian Adventism. It should perhaps be reiterated here, that although Ellen G. White stressed the importance of order frequently, she did not propose a specific system.[2] That was left to her husband and his colleagues to discover through Bible study and to hammer out in debate in the face of practical exigencies.[3]

In discussing the theological basis of Seventh-day Adventist church order we have made a distinction, for the sake of convenience, in the outline of this section between the mission of the church and its doctrinal and organizational unity. However, we would suggest that in fact, in the minds of early Seventh-day Adventists including Ellen G. White, the unity of the church which had been achieved through organization was an essential part of the church's witness. Thus, mission could not be accomplished without order, nor could there be a message.[4]

---

[1]Ellen G. White, MS 30, 1900.

[2]Cf. above, pp. 191-192.

[3]It should be noted that Loughborough (The Great Second Advent Movement, p. 349) and Graham ("Ellen G. White: An Examination of Her Position and Role in the Seventh-day Adventist Church" [1977], p. 72) ascribed a more crucial role to Ellen G. White's leadership in the development of Seventh-day Adventist church organization than we have discovered in this study.

[4]Other Seventh-day Adventist writers continued the theme of

Early Seventh-day Adventist Reflections
on the Nature of the Church

As has been noted,[1] the Millerite movement received its
impetus from the principles of biblical interpretation laid down by
Miller and his associates. They placed particular emphasis on the
apocalyptic books of Daniel and Revelation. Building upon the
Millerites' work, Sabbatarian Adventists regarded the same biblical
books as foundational to their unique sense of identity as expressed
in the three angels' messages of Rev 14.[2]

It is not surprising therefore, in view of the eschatological
nature of their mission, that Seventh-day Adventists looked for
motifs in biblical apocalyptic literature which would assist in
articulating their understanding of the nature of the church. The
remnant motif, as has been indicated,[3] was expressive of the fact
that Seventh-day Adventists saw themselves as the church in the last
generation of history before the return of Christ.[4] The term
"remnant" also implied the obedience to the ten commandments of the

---

doctrinal unity in the "remnant" church made possible by organization. See, e.g., Loughborough, The Church: Its Organization, Order,
and Discipline, p. 60; Crisler, Organization, pp. 17-32; W. A.
Spicer, Gospel Order: A Brief Outline of the Bible Principles of
Organization (Washington, D.C.: Review and Herald Pub. Assn, n.d.),
pp. 1-2.

[1]See above, pp. 35-36.

[2]On the three angels' messages, see above, pp. 95-97, 196-
199.

[3]See above, pp. 199-200.

[4]White, "Signs of the Times," p. 75. On the remnant motif,
see also Damsteegt, Foundations, pp. 243-244.

true church in contrast to the false doctrines of "Babylon" (cf. Rev 12:17).

Sabbatarian Adventists came in time to identify themselves with the Laodicean church described in Rev 3:14-22.[1] Early interpretations of the messages to the seven churches of Rev 2 and 3 had identified Sabbath-keeping Adventists with Philadelphia, the church of brotherly love. The lukewarm Laodiceans were considered to be those who had gone back on their belief in the Seventh Month movement and denied the validity of the Millerite message preached prior to October 22, 1844.[2] In 1856 White suggested that, in view of the declining spirituality of Sabbatarian Adventists, they themselves were in a lukewarm Laodicean condition and in need of revival.[3] Damsteegt suggests that "this shift in ecclesiological self-understanding from a triumphalistic to an anti-triumphalistic attitude was immediately accepted and provided a powerful incentive to awaken believers to participate in missionary activity."[4]

Other figures applied to the Seventh-day Adventist Church, though not in an extended way, included a school, an army, and a fort. Butler's 1874 series on church government likened the members of the church to "apt pupils who will be in submission to proper

---

[1]Cf. above, pp. 140-141. Cf. also Damsteegt, Foundations, pp. 244-248.

[2]See, e.g., Bates, "The Laodicean Church," pp. 7-8.

[3]White, "The Seven Churches," pp. 188-189, 192.

[4]Damsteegt, Foundations, p. 245.

discipline."[1]   In the same series, and with the same intent, he
compared the efficient organization and discipline of an army with
the strict order expected of God's church.[2]   White regarded the
church as a fort "in which we may intrench ourselves for protection
and self-defense."[3]

It is worth noting that the early Seventh-day Adventist
pioneers almost ignored the metaphor of the church as the body of
Christ. The subject did not appear in discussions over congregational or centralized administration,[4] nor in White's presentations
on spiritual gifts,[5] a subject of particular interest to Sabbatarian
Adventists in the light of Ellen G. White's prophetic ministry. It
would seem that Paul's figure of the body of Christ (cf. Eph 4:4-16;
Col 1:18) might well have informed their deliberations. There is
little reference, for example, to the Christian's relationship to
Christ as the Head, to the life the believer finds in unity with the
Son of God, or to the nurture and spiritual growth one may experience
through union with the risen Savior.

The analogies used to describe the church (remnant, Laodicea,
army, school, fort) as well as those which were not employed are
significant. The fact that the more extended figures were drawn from

---

[1]Butler, "Thoughts on Church Government," RH, August 4, 1874, p. 60. Cf. above, p. 176.

[2]Ibid., August 18, 1874, p. 68.

[3][White], "Conference Address" (1873), p. 180.

[4]One thinks, e.g., of White's discussions with Cottrell (see above, pp. 135-149).

[5]See, e.g., White's 4-part series "Unity and Gifts of the Church," RH, December 3, 1857-January 7, 1858.

the book of Revelation reveals the importance of the Seventh-day Adventist Church's eschatological self-understanding. The use of commonplace metaphors such as army, fort, and school suggests the pragmatic, down-to-earth attitudes of early Seventh-day Adventists. The absence of some rather prominent images of the church in Scripture, such as the body of Christ, indicates that the concerns that occupied much of the attention of Seventh-day Adventist pioneers, namely, the need for proper discipline and efficiency, did not give rise at this stage to systematic thought about the mystical union between the church and Jesus Christ. An army equipped for battle obediently following the commands of its experienced leaders (under Christ) perhaps served as a more effective figure of speech for their purposes. The fact that the organization of the General Conference took place in the midst of the American Civil War (1861-1865) perhaps brought military analogies readily to mind.

In summary, we would suggest that the theological basis which undergirded Seventh-day Adventist church order developed in response to the changing situation in the church and in the world, and expressed itself in various fashions. It was essential that the form of organization be adjusted from time to time in order that it might remain appropriate to present needs. The organizational requirements of a "little flock" of a few hundred members were obviously different from those demanded by an international church with a variety of institutions to carry out its mission. At the time of White's death in 1881, the Seventh-day Adventist Church was faced with several challenges which could not have been envisaged thirty years earlier. These challenges included caring for the needs of an increasingly large and diverse membership,[1] planning for a truly global mission of proclaiming the three angels' messages, encouraging the development of several medical, educational, and publishing institutions, maintaining the unity of the faith and authority of the leaders of the church while at the same time guarding against distortion or misapplication of the original principles of organization.

No church, if it is to accomplish its mission, can lose sight of its origins and reason for existence; neither can it afford to remain static and fail to adjust to meet new circumstances. The continued growth of the Seventh-day Adventist Church in the years under study (1844-1881) would seem to indicate that the pioneers of the denomination succeeded, to a certain extent at least, in keeping a necessary balance between a strong regard for past experiences on the one hand and living in the present and dynamically developing in the face of modern circumstances on the other. The system of church order established in the Seventh-day Adventist Church played a significant role in this success. It was not so rigid that it could not be modified if necessary. It enabled the pioneers of Seventh-day Adventism, who sought to follow Scripture as a guide in every aspect of their lives, to conform to a pattern seen to be in harmony with general principles of biblical order while still allowing room for development and modification to meet new situations. Finally,

---

[1]In 1880 church membership numbered 15,570; there were twenty-four conferences, including one in Europe (Denmark), and eight missions, three of them in Europe ("G.C. Statistics, 1880," p. 280).

organization provided the framework and instrumentality whereby the church could continue to effect its mission.

Early Discussions About Order as
Found in Scripture

Dialogue on the New Testament Material

As has been indicated,[1] Seventh-day Adventist pioneers responded to practical considerations by referring to the pattern of the New Testament church as they perceived it. In their study of Scripture, they followed a hermeneutical method derived from their 19th-century religious heritage. Considerable attention has been devoted to Miller's principles of prophetic interpretation which undergirded his apocalyptic eschatology,[2] but less has been paid to his general rules of biblical interpretation. These rules reveal that he regarded the Bible as the only safe guide in every aspect of Christian life and that those who approached the Scriptures in faith and diligence could not be in error.[3] We have documented above that

---

[1]See above, pp. 155-157. Cf. also below, p. 268.

[2]See, e.g., Froom, Prophetic Faith, 4:443-737; Damsteegt, Foundations, pp. 57-100.

[3]Miller's fourteen rules of biblical interpretation may be found in Bliss, Memoirs of William Miller, pp. 70-71. Key excerpts from the first five rules, which deal with general principles, are as follows: (1) "Every word must have its proper bearing on the subject presented in the Bible." (2) "All Scripture is necessary, and may be understood by a diligent application and study." (3) "Nothing revealed in Scriptures can or will be hid from those who ask in faith, not wavering." (4) "To understand doctrine, bring all the Scriptures together on the subject you wish to know; then let every word have its proper influence; and if you can form your theory without a contradiction, you cannot be in error." (5) "Scripture must be its own expositor. . . ."

Seventh-day Adventist pioneers adopted the same approach to Scripture.[1]

When White first proposed a relatively simple system of organization, no recorded opposition to his proposals appeared in the pages of the Review. It was assumed that a pattern of church order relevant to the church in all ages was to be found in the New Testament. It was when White suggested that the New Testament contained only the basic principles of church organization that opposition arose, especially in the person of Cottrell.[2]

We have suggested that White's proposals from the earliest days of Sabbatarian Adventism went beyond mere congregationalism.[3] Cottrell and Frisbie in particular did not agree with these proposals. Frisbie expressed the opinion that the New Testament concept of the church never went beyond the confines of a local congregation.[4] Cottrell feared centralized organization partly because it carried with it legal incorporation which would require illegitimate involvement of the church with the state.[5] In the end

---

[1]See above, pp. 126-128. Studies of Seventh-day Adventist principles of biblical interpretation include: Neufeld, "Biblical Interpretation in the Advent Movement," pp. 109-125; Committee on Problems in Bible Translation, Problems in Bible Translation (Washington, D.C.: Review and Herald Pub. Assn, 1954), pp. 79-127; Froom, Movement of Destiny, pp. 91-106; Walter E. Read, The Bible, The Spirit of Prophecy, and the Church (Washington, D.C.: Review and Herald Pub. Assn, 1952), pp. 41-62; Gerhard F. Hasel, Understanding the Living Word of God (Mountain View, Calif.: Pacific Press Pub. Assn, 1980).

[2]On the debate between White and Cottrell, see above, pp. 135-153.

[3]See above, p. 136.   [4]See above, pp. 135-137.

[5]See above, pp. 143-153.

Cottrell, Frisbie, and the Seventh-day Adventist Church as a whole accepted the necessity of centralized organization, as advanced by White. Cottrell, Frisbie, and most Seventh-day Adventists still believed, however, that the Bible provided a complete pattern for Seventh-day Adventist church order, but were convinced (presumably by White's arguments and the sessions of group Bible study on church organization) that the New Testament model of the church did indeed go beyond the local congregation to allow for churches to be joined together on a geographical basis.

It is worth noting the modification in Cottrell's thinking as revealed in the Review. In June 1860 he urged that "the combination of churches into bishoprics led to the great apostasy" in the early Christian church.[1] At the Battle Creek Conference of September 28 to October 1, 1860, at which the name "Seventh-day Adventist" was chosen and which Cottrell was unable to attend, a letter from him was read to the delegates. In it he reasoned that, as the church was already organized according to the gospel, any change in church order to hold property legally would require it to give up its present system of organization. An alternative form of order could, therefore, no longer be scriptural. It might not be anti-scriptural, he added, but it would be unscriptural and hence unacceptable.[2]

Most of the objectives White had in mind for church organization were achieved at this conference, contrary to the wishes

---

[1]Letter, R. F. Cottrell to James White, RH, June 19, 1860, p. 36.

[2]See "Business Proceedings of the B.C. Conference," RH, October 9, 1860, p. 163. Cottrell's letter may be found in the minutes of the conference session as recorded in the Review.

of Cottrell as expressed in his letter.[1] Apparently, Cottrell was willing to admit when he was wrong, as indicated by his compliance with the majority decision. A couple of comments by him in the two succeeding years provides a hint that his point of view was changing. In October 1861 he wrote, "I see no objection against different churches co-operating in the spread of truth."[2] A year later he was even more definite, admitting that systematic work was impossible without the organization of conferences.[3] In the same context he reiterated his belief that only New Testament organization was acceptable. One can only presume how the change took place in Cottrell's mind. Clearly he had come to see White's conviction of the need for more extensive organization. There is no indication from Cottrell's pen, however, that he agreed with White that the Scriptures provide only general principles of church order.

It is the opinion of this writer that the majority of Seventh-day Adventist leaders at that time shared Cottrell's opinion that the New Testament provided the only legitimate pattern of church organization. One might cite the resolution of the September 28 to October 1, 1860, conference: "That we are highly favorable to such organization, and such only, as the Bible authorizes and recognizes."[4] Fourteen years later, Butler offered the opinion that

---

[1]See above, p. 148.

[2]Letter, R. F. Cottrell to James White, RH, October 8, 1861, p. 151.

[3]Cottrell, "System--Order," pp. 165-166.

[4]"Business Proceedings of the B.C. Conference," RH, October 9, 1860, p. 161. A comparison of statements by White and Cottrell indicates clearly that the resolution passed by the conference was

the role of the General Conference corresponded to the authoritative function of the Jerusalem Council described in Acts 15, and local conferences might be compared to the geographical subdivisions of Judea, Galatia, and Asia Minor, etc. An additional similarity, he added, lay in the identical offices that could be found in local churches of both the New Testament era and the Seventh-day Adventist Church.[1] Even in the last year of his life White, in contrast to Butler, did not attempt to defend the concept that every element of Seventh-day Adventist church government had an exact precedent in the New Testament. The systems of organization among the Jews in the Old Testament and in the New Testament church, he said, provided "all that Infinite Wisdom saw necessary for the Christian church."[2]

It would seem that White was successful in accomplishing all of his major church organizational goals.[3] The opposition he received from Cottrell and Frisbie, among others, delayed the implementation of certain practices, but may not have been a wholly negative factor.[4] It is likely that the interaction between White

---

closer to Cottrell's view than White's. The latter wrote, "All means which . . . are not forbidden by plain scripture declarations, should be employed" (White, "Making Us a Name," RH, April 26, 1860, p. 180). Cottrell's letter to the delegates read, "I think we should fear an organization as a church which has no warrant from the Scriptures, while we hold the Bible and the Bible alone as the rule of our faith and practice" ("Business Proceedings of the B.C. Conference," RH, October 9, 1860, p. 163). While White's position was inclusive, Cottrell's and that of the delegates was exclusive of anything not specifically approved in the New Testament.

[1]Butler, "Thoughts on Church Government," RH, August 18, 1874, pp. 68-69.

[2]White, "Organization and Discipline," p. 8.

[3]Cf. above, pp. 158, 171.   [4]Cf. above, pp. 135-153.

and other Seventh-day Adventist leaders succeeded in refining the finished product of church order and perhaps helped to avoid some potential pitfalls.[1] White was less successful, however, in changing the conviction of most Seventh-day Adventists that the system of church order adopted by them was patterned exactly after the New Testament church.[2]

Office and Leadership in Seventh-day Adventism

The dialogue by early Seventh-day Adventist leaders on the New Testament precedent (or lack of it) for centralized administration was accompanied by other discussions on the New Testament data concerning office and leadership. Three separate articles, written in 1853, 1861, and 1873, have been chosen as representative of the development of Seventh-day Adventist understanding on the subject.[3] White, writing in December 1853, at which time he

---

[1]Butler's series on the authority of church leaders comes to mind. It would seem that Seventh-day Adventists sought to build into their system not only sufficient authority for their leaders to function effectively, but also (as White recognized) certain checks against the abuse of that power (cf. above, pp. 175-178). Perhaps this balance derived from the extended discussions prior to 1863.

[2]As indicated above, Butler, Cottrell, and Frisbie continued to hold the view that Seventh-day Adventist organization was built upon the example of New Testament church order. One can also find in the writings of Ellen G. White support for the concept that local congregations may find a model for their organization in the New Testament. However, she recognized that when dissension arose in a local church "and the believers were unable to come to an agreement among themselves, such matters . . . were referred to a general council of the entire body of believers, made up of appointed delegates from the various local churches. . . ." (Ellen G. White, The Acts of the Apostles, pp. 91-96).

[3]These articles illustrate the change in Seventh-day Adventist understanding of church organization in three separate decades. In 1853 Sabbatarian Adventism was still very much a fledgling movement. By 1861 it had grown to the extent that its

still held to the idea that the New Testament provided a perfect pattern for church order,[1] equated the calling of Sabbatarian Adventist ministers to preach with Christ's appointment of the twelve apostles. There is no hint in this context that White regarded the office of apostle as unique to the New Testament era. It is God who calls a minister, White continued, the (local) church recognizing that call in setting him apart through ordination done on behalf of the church by other ministers. The purpose of "setting apart" an ordained ministry was "to shut the door against Satan," that is, to counteract the influence of false and unauthorized teachers. An additional advantage of an ordained and properly recognized ministry, he added, was that the ministers would be confident in the knowledge of the church's support. "Union is strength" was White's motto.[2] When someone was ordained to the ministry on behalf of a local church, other churches were to be informed of the action, according to White, so that all might know who had authority to teach and who did not.[3] At this point there are three aspects that should be noted: (1) White did not regard the apostolate as a unique

---

leaders were in the midst of vigorous discussions concerning the necessity of centralized administration. The third example is drawn from a time of consolidation. Central organization was an accomplished fact in 1873 and attention had shifted to new concerns, such as the authority of the ministry.

[1]White wrote, "The divine order of the New Testament is sufficient to organize the church of Christ" ([White], "Gospel Order," RH, December 6, 1853, p. 173). Cf. above, pp. 126-128.

[2][White], "Gospel Order," RH, December 20, 1853, p. 189.

[3]Ibid.

office,[1] (2) a minister's calling was to be recognized by a local church through ordination, and (3) ordination provided him with authority to teach in all churches.

Eight years later a committee comprised of Loughborough, Hull, and Cornell was appointed to study the office of the ministry and report its findings in the Review.[2] Its interpretation of the New Testament identified four main categories of leaders--apostles, evangelists, elders (synonymous with bishops, pastors, and over-seers), and deacons. The term apostle referred to the original twelve in "a pre-eminent sense," but the office was not confined to them or to that age. Evangelists corresponded to Seventh-day Adventist travelling preachers. Elders and deacons were appointed by the local church to serve its spiritual and temporal needs, respec-tively, and their authority was limited to the congregation to which they were appointed. The committee's report specifically stated that apostles and evangelists (the ministry) on the one hand, and elders and deacons (local officers) on the other, represented two separate classes. Apostles and evangelists held their offices by virtue of "an especial call from God," while elders and deacons were chosen by the church.[3] It was on this basis that the committee recommended that "no person by virtue of a lower office can fill a

---

[1]White and his associates apparently did not use the term "apostle" of ordained ministers (cf. above, p. 126).

[2]Loughborough, Hull, and Cornell, "Conference Address. Organization," pp. 156-157. The report of the committee is discussed in greater detail above, pp. 155-157.

[3]Loughborough, Hull, and Cornell, "Conference Address. Organization," p. 156.

higher one; but anyone filling a higher office, can by virtue of that office, act in any of the lower."[1]

According to the report of the committee, therefore, which was accepted by the church at large, there was a threefold hierarchical structure of ministry in the New Testament (evangelists, elders, and deacons) which would correspond to the travelling ministers, local elders, and deacons in Seventh-day Adventism. New Testament evidence cited for this viewpoint included the fact that the apostle Peter referred to himself as an elder (1 Pet 5:1), and the apostle Paul performed the office of deacon (2 Cor 8:4).[2] In each instance, in the opinion of Loughborough, Hull, and Cornell, it was the case of a holder of a higher office filling a lower one. They apparently did not intend to imply that the various titles referred to different, yet equal, spheres of ministry, or that the names were descriptive of function rather than office. It seems, therefore, that a hierarchical view of leadership developed at an early stage within Seventh-day Adventism and that the authority of the ministry was deemed necessary to meet the crises of the time, such as problems caused by a rapidly growing but scattered membership and the need to maintain doctrinal unity.

Butler's article on leadership in 1873 reveals further development in the concept of the authority of the ministry, although

---

[1]Ibid., p. 157.

[2]It is recognized that Paul used διακονία rather than διάκονος in 2 Cor 8:4. The committee, however, applied the text to the office of deacon: "Paul, carrying the liberalities of the brethren up to Jerusalem (Acts 11:30) might with equal propriety be called a deacon. In 2 Cor 8:4, he is spoken as performing the office of a deacon" (ibid., p. 156).

one must bear in mind that the church in time came to recognize that his opinions tended to the extreme.[1] He too, like White and the Loughborough, Hull, and Cornell committee before him, built his case for the authority of the ministerial office upon the authority Christ bestowed upon the apostles. Butler assigned apostolic authority to Seventh-day Adventist leaders on the basis of several facts: (1) even in New Testament times individuals other than the twelve disciples were described as apostles (Acts 13:2, 14:14; Phil 2:25; 2 Cor 8:23), (2) the gifts of the Spirit, which were to continue in the church in all ages, included apostleship (1 Cor 12:28; Eph 4:11), (3) the priority of "apostles" in 1 Cor 12:28 refers to their "authority or position,"[2] and (4) even leaders who were not apostles were appointed to positions of authority in the church (Heb 13:17; 1 Tim 5:17, 20; 2 Tim 4:1-2; Titus 1:13, 2:15).

In the opinion of early Seventh-day Adventist leaders, therefore, the role if not the office of apostle continued in the Christian church after the New Testament era. In their view it was a role that should be fulfilled in the Seventh-day Adventist Church by the ministry.

It is noteworthy that none of the three articles reviewed examined in depth the meaning of ordination. We have observed that a distinction was made between the calling of the minister and the

---

[1]Butler, "Leadership," pp. 180-181. On the church's eventual rejection of Butler's more extreme views, see above, pp. 178-179.

[2]We have already indicated (p. 156) that Seventh-day Adventist pioneers viewed the continuity of the apostolate in terms of function rather than authority or office.

choice of the elder and deacon by the church, but an extensive

discussion on the significance of ordination does not appear in early

Sabbatarian Adventist writings. One of the most revealing statements

from White's pen appeared in 1853:

> Men who are called of God to teach and baptize, should be
> ordained, or set apart to the work of the ministry by the laying
> on of hands. Not that the church has power to call men into the
> ministry, or that ordination makes them ministers of Jesus
> Christ; but it is the order of the gospel that those who are
> called to the ministry should be ordained, for important
> objects.[1]

The intent of White's statement seems to be that ministers,

in contrast with elders and deacons, were called by God to a special

work which set them apart from other church officers. The local

congregation, he added, would recognize or "feel it," if God had

chosen one of their number to the ministry.[2] Before the organization

of the General Conference in 1863 the decision to ordain someone to

ministerial work seems to have been taken by the local congregation

and the act of ordination carried out by ministers.[3] At one of the

first ministerial ordination services, for example, White and

Joseph Baker (a former Millerite preacher) "performed the solemn

---

[1]White, "Gospel Order," RH, December 20, 1853, p. 189. The
objects of ordination were, according to White: to give assurance to
those ordained of support by their local congregation as they went
out to preach, to produce and secure union in the church, and to
guard against false teachers (cf. above, pp. 125-126).

[2]Ibid.

[3]Before the first Sabbatarian Adventist ministerial ordinations in 1853, ministerial functions were carried out by men such as
White, Byington, and Buck, who had been ordained in other denominations (cf. above, p. 125).

duty" with the "unanimous expression" of approval by all present.[1] Once conferences came into being, however, the authority to ordain to the ministry lay with the local conference.[2]

The proposal of the committee appointed to study organization in 1861 was that the local congregation choose elders and deacons "by informal ballot," who would then be ordained by the minister.[3] By 1874, according to Butler, the General Conference recommended that a committee--made up of a minister and two others named by him-- nominate local officers. Butler acknowledged that the church was "not obliged to sanction the action of the nominating committee." Nevertheless, it would seem that the appointment of lay leadership in local churches came to be carefully controlled by the ordained ministry.[4]

The Servanthood of Church Leaders

It is clear that the questions of authority and leadership became prominent issues among Seventh-day Adventists in the 1870s. Butler's pamphlet on leadership in 1873 and his series in the Review, between July 28 and October 13, 1874,[5] represented the most notable

---

[1][White], "Eastern Tour," RH, November 15, 1853, p. 148. Cf. also his comment concerning another ordination the same year: "The church was in one accord in this matter" (White, "Eastern Tour," RH, September 20, 1853, p. 85).

[2]See above, p. 184.

[3]Loughborough, Hull, and Cornell, "Conference Address. Organization," p. 157.

[4]Butler, "Thoughts on Church Government," RH, September 1, 1874, p. 85.

[5]Butler, Leadership; "Thoughts on Church Government," RH, July 28, 1874-October 13, 1874.

interpretation of the authority of church leaders (especially White). Even though Butler's thesis was rejected later by the church as overstated--partly as a result of the urging of White--the writings of church leaders during the 1870s frequently touched on the authority of church leadership.

Partly in response to Butler's somewhat exaggerated views on the authority of church leaders, White emphasized the servant role of Christian ministers. In 1873 he wrote:

> No man capable of filling any office in the cause of God, will feel exalted by such promotion. The true principle bearing upon this subject is expressed by our Lord in these words: . . . "whosoever will be chief among you, let him be your servant."[1]

The following year, in response to Butler's articles on leadership, White added, "Christ's ministers are shepherds of the flock, and leaders of the people in a subordinate sense."[2] Taking Christ as the example, he affirmed that "mutual submission is demanded of all in the spirit of humility" and "officers were not ordained in the Christian church, to order, or to command the church, and 'to lord it over God's heritage.'"[3]

White returned to the topic of service in some of the last articles published before his death in 1881. He recognized that however important organization was to secure unity and "protection from imposters," it must not obscure the primary consideration that

---

[1]White, "Organization" (1873), p. 60.

[2]White, "Leadership" (1874), p. 180.

[3]Ibid.

"'the head of every man is Christ'" and "must not come in to take the disciple from the hands of the Master."[1]

Among White's associates, Haskell and Loughborough expressed the same view. They urged ministers to emulate the example of Christ, who took the form of a servant.[2] Ellen G. White also supported her husband's words on this point:

> In His life and lessons Christ has given a perfect exemplification of the unselfish ministry which has its origin in God. . . .
> Jesus was given to stand at the head of humanity, by His example to teach what it means to minister. His whole life was under a law of service. He served all, ministered to all.[3]

We would suggest that White and others came to recognize that the servanthood of the church's ministry had become a necessary balance against the concept of church authority. As the church sought to keep in proper relationship the expectancy of Christ's imminent return with the prospect of a great and largely uncompleted mission, so it also had to recognize that considerations other than efficiency and pragmatism were equally important, namely, proper pastoral care of the flock, which could only be achieved by emulating the example of Christ as a humble servant. In other words, only when the church had come to recognize that the Second Advent might be

---

[1]White, "Organization and Discipline," p. 8. Cf. also the following statement: "Christ is Lord and Master of all, and yet he is servant of all. He is the Chief Shepherd of the flock, and, in a subordinate sense, his ministers are shepherds, guides and guardians of the sheep of his fold. Was Christ servant of all? Much more should his chosen servants willingly and faithfully serve the church" (White, "Christ and His Ministers," p. 248).

[2]Haskell, "Responsibility of Christ's Ministers," p. 395; Loughborough, The Church: Its Organization, Order, and Discipline, pp. 26-30; The Great Second Advent Movement, p. 346.

[3]Ellen G. White, The Acts of the Apostles, p. 359. Cf. also Ellen G. White, MS 165, 1898; MS 26, 1889.

delayed and church members would require careful nurture over an extended period of time did the idea of service arise, not to replace the properly constituted authority of church leaders but to stand alongside and strike a balance with it.[1]

In summarizing the manner in which early Seventh-day Adventists wrote about New Testament practices in their establishment of church order, it would seem that they sought to copy as closely as possible what they perceived to be the New Testament norm. This we say in spite of White's declarations that Scripture does not provide all the specifics of organization. Even the pragmatic approach of the Seventh-day Adventist Church in adapting to meet certain needs is not out of harmony with the flexibility apparent in the New Testament church, which also modified and developed its organizational system as time passed.[2] The Seventh-day Adventist Church sought to remain faithful to the scriptural ideal by adopting a system of church order appropriate to practical requirements within the framework of their theological presuppositions. Behind statements of a pragmatic nature

---

[1]The servanthood of the church of Christ has been addressed frequently by Seventh-day Adventist writers in recent years. See, for e.g., Robert E. Firth, ed., Servants for Christ: The Adventist Church Facing the '80s (Berrien Springs, Mich.: Andrews University Press, 1980). See especially the chapter by Walter B. T. Douglas, "The Church: Its Nature and Function," pp. 53-85. Cf. also Rex Edwards, Every Believer a Minister (Mountain View, Calif.: Pacific Press Pub. Assn, 1979), pp. 58-68; Damsteegt, Foundations, p. 258. Two papers presented at a theological consultation for Seventh-day Adventist Administrators and Religion Scholars held at Glacier View, Colorado, August 15-19, 1980, also stressed the servant nature of the work of the entire church. See, Veltman, "The Role of Church Administrators and Theologians" (1980), pp. 17-25; Bradford, "A Theology of Church Organization and Administration" (1980), p. 16.

[2]Bates expressed the point of view that there was development in organizational methods in New Testament times ("Church Order," p. 22). Cf. above, p. 134.

lay a fundamental concern that the church fulfill its unique role in history as the remnant church. This could only be accomplished, in the view of early Seventh-day Adventists, by developing a structure that encouraged unity of faith and action.[1]

Congregational, Presbyterian, or Methodist?

As has been mentioned,[2] Puritanism was a potent force in the United States in the 19th century, especially in the north-eastern part of the country--the same area where Millerism flourished and Seventh-day Adventism began. Although the Congregational, Presbyterian, Baptist, and Methodist Churches each followed its own particular system of church organization, Puritan influence may be seen in the polity of each.

A brief survey of the organizational methods of the four denominations just mentioned is undertaken here in order to compare the polity of these churches with Seventh-day Adventist order as it developed and existed during the lifetime of White and to determine to what extent, if any, Seventh-day Adventists consciously imitated, adapted, or avoided systems of church government which were prevalent at the time.[3]

---

[1]On the theological foundations of Seventh-day Adventist organization, see above, pp. 195-217. A discussion of Seventh-day Adventist pragmatic concerns appears below, pp. 267-272.

[2]See above, pp. 21-22.

[3]The Protestant Episcopal Church seems to have had little direct influence on the development of Seventh-day Adventist organization. Before the American Revolution, the center of Anglican strength in the American colonies had been Virginia. The limited influence of Anglicanism in New England (where Seventh-day Adventism originated) was severely weakened by the Revolution and continued to

The Congregationalists

The beginnings of Congregationalism may be traced back to Puritan members of the Church of England who wished to see the English church complete the theological and ecclesiological reforms begun when the Anglican Church broke away from Roman Catholicism.[1]

The Savoy Declaration, a statement of Congregationalist Principles drawn up in 1658, is considered the basic English Congregational declaration of doctrinal beliefs and rules for church

---

diminish after the war. It was not until the time of Bishop John H. Hobart (d. 1830) that the fortunes of the Protestant Episcopal Church began to revive. Even then, because Hobart vigorously opposed the inter-denominational cooperation and voluntary societies characteristic of the Second Great Awakening, it is doubtful that episcopal polity had a significant impact on Seventh-day Adventism. See H. Shelton Smith, Robert T. Handy, and Lefferts A. Loetscher, American Christianity: An Historical Interpretation with Representative Documents, 2 vols. (New York: Charles Scribner's Sons, 1960), 2:74-79; Hudson, Religion in America, pp. 32-36, 116-117, 171-173.

[1]Robert Browne (1550-1633), an English Separatist, has been identified as the founder of Congregationalism. More recent studies have drawn the conclusion that Congregationalists were not followers of Browne and did not seek separation from the Church of England, but rather identified Henry Jacob (1563-1624) as the one who originated Congregational Puritanism. Examples of exponents of the former viewpoint include Henry M. Dexter, Congregationalism of the Last Three Hundred Years As Seen in Its Literature (Boston, 1880; reprint ed., Westmead, Farnborough, Hants., England: Gregg International Publishers, 1970), pp. 61-128; Williston Walker, Creeds and Platforms of Congregationalism (New York: 1893; reprint ed., Boston: Pilgrim Press, 1960), p. 10. See Champlin Burrage, The Early English Dissenters in the Light of Recent Research, 1550-1641, 2 vols. (New York: Russell & Russell, 1912; reprint ed., 1967), 1:281-311; Perry Miller, Orthodoxy in Massachusetts, 1630-1650 (Cambridge, Mass.: Harvard University Press, 1933), on the more recent theory of the origins of Congregationalism. An account of the debate on the early history of Congregational Puritanism and additional bibliography may be found in Smith, Handy, and Loetscher, American Christianity, 1:82-89, 140-142.

polity.[1] It was in three parts: a confession of faith almost identical to the Calvinistic Westminster Confession (1648), a platform of discipline, and a plea for toleration for a congregational form of church government.[2]

Congregationalism rested on the fundamental principle that Christ is the supreme Head of the church.[3] Each local congregation drew "immediate and full power to order its entire life" directly from Jesus Christ and not from any intermediate controlling body.[4] Several other rules of church government were derived from this underlying tenet of Christ's sole leadership. As each local church was independent and autonomous, Congregationalists believed in the equality of all believers, both laity and clergy. The minister's work--teaching, preaching, exhorting, and visitation--was indeed regarded as important, but "to the Congregationalist, the real Church was the laity."[5] When it came to matters involving rulership of the

---

[1]The Savoy Declaration of Faith may be found in Walker, Creeds of Congregationalism, pp. 354-402. On the polity of the Savoy Assembly, see also Arthur A. Rouner, Jr., The Congregational Way of Life (Englewood Cliffs, N.J.: Prentice-Hall, 1960), pp. 29-36.

[2]See the comparison between the Savoy Declaration and the Westminster Confession in Philip Schaff, The Creeds of Christendom, 3 vols., 4th ed., rev. and enl. (New York: Harper & Bros, 1919), 3:718-723. Cf. "Savoy Declaration," Oxford Dictionary of the Christian Church (1974), p. 1239.

[3]See Article I of the Savoy Declaration (Walker, Creeds of Congregationalism, p. 403), which reads: "By the appointment of the Father all Power for the Calling, Institution, Order or Government of the Church is invested in a Supreme and Soveraign maner [sic] in the Lord Jesus Christ, as King and Head thereof."

[4]Smith, Handy, and Loetscher, American Christianity, 1:84.

[5]Leonard J. Trinterud, The Forming of an American Tradition: A Re-Examination of Colonial Presbyterianism (Philadelphia: The Westminster Press, 1949; reprint ed., New York: Books for Libraries

church, as opposed to ministry of the Word, all decisions were made by the "brotherhood" alone, which consisted of all male members of the congregation. The minister held his place in this "brotherhood" only as an equal. Issues that might come before this ruling body were "'the keys of the Kingdom' [entrance to the Church] or church discipline, decency and expedition."[1]

Another significant feature of Congregationalism, as expressed at Savoy, was its concept of the "gathered" church.[2] As the church was considered to be only a particular, visible congregation, "never a diocesan or national body,"[3] it was considered essential that only holy and regenerate believers be permitted to belong. This required careful examination of any prospective member, pastoral concern by the whole congregation for each individual's spiritual condition, and strict discipline in cases of moral deficiency. Congregationalists did not consider themselves to be infallible in making such judgments, but had no doubt that such decisions must be made and acted upon as well as possible.[4]

Press, 1970), p. 18. Rouner agrees with Trinterud. He writes that the congregational way of life is "essentially a layman's church" (The Congregational Way of Life, p. 32). One should note that in later years greater authority was attributed to the ministry. The Saybrook Articles (1708) are a case in point, considerably extending the disciplinary powers of regional associations of local churches and of the ministry (see below, pp. 239-240).

[1]Trinterud, An American Tradition, p. 18.

[2]See Articles 2 and 3 (Walker, Creeds of Congregationalism, p. 403).

[3]Smith, Handy, and Loetscher, American Christianity, 1:84.

[4]Cf. Trinterud, An American Tradition, p. 17.

A natural corollary of the local congregation as the "church" was the doctrine of the invisible church in which all converted Christians are one. As Congregationalists believed that the true church could only be identified either with the local congregation or the universal, invisible church, never with a denomination, they greatly encouraged inter-denominational cooperation.[1]

Generally speaking, Congregationalists have, because of their dissatisfaction with denominationalism, also opposed setting up creedal tests for church membership. While this has been a strength in terms of understanding and tolerance, it can be said that it has also been a weakness, leaving Congregationalists open to liberal and modernistic teaching.[2]

A great wave of Puritan migration to America took place in the 1630s during the reign of Charles I. Puritan hopes of continuing reform of the Church of England declined under the repressive leadership of Archbishop Laud. Even so, the settlers in Massachusetts Bay did not specifically seek separation from the Church of England, but hoped to provide a suitable example of a properly governed church that the world could see.[3] The need to clarify their position was made more urgent in the 1640s by the

---

[1]Cf. Smith, Handy, and Loetscher, _American Christianity_, 2:66-67. One is reminded that the Christian Connection, which was also congregationally organized, held a similar unfavorable view of denominational divisions (cf. above, pp. 29-32).

[2]Gilbert W. Kirby, "Congregationalism," _New International Dictionary of the Christian Church_ (1978), pp. 252-253. Once again, the anti-creedal stance of the Christian Connection comes to mind (cf. above, pp. 30-31).

[3]Cf. Ahlstrom, _A Religious History_, pp. 93, 132-134.

debates taking place in the Westminster Assembly and by a desire to distinguish their ecclesiology from the Brownists or Separatists on the one hand and the Presbyterians on the other.[1] Representatives gathered for a synod, therefore, at Cambridge, Mass., and produced in 1648 what is known as the Cambridge Platform, which limited itself to matters of church order. Recognizing the need for a confession of faith, they agreed to adopt the one just issued by the Westminster Assembly.[2]

Although the Cambridge statement reiterated the Congregationalist principles that each local church is distinct and all congregations and members equal, some Presbyterian ideas were embodied in the Platform.[3] The office of the ruling elder was recognized and both Congregationalist and Presbyterian views on the appointment and ordination of ministers allowed. Congregationalists believed that the brethren--male members of the local church-- should ordain their own minister. Presbyterians held that he should be ordained by other ministers.[4] The Cambridge delegates also agreed that there should be communion among congregations "for mutual advice and counsel; admonition concerning church offences; inter-congregational sharing in the Lord's Supper; aid to needy churches;

---

[1]Smith, Handy, and Loetscher, American Christianity, 1:128. On the development of American Congregationalism, see also Gaius G. Atkins and Frederick L. Fagley, History of American Congregationalism (Boston: Pilgrim Press, 1952).

[2]Smith, Handy, and Loetscher, American Christianity, 1:129. The main part of the text of the Cambridge Platform is reproduced in the same volume, pp. 129-140.

[3]On Presbyterian order, see below, pp. 241-248.

[4]Cf. Trintrud, An American Tradition, p. 21.

organization of new churches; inter-church participation in the calling and settlement of ministers."[1]

Provision was also made at Cambridge for the convening of synods to settle doctrinal controversies, to give scripturally based direction for proper forms of worship, and to deal with matters of church government. Jurisdiction over discipline was specifically denied the synod and left to the local congregation. It was also recognized that such synods were, under normal circumstances, not absolutely necessary, but "through the iniquity of Men, and perverseness of Times, necessary to the Well-being of Churches. . . ."[2] This provision is particularly relevant to the present study. The New England Congregationalists concluded that man's sinful condition and the declining spirituality within and outside the church demanded stricter discipline and wider jurisdiction than local congregations could provide. Worldliness meant increased centralization, even for Congregationalists.

It should also be noted that the Cambridge Platform contained prolific scriptural citations, witnessing to the importance of the perceived congregational pattern to be found in the New Testament.[3] The importance of Scripture as the basis for church order may also be seen in instructions given for the appointment of church officers. The framers of the Platform distinguished between extraordinary and

---

[1]Smith, Handy, and Loetscher, American Christianity, 1:138.

[2]See chapter 16 of the Cambridge Platform (Smith, Handy, and Loetscher, American Christianity, 1:139).

[3]For the sake of conciseness the scriptural references are omitted from the text reproduced by Smith, Handy, and Loetscher.

ordinary officers. The extraordinary officers--apostles, prophets, and evangelists--were called by Christ and their office ended with themselves. Ordinary officers were the elders and deacons who, as with their New Testament counterparts, were appointed to feed only "the particular Flock of God over which the holy [sic] Ghost had made them Over-seers."[1] A further distinction was seen between the call of apostles, prophets, and evangelists on the one hand and elders and deacons on the other. As has been stated, the extraordinary officers received their commission directly from Christ. The call of the ordinary officers was "mediate," that is, by the local church.[2]

The Articles of the Saybrook Platform (1708) were another important development in the history of New England Congregationalism. Representing the decision of Connecticut Congregationalists, this document introduced "a centralizing principle of far-reaching consequences"[3] and replaced the Cambridge Platform as the "most important confessional document of New England."[4]

Perhaps the most significant change in the Saybrook Articles from the Cambridge Platform was to extend authority in matters of church discipline to regional "consociations" instead of confining disciplinary matters to the local body as affirmed at Cambridge. Any

---

[1]Cambridge Platform, chapter 3 (Smith, Handy, and Loetscher, American Christianity, 1:131).

[2]Cambridge Platform, chapter 8 (Smith, Handy, and Loetscher, American Christianity, 1:134).

[3]Smith, Handy, and Loetscher, American Christianity, 1:225. The text of the Saybrook Articles appears on pp. 226-229.

[4]Donald M. Lake, "Saybrook Platform (1708)," New International Dictionary of the Christian Church (1978), p. 881.

church or individual refusing to accept decisions of such a consociation would be guilty of "Scandalous Contempt."[1] County-wide associations of ministers were also set up "with authority to examine and recommend ministerial candidates, and to ferret out and bring before councils suspected heretics and others guilty of scandalous conduct."[2]

Like the Cambridge Platform, the Saybrook Articles decided that greater centralization was necessary to revitalize religion and to deal more effectively with problems encountered because of the declining spirituality in church and society.[3] The success of the Saybrook provisions in improving the sinful situation would be difficult to determine; but Sweet, for one, has observed that the greater degree of centralization within Connecticut Congregationalism as a result of the Saybrook Platform, enabled it to become "the most aggressive and effective" in westward missionary enterprises.[4]

At the close of the War for Independence the Congregationalists were the largest and most influential religious body in America.[5] The prominent role played by Congregationalist clergy in winning independence stood them in good stead in the years immediately following. Yet this involvement in public affairs may in the end have proved detrimental, as Congregational ministers came to

---

[1]See Smith, Handy, and Loetscher, _American Christianity_, 1:225.

[2]Ibid.   [3]Ibid., pp. 224-225.

[4]William Warren Sweet, _Religion on the American Frontier, 1783-1850: A Collection of Source Materials_, vol. 3: _The Congregationalists_ (Chicago: University Press, 1939), p. 12.

[5]Ibid., p. 3.

be regarded by many as political rather than religious leaders.[1]

Sweet also identifies the relative lack of centralization among Congregationalists as a serious factor in their later failure to capitalize upon the advantageous position in which they found themselves at the close of the War for Independence. It seems that opposition to increased centralization was particularly strong about the end of the 18th century, in reaction to the kind of consociations established in Connecticut in 1708.[2]

In May 1801, a Plan of Union was adopted by the General Assembly of the Presbyterian Church and by the Congregational General Association of Connecticut a month later. This Plan had important implications for the church order practiced by both bodies. However, it is necessary to survey the historical development of Presbyterianism up to this time, before we describe the impact of the Plan of Union upon Congregationalists and Presbyterians.

The Presbyterians

The presbyterian system follows the model established by John Calvin in Geneva.[3] It is built upon the practice of the Old

---

[1]Ibid., pp. 4-11.

[2]Ibid., pp. 11-12. Sweet cites the formation of state associations in Massachusetts in 1803, similar to the Connecticut Consociations in 1708, as a catalyst for this opposition. One of the leaders, Nathaniel Emmons, minister in Franklin, Mass., from 1773 to 1827, stated: "Association leads to Consociation; Consociation leads to Presbyterianism; Presbyterianism leads to Episcopacy; Episcopacy leads to Roman Catholicism; and Roman Catholicism is an ultimate fact" (p. 12).

[3]Cf. John Calvin, Institutes of the Christian Religion, 2 vols. (Grand Rapids, Mich.: William B. Eerdmans Pub. Co., 1962), 2:315-326. Of the many biographies and analyses of Calvin's

Testament synagogue, which was governed by a group of elders. Calvin recognized four officers in the church: the pastor, whose primary duty was to preach the Word; the teacher, who instructed in doctrine in a more formal way; the deacon, who cared for the material needs of the flock; and the elder or presbyter, who had oversight of the spiritual needs and life of the congregation. Under presbyterian order, there is no elite group with extraordinary powers or authority. Those who govern are chosen by all the church members. The local congregation is governed by the board, which is comprised of the elders and local minister. Each congregation appoints two representatives, an elder and a pastor, to the presbytery, which is comprised of local congregations within a given geographical area. Each presbytery appoints two individuals, an elder and a pastor, to the next level of government, the synod.[1] The synod in turn appoints an elder and a pastor to the General Assembly. Thus, each administrative body is comprised of an equal number of clergy and laity.

---

theology, three works provide particularly useful discussions of his doctrine of the church: Benjamin C. Milner, Jr., Calvin's Doctrine of the Church (Leiden: E. J. Brill, 1970); Wilhelm Niesel, The Theology of John Calvin, trans. Harold Knight (Guildford, England: Lutterworth Press, 1956; reprint ed., Grand Rapids, Mich.: Baker Book House, 1980), pp. 182-210; G. D. Henderson, Presbyterianism (Aberdeen: University Press, 1954). The latter work contains lectures delivered by the author for the Chalmers Lectureship, 1948-1952. Lectures three and four on "The Rejection of the Bishop in the Sixteenth Century" and "Origins of the Eldership" (pp. 32-71) show how English-speaking Presbyterians adapted Calvin's principles of church polity to their own particular situation. The development of colonial Presbyterianism is described in Trinterud, An American Tradition.

[1]Apparently, the synod has become less important in the structure of the Presbyterian Church because of the improvement of modern communications (W. S. Reid, "Presbyterianism," New International Dictionary of the Christian Church (1978), p. 801.

Any change proposed by the General Assembly must be referred back to the local church for approval.[1]

G. D. Henderson comments on the perceived effectiveness of presbyterian or reformed order. In contrast to an episcopal system, the minister "is no delegate of a bishop, but by right of ordination proclaims the Word, and celebrates the sacraments, and directs public worship as representing the congregation."[2] On the other hand, he is not an employee of the congregation, as might be said of ministers of Independent or Congregationalist churches. He is therefore "free to speak and act as he believes he ought. . . ."[3]

The role of the layman as supervisor of the church's spiritual affairs is another essential of the presbyterian system. As James Moffatt has rightly said: "It is on the efficiency of the elders that the Presbyterian Church in any community largely depends."[4] In Henderson's opinion, the eldership "gives to the laity

---

[1]Ibid., pp. 800-802. Cf. the authority of church synods and councils as expressed in the Westminster Confession of Faith, chap. 31:3: "It belongeth to synods and councils ministerially to determine controversies of faith, and cases of conscience; to set down rules and directions for the better ordering of the publick worship of God, and government of his church; to receive complaints in cases of mal-administration, and authoritatively to determine the same: which decrees and determinations, if consonant to the word of God, are to be received with reverence and submission, not only for their agreement with the word, but also for the power whereby they are made, as being an ordinance of God, appointed thereunto in his word" (The Confession of Faith; the Longer and Shorter Catechisms [n.p.: Publications Committee of the Free Presbyterian Church of Scotland, 1976], p. 122).

[2]Henderson, Presbyterianism, p. 162.

[3]Ibid.

[4]James Moffatt, quoted in Henderson, Presbyterianism, p. 162.

a fuller share of opportunity and responsibility than do the Church of Rome and the Church of England."[1]

One should not conclude that the presbyterian system is without any potential difficulties. Henderson is concerned that the eldership may not be sufficiently representative. The elders of the church may indeed become "too clerical" in their practice and not be sufficiently sensitive to the wishes of the rest of the laity whom they represent. There are other dangers: that some ministers may prefer "acquiescent nonentities for elders"; elders may be sometimes "unvocal" or "maintainers of the status quo."[2] The adequacy of the presbyterian system is dependent, therefore, on the quality of those who serve as elders.[3]

While "Presbyterian sentiment was constantly cropping out in early New England," it was the large wave of Scottish-Irish immigration after 1720 that established Presbyterianism as an important force in the North American colonies.[4] The Presbyterian immigrants who settled in New England tended to join one of the already established Congregational churches, many of which showed

---

[1]Henderson, Presbyterianism, p. 165.

[2]Ibid., p. 167.

[3]One might well remark that the same is true of any system. The effectiveness of any form of church order is principally subject to the ability and dedication of those holding positions of authority. Perhaps one important consideration in determining the appropriateness of a particular method of church government is its adequacy in limiting or controlling possible abuses of power by frail and sinful human beings.

[4]Hudson, Religion in America, p. 42. Cf. also Trinterud, An American Tradition, p. 15; Sweet, The Presbyterians, pp. 3-20; Ahlstrom, A Religious History, pp. 265-272.

pronounced presbyterian leanings, especially in Connecticut.[1] The
largest number of Presbyterian congregations at the opening of the
War for Independence were to be found, therefore, in New York, New
Jersey, Pennsylvania, Western Maryland, and Virginia; not in New
England.[2] This point is significant when one attempts to evaluate
the influence of Presbyterianism on Seventh-day Adventist church
order. The Presbyterians were not predominant where Seventh-day
Adventism first flourished, a fact which may have limited the impact
of the presbyterian form of government on Seventh-day Adventist
polity.

At the close of the War for Independence, the Presbyterians,
like the Congregationalists, stood in an advantageous position.
They, too, had supported the movement for independence and
immediately after sought to organize the church on a national basis.
This they accomplished at the Philadelphia Synod in May 1788.[3]
Sweet suggests that the Presbyterian Church had the best chance at
that time of becoming the greatest of American churches in terms of
numbers and influence. Their presbyteries, churches, and ministers
were to be found farthest west, he adds, and their leaders "imbued
with the sturdy spirit of the pioneers."[4]

---

[1]See above, pp. 239-240.

[2]Sweet, _Religion on the American Frontier_, Vol. 2: _The_
Presbyterians (New York and London: Harper & Bros., 1936), p. 5.
Additional sources on American Presbyterianism may be found in M. W.
Armstrong, Lefferts A. Loetscher, and C. A. Anderson, eds., _The_
Presbyterian Enterprise: Sources of American Presbyterian History
(Philadelphia: Westminster Press, 1956).

[3]Sweet, _The Presbyterians_, pp. 10-11.

[4]Ibid., p. 23.

Presbyterian hopes, however, were not realized. Their failure to capitalize upon their favorable situation is all the more puzzling when one remembers the Connecticut Congregationalist-Presbyterian Plan of Union, mentioned earlier, which was proposed in 1801 and seemed to benefit the Presbyterian Church more than Congregationalist churches.[1] The Plan of Union made four key provisions: (1) "Mutual forbearance" should be encouraged on both sides, (2) a Congregational church with a Presbyterian minister should follow congregational methods of order, (3) if the opposite situation obtained (a Congregational minister serving a Presbyterian church), presbyterian regulations should be followed, and (4) in a congregation made up of Congregationalists and Presbyterians a standing committee, chosen by the church, would have oversight of all members.[2]

According to Sweet, the Plan of Union was so beneficial to the Presbyterians that by 1825 "Presbyterianism had become completely triumphant in those regions where the Plan of Union had been most fully in operation."[3] He suggests two factors which help to account for this development. In the first place, even some Congregationalists felt that the presbyterian system was more effective in the rough, unstable frontier situation. Second, he

---

[1]Sweet's discussion of the Plan of Union is particularly helpful (The Presbyterians, pp. 39-47; The Congregationalists, pp. 13-42).

[2]Sweet, The Presbyterians, pp. 41-42.

[3]Ibid., p. 46.

indicates that Presbyterian ministers clung to their polity with more tenacity than the Congregational clergy.[1]

The Presbyterian Church in America did indeed grow with "amazing rapidity" during the first third of the 19th century, but the rate of growth was not maintained. Between 1834 and 1837 a series of discords arose which led to an actual decrease in membership.[2] The first cause of dissension was concern on the part of conservatives who feared that the Plan of Union had led to laxity in observing Presbyterian standards of polity. A second source of discord was increasing rivalry between the American Home Missionary Society and the Assembly's Board of Missions. Both of these organizations were supported by Presbyterians and carried on the same kind of work in the same territory.[3] A third bone of contention lay in the heretical opinions that some of the stricter Calvinist Presbyterians felt were creeping into the church from New England and Congregational sources. They perceived a radical and dangerous modification of Calvinist theology's entering the Presbyterian Church through the revivals of the Second Great Awakening.[4] In particular, emphasis upon human responsibility by the revivalists was seen to be contrary to the Calvinistic doctrines of election and the nature of man. Finally, the issue of slavery came to a head in the 1830s within Presbyterianism. In 1818 the General Assembly had

---

[1]Ibid., pp. 46-47.   [2]Ibid., p. 99.

[3]Sweet describes the rivalry between these two organizations in The Presbyterians, pp. 102-106.

[4]On the Second Great Awakening, see above, pp. 17-21.

unanimously denounced slavery, but in the 1830s anti-slavery agitation called for immediate emancipation. Some Presbyterians regarded such demands as precipitous. The conflict resulted in distinct anti-slavery and pro-slavery wings forming within the denomination by 1836.[1]

To conclude this survey of Congregationalism and Presbyterianism some observations on the effectiveness of their respective systems of church polity are in order. It has been observed that both religious bodies appeared to be on the verge of success and expansion at the close of the War for Independence. Both failed, in varying degrees, to meet expectations of numerical growth and geographical expansion, as neither experienced continuing spiritual well-being.

It does seem that the more centralized presbyterian form of government was better suited to the frontier situation. It also appeared more effective in carrying out a vigorous missionary enterprise, as evidenced by the fact that of the New England Congregationalists, the Connecticut branch (which has been described as "semi-Presbyterian"[2] anyway) was most successful in its endeavors to expand westward. Additionally, even some Congregationalists found their form of government to be inadequate in maintaining doctrinal unity.[3]

---

[1]On the Presbyterian controversies of the 1830s, see Sweet, The Presbyterians, pp. 100-120.

[2]Smith, Handy, and Loetscher, American Christianity, 1:523.

[3]Rouner, e.g., while holding to the excellence of the "Congregational Way," admits that members of Congregational churches frequently confess that their "faith is too vague" (Rouner, The

Having made these remarks about the apparent advantages of the presbyterian system, it also needs to be recognized that there are undoubtedly factors other than structural pattern in the prosperity of any religious body. New England Congregationalism suffered, not only from lack of centralization, but from "smug provincialism," the involvement of its ministers in political rather than spiritual matters, and from the fact that it came to be regarded as the religion of the privileged rather than of the masses.[1] Presbyterianism ultimately declined in the 1830s as a result of doctrinal and political controversies, and because its theology was unsuited to the revivalism and optimism of the age.

The Baptists

It is not necessary to describe Baptist origins or polity as fully as congregationalist and presbyterian order have been delineated, because the Baptists were also congregationally organized.[2] However, there are a few characteristics of Baptist belief and practice which deserve to be pointed out.

Prior to the First Great Awakening (c.1725-c.1760), Baptists in North America were few. The revivals of the 18th century and the traditional Baptist stand on religious liberty and separation of

---

Congregational Way of Life, p. 39). Cf. also, Kirby, "Congregationalism," International Dictionary of the Christian Church (1978), pp. 252-253; Hudson, Religion in America, p. 120; above, p. 236.

[1]Cf. Sweet, The Congregationalists, pp. 5-12.

[2]On the beginnings of the Baptists in North America, see Ola E. Winslow, Master Roger Williams (New York: Macmillan Publishing Co., 1957); Perry Miller, Roger Williams: His Contribution to the American Tradition (Indianapolis: Bobbs-Merrill & Co.,

church and state during the War for Independence greatly increased their numbers and influence. Perhaps partly as a consequence of their congregational polity, several Baptist movements emerged. Some--the General Baptists--were Arminian in theology, but the Calvinistic Baptists, or Particularists, became the major Baptist body.[1] Whatever the considerable differences among the Baptist groups, they held five essential principles in common:

> (1) Separation of church and state; (2) Conversion as a condition of church membership; (3) Individual responsibility to God; (4) Congregational church government; and (5) Immersion as the only Scriptural form of Baptism.[2]

Baptist congregational polity was based on a strong desire to follow the perceived New Testament pattern, adhering to the "historic Baptist emphasis on strict biblicism."[3] It was accompanied by equally strict discipline, especially in frontier areas where rigorous standards were considered essential to keep order in society.[4]

Most Baptists shared with Congegationalists and Presbyterians a theology based upon the Westminster Confession, and Baptist polity

---

1953). General histories include: Norman A. Baxter, History of the Freewill Baptists: A Study in New England Separatism (Rochester, N.Y.: American Baptist Historical Society, 1957); Robert G. Torbet, A History of the Baptists (Philadelphia: Judson Press, 1950); Sweet, Religion on the American Frontier, Vol. 1: The Baptists (New York: Henry Holt & Co., 1931). The latter work contains an introduction by Sweet and a collection of source materials.

[1]Cf. ibid., pp. 3-17; Hudson, Religion in America, pp. 43-45.

[2]Sweet, The Baptists, p. 43.

[3]Smith, Handy, and Loetscher, American Christianity, 1:269.

[4]Sweet, The Baptists, p. 49.

was essentially the same as American Congregational order. However, whereas Congregationalists and Presbyterians failed to maintain growth and even declined in number, Baptist membership mushroomed, so that by the end of the Second Great Awakening they stood with the Methodists as the leading religions of the frontier.

What enabled Baptist churches to succeed in their evangelistic efforts? Ahlstrom stresses that their growth was not due to a popular "frontier faith," namely, one built on a doctrine of human freedom and an optimistic view of human nature. Baptist preachers proclaimed a basically Calvinistic theology requiring evidence of a firm conversion experience in prospective members and administering strict discipline within the church.[1] The increase in Baptist membership was a consequence of "their spiritual vitality and their individualistic emphasis on conversion."[2] One might add that Baptists prospered because they were not restricted by a rigid, centralized polity, or strict educational requirements for their ministers, but depended upon the farmer-preacher for their evangelistic work. A farmer who felt called to preach might obtain a license and eventually be ordained, sometimes by a church which he

---

[1] Ahlstrom, A Religious History, p. 442. He also warns against the simplistic view that Particular Baptists and Methodists taught opposite and conflicting theologies. He points out that both theologies were built on "the sovereignty of God and the depravity of man." He continues, "No one spoke more forcefully of man's abject need for divine grace than Wesley, and the true Methodist demand for repentance--or, more often, penitential conflict--stems from the heart of the Puritan movement. Arminianism in this context meant not an optimistic view of human nature . . . but a reinterpretation of the strict Calvinistic understanding of atonement, grace, and the sanctifying work of the Holy Spirit" (p. 438).

[2] Ibid., p. 443.

himself had gathered.[1] It is also significant that Methodist order
(discussed below) which, having strict centralized control and
authority, was quite different from Baptist order, proved to be even
more successful in terms of stimulating spiritual vigor and numerical
growth.

Baptists also grew because they sprang from and appealed to
the largest class of Americans--"the common people of the country and
small towns--and they spoke to the people with simplicity and power,
without pretense or condescension."[2] Their work was aided, too, by
the effective use of revivalistic methods and camp meetings.[3]

The Methodists[4]

The stamp of John Wesley's personality can be seen in
Methodism in England and America. Methodism began in England as a
paternal system completely under his control and continued to be so
there to the end of his life. However, Wesley was not able to
exercise the same control over American Methodism, although the
general features of his organizational methods--field preaching,
social prayer meetings, lay preaching, itinerancy, conferences--were
perpetuated in North America.[5]

The formation of the American Methodists as a separate

---

[1]Cf. ibid.   [2]Ibid.

[3]Cf. above, pp. 17-21.

[4]On the history and organization of American Methodism, see
Sweet, Religion on the American Frontier, Vol. 4: The Methodists,
(Chicago: University Press, 1946). For additional bibliographical
information see p. 27, footnote 1. See also our discussion on the
contribution of Methodism to the Millerite movement, pp. 26-28.

[5]See Scudder, American Methodism, pp. 98-121.

ecclesiastical organization took place in Baltimore in 1784 at the
so-called Christmas Conference.[1] According to Sweet, this meeting
determined what course Methodism would take in an independent
America. It was also, he adds, a new kind of Methodist conference,
in that it was not an advisory body such as Wesley would have
preferred, but was one that decided all matters by majority vote,
introducing "the governing conference into the American Methodist
system."[2]

At Baltimore, Francis Asbury was ordained deacon, elder, and
joint superintendent on successive days.[3] In the 1787 edition of the
"Form of Discipline" he took the title "bishop," against Wesley's
wishes. The members of the newly independent church described it as
a moderate episcopacy, under the direction of bishops, elders,
deacons, and preachers.[4] In 1785 the Methodist Conference met
in three sectional meetings. These meetings were not separate
conferences but sections of one undivided conference held in
different localities for the convenience of the members. By 1791, as
a result of rapid growth, there were seventeen sectional conferences.
Further growth necessitated making the conferences delegated bodies

---

[1]On the Christmas Conference, see Sweet, The Methodists, pp. 38, 100-121; Scudder, American Methodism, pp. 211-229. Excerpts of the minutes of the Conference, drawn up and revised in more readable form in 1788, may be found in Smith, Handy, and Loetscher, American Christianity, 1:456-459.

[2]Sweet, The Methodists, p. 38.

[3]Francis Asbury had been named by John Wesley as joint leader of American Methodism with Thomas Coke.

[4]"Form of Discipline," Section 3 (Smith, Handy, and Loetscher, American Christianity, 1:457).

in 1808, and provision was made for a General Conference to meet every four years. This general meeting had authority to make all rules and regulations for the church, which might be altered with a joint recommendation by the annual local conferences and a two-thirds majority vote at the next General Conference.[1]

Methodism was also carefully organized on the "lower" levels. The basic unit of the local church was the class, which was made up of about twelve believers in a given community. The class leader's responsibility was to inquire into the spiritual condition of the members and to reprove, comfort, and exhort when necessary. The exhorter was the next step up in the local church, and above him was the local preacher. After 1789 provision was made for the latter to be ordained as a deacon, and after 1812 deacons were made eligible for the office of elder. Over all of these was the circuit-rider, who supervised those in his care through a quarterly conference of class leaders, exhorters, and local preachers from each circuit.[2]

Evidence of the flexibility of the Methodist system may be seen in the establishment of a new office--the presiding elder--in 1792, to keep pace with the demands of growth. He fulfilled a role as director of a district made up of several circuits under the overall direction of the bishop.[3] This adaptability of Methodism was

---

[1]See Sweet, The Methodists, pp. 38-41.

[2]Ibid., pp. 47-48.

[3]Some of the presiding elder's responsibilities included: oversight of circuit-riders and local preachers in a district; authority to change, appoint, and suspend travelling preachers in the absence of the bishop; attendance at quarterly meetings of the

perhaps one of its greatest strengths. If increased growth or
demands of the frontier situation created new challenges, a new
office, such as presiding elder, or a new section of the conference
could be established to meet the need. Sweet has suggested that it
was the youthfulness of the attendees at the Christmas Conference
that enabled them, perhaps from a lack of knowledge of other forms of
church polity, to turn their backs on precedent and create innovations in church government.[1]

It is perhaps not surprising, in view of their pragmatic
approach to organizational needs, that Methodists did not believe
that only one form of church government was prescribed in Scripture.
Such a belief harmonized with that of Wesley himself, who
wrote: "I think . . . that neither Christ or His Apostles prescribed
any particular form of Church government."[2] Methodists may not have
believed that their economy was prescribed in Scripture, but they
were in no doubt that the efficiency of the system was "one of the
most powerful elements in the religious prosperity of the United
States,"[3] and that Methodism's growth by the 1840s into the largest

---

circuits in his district; and right to preside at the district
conference in the absence of the bishop (ibid., p. 40).

[1]Ibid., p. 20.

[2]John Wesley to James Clark, July 3, 1756 (quoted in Sweet,
The Methodists, p. 31). Cf. also "Methodist Churches," Oxford
Dictionary of the Christian Church (1974), p. 909.

[3]Robert Baird, Religion in America, or an Account of the
Origin, Relation to the State and the Present Condition of the
Evangelical Churches in the United States, with Notice of the Unevan-
gelical Denominations (1st ed., 1843; New York, 1856), pp. 496-497.

Protestant body in America proved the "remarkable superiority of the Methodist economy."[1]

Methodist polity was effective not only because of its ability to adapt to the needs of society; it was also considered the ideal form of organization for a "holiness" church in which the members were actively "seeking the power of godliness."[2] Scudder, at least, was sure that "no ecclesiastical system has furnished better appliances to aid men to live holy."[3]

The effectiveness of the Methodist system may have been ideal, but even more important was the devotion of its leaders. The "burning zeal" of the circuit-riders, in particular, was one of the main reasons for the growth of Methodism and the success of its revivals.[4]

There developed concern among Methodists that an authoritarian, centralized form of government such as theirs, while suitable for "a holy people," might be a means of abuse and despotism should the church become "a strong establishment." Scudder wrote in 1867:

> There is no church organization in existence that has in it such elements of weakness, division, and ruin as the Methodist Church. Its grand system of centralized power, and the authority it gives to individuals for the supervision and direction of both ministers and members, perverted, would be like aroused Samsons in the temple of the Philistines. . . .[5]

---

[1]Abel Stevens, _An Essay in Church Polity_ (New York, 1847), p. 148 (quoted in Sweet, _The Methodists_, p. 45).

[2]Scudder, _American Methodism_, p. 101.

[3]Ibid.

[4]Sweet, _The Methodists_, p. 52. Cf. Smith, Handy, and Loetscher, _American Christianity_, 1:562.

[5]Scudder, _American Methodism_, p. 102.

Perhaps Scudder's observations were based on trends already apparent in Methodism. Sweet, for example, states that there was a growing tendency toward a "stationed ministry" by the end of the third decade of the 19th century when it came to be generally believed that the itinerant circuit-rider was not suited to the larger towns and cities.[1]

Comparison With Seventh-day Adventist Order

A comparison of the principles of early Seventh-day Adventist organization, as presented in the previous chapter, with the systems of church government practiced by Methodists, Presbyterians, Congregationalists, and Baptists reveals a number of parallels and differences.

The centralized system of the Presbyterian Church proved effective in maintaining doctrinal unity and discipline on the frontier, and in carrying out the evangelistic mission of the church. Seventh-day Adventists adopted centralized church order for similar reasons.[2] Considerable differences are apparent, however, in the methods of representation utilized by the two churches. Presbyterians allocated an equal number of ministers and elders to the presbyteries, synods, and General Assemblies. The Seventh-day Adventist Church, in contrast, has not normally made provision for representation by a certain percentage of elders or laity at the

---

[1]Sweet, The Methodists, pp. 46-47.

[2]Cf. above, pp. 171-175.

sessions of the local or General Conference levels.[1] The elder's role is more vital, therefore, to the proper functioning of Presbyterianism than is the local elder in a Seventh-day Adventist congregation. Not only does the former have an equal voice with the minister at representative sessions but he also plays a key role in "ruling" the local church. As has been observed, the 1863 constitution of the Seventh-day Adventist Church made no distinction between a local elder and other members of the church when it came to representation at conference sessions. Additionally, the function of the elder as ruler of the local church has been taken over within Adventism by the church board, of which the minister is usually chairman and the elder a member with no greater voice than other lay board members.[2]

Seventh-day Adventist church order as adopted in 1863 seems to be closest to the Methodist economy in several respects. Both denominations were governed by General Conferences, which were delegated bodies convened at regular intervals to conduct the business of the church.[3] The constituent parts of the General Conference in the Methodist system were called sectional conferences, which were not separate units but sections of one undivided

---

[1]Proposals have recently been put forward to increase the level of lay representation. See, e.g., Task Force Report, "Defining Participation," pp. 25-35.

[2]See SDA Church Manual (1981), pp. 77-87, 104, on the duties of the elder and composition of the church board.

[3]On the organization of the Seventh-day Adventist General Conference in 1863, see above, pp. 161-162.

conference.[1] The Seventh-day Adventist local conferences corresponded to the sectional conferences of Methodism. From 1863 to 1901
the local conferences served as the constituent parts of the General
Conference. After 1901, union conferences (the grouping together of
several local conferences on a geographical basis) were introduced as
the constituent elements of the General Conference.[2] One does not
find a corresponding development to union conferences in 18th- or
19th-century American Methodism, but the flexibility of Seventh-day
Adventist organization which enabled the delegates to the General
Conference in 1901 to introduce an additional level of government,
which the growth of the church required, resembled the adaptability
of the Methodist economy. As the denomination grew, Methodists
created additional sectional conferences to meet the new situation.[3]
Both the Seventh-day Adventist and Methodist Churches were characterized by a pragmatic approach to organizational matters and cited
the effectiveness of their respective polities as evidence of the
superiority of their systems.[4]

Of the four churches compared above, the Methodist Church was
the only one to suggest that Scripture does not prescribe one

---

[1]On Methodist sectional conferences and their relationship to
the General Conference, see Sweet, The Methodists, pp. 38-42. Cf.
also above, pp. 253-254.

[2]Seventh-day Adventists eventually created four administra-
tive levels--local church, conference, union, and General Conference.
For accounts of the 1901 General Conference session when unions were
established, see Jorgensen, "Administrative Reorganization of the
General Conference" (1949); Crisler, Organization, pp. 135-176;
Schwarz, Light Bearers, pp. 267-281.

[3]See above, p. 255.

[4]Cf. above, pp. 171-175, 255-256.

particular form of church government.[1] It was this belief, perhaps,
that enabled Methodists to maintain a flexible approach to organizational matters. Seventh-day Adventists were not quite as ready to
agree that the Bible did not set forth a specific system of order;
but White, at least--the most influential individual in matters
concerning church organization among early Seventh-day Adventists--
declared on more than one occasion that Scripture only provided
general principles of organization.[2]

One might also suggest that efficient systems of Methodism
and Seventh-day Adventism were appropriate to their shared understanding of the church as a gathered community. Strict discipline
was administered in the congregations of both denominations in
keeping with their belief that only the regenerate should be admitted
into membership.[3]

Much of the success of Methodism, especially until the end of
the third decade of the 19th century, depended upon the work of the
itinerant preacher, the circuit-rider.[4] The "travelling brethren"
among Sabbatarian Adventists filled a similar role. While their
parishes or circuits were perhaps not as clearly defined as the
Methodist preachers', early Sabbatarian Adventist visiting preachers

---

[1]See above, p. 255.

[2]See above, pp. 130-131, 144-145, 189-190.

[3]On the suitability of Methodist order to its self-
understanding as a "holiness" church, see above, p. 256. The role
of the "travelling brethren" in maintaining discipline in the early
days of Sabbatarian Adventism also comes to mind (see above, pp. 119-
120).

[4]Cf. above, p. 256.

sought to exercise discipline, to encourage the leaders of local congregations, and to maintain links with congregations in other areas in much the same way as the circuit-rider.[1]

Differences between Seventh-day Adventist and Methodist organization are relatively few but deserve to be pointed out. An obvious difference was the avoidance of the term "bishop" by Seventh-day Adventists.[2] The disparity between the roles of circuit-riders and travelling brethren has already been mentioned. But it is perhaps on the level of the local congregation that the greatest dissimilarities between Seventh-day Adventist and Methodist order may be seen. Local officers of the Methodist Church included class leaders, exhorters, and preachers whose responsibilities seemed to have been fairly well defined.[3] In early Sabbatarian Adventism, officers were normally limited to elders and deacons whose roles seemed to be more fluid than Methodist local officers, perhaps varying according to the abilities of the elder or deacon in question. One might also point out that among Methodists, elders were classified as supervising preachers and administrators rather than as officers of a local church.[4]

The differences between Seventh-day Adventist and Methodist church order at the congregational level may be partly due to the

---

[1]Cf. above, pp. 119-120.

[2]Seventh-day Adventists considered the terms "elder" and "bishop" to be synonymous, but chose to employ the former as title for the ordained minister (cf. above, p. 156).

[3]See, e.g., Sweet, The Methodists, pp. 47-48.

[4]Ibid, pp. 40-41. Sweet also points out that after 1789 local preachers were ordained as deacons (p. 48).

fact that Seventh-day Adventists retained some congregational principles of local church organization. It seems that the importance of unity of doctrine and a common sense of mission to proclaim the imminent return of Christ required, in the view of early Seventh-day Adventists, greater cooperation and harmony than could be achieved through congregational government.[1] However, Seventh-day Adventists also desired that organization should be as simple as possible and for that reason, at least, retained the authority of the local church in matters of discipline and the acceptance of converts into church membership.[2] In this respect the organization of the Seventh-day Adventist Church possesses some similarities to the polities of Baptists and Congregationalists.

Discovering a certain resemblance between Seventh-day Adventist and Methodist organization does not demonstrate conscious imitation, or even awareness, on the part of Seventh-day Adventist pioneers of the Methodist economy. Undoubtedly, there was general knowledge of Methodism, as the Methodist Church was the largest in North America by the mid-19th century and approximately 44 percent of the Millerite preachers identified by Dick were Methodist.[3] However, in the recorded discussions on church order, at least, there is little evidence of awareness of any existing form of denominational polity, let alone reference to actual

---

[1]Cf. above, pp. 195-211.

[2]See, e.g., SDA Church Manual (1981), pp. 62-68. Cf. also below, p. 267.

[3]Cf. above, p. 26.

copying. This is hardly surprising. It is unlikely that a movement which at its inception experienced separation and alienation from the established churches would be inclined to imitate any current denominational structure.

In conclusion, it would seem that the resemblance of Seventh-day Adventist organization to the Methodist economy may be attributed to the following factors:

1. Common knowledge and application of scriptural principles of church order by Methodists and Seventh-day Adventists.

2. Similar value placed by the two denominations upon doctrinal unity and church discipline.

3. The same pragmatic approach to carrying out as efficiently as possible the mission of the church.

4. General awareness (without conscious imitation) by Seventh-day Adventist leaders of Methodist organizational principles.

Personal and Pragmatic Factors

The prominence of White in the early history of Seventh-day Adventism is obvious. The system of order established in 1863 and the present organization bear the mark of his personality. This does not mean that an interpretation of the rationale for Seventh-day Adventist church organization can be attributed to his influence alone, but it does mean that his life and the experience of the church were so closely interwoven that the formulation of church order was necessarily conditioned by his opinions and the ideas of others as they interacted with him.

We have characterized White's style of leadership as

aggressive, resourceful, and energetic.[1] When he was in charge, administrative matters seemed to prosper. Other Seventh-day Adventist leaders were not, it seems, as effective as he. As he did not always trust the efficiency of his associates, he was inclined to maintain direct oversight of all aspects of church work. With the growth of the denomination, personal involvement in everything became virtually impossible and the resulting overwork may have contributed to the breakdown of White's health. There was also a tendency among his co-workers, in the face of his censures, to let him do everything himself.[2]

Centralized Authority

What facets of Seventh-day Adventist organization reflect more particularly the influence of White's personality? The move toward centralization of authority seems to give evidence of his concern for adequate supervision. Could it be that the decision to invest the General Conference with far-reaching authority over state conferences evinced not only a desire to maintain doctrinal unity, but a lack of trust in the ability of those on lower levels of

---

[1]On White's leadership style, see above, pp. 168-169.

[2]After his stroke in 1865 (see above, p. 164), White became increasingly censorious of others who held positions of leadership. His wife, for example, wrote in 1872: "While standing under these burdens that no one else would venture to take, my husband has sometimes, under the pressure of care, spoken without due considera- tion and with apparent severity. He has sometimes censured those in the office because they did not take care" (Testimonies for the Church, 3:86). Robinson, White's biographer, commented: "He did not hesitate to censure those who failed to do all he thought they should. As a result, for fear of incurring his displeasure, workers were inclined to sit back and let him do the job his own way" (James White, p. 290).

leadership to carry out their responsibilities effectively without close direction?

Perhaps White's question, "Must not the General Conference be the great regulator?" implied more than simply the equitable territorial assignment of ministers.[1] The General Conference executive committee was also the final earthly authority in matters of discipline, doctrinal unity, and the settling of disputes. The original provision that at least one member of the General Conference executive committee must be present at the session of every local conference seems to reflect in part White's tendency to maintain direct personal supervision over all phases of Seventh-day Adventist work.[2]

The constitution of the General Conference, voted in May 1863, is a suitable example of the relationship between state conferences and the General Conference.[3] The General Conference was given responsibility for "the general supervision of all ministerial labor," and its proper distribution. It was invested with similar power to assign to their tasks non-ministerial workers and all others (whether ministers or not) working in territories outside constituted state conferences.[4] Furthermore, a minister visiting from another state could appeal to the General Conference executive committee if, on arriving at his appointed place of labor, he found

---

[1][White], "General Conference," p. 172. Cf. above, p. 162.

[2]"Fourth Annual Session," pp. 196-197.

[3]Byington and Smith, "Report of General Conference," pp. 204-206.

[4]Ibid., p. 205.

inefficiency in the operation of the state conference. Conversely, a conference could appeal to the same authority if it was unhappy with the work of a visiting minister.[1]

The 1863 constitution formally established the authority of White, Bates, Byington, and other experienced leaders of the church to supervise the work force and to exercise jurisdiction in matters of doctrine and discipline. It should be observed, however, that as soon as Sabbatarian Adventism had come to a sense of unity of doctrine by the time of the 1848 conferences, and to a common conviction concerning the mission of the church shortly afterwards, Seventh-day Adventist leaders (especially White) upheld the authority of those who had been appointed as "travelling brethren" to teach and to advise in matters of discipline, on the grounds of their wide experience.[2] As the church grew, the means by which discipline and authority might be applied increased as well. However, the assumption that it is the duty of a properly appointed, ordained ministry to direct all phases of the work of the church was never in question. In this sense Sabbatarian Adventists never followed a congregational system of government. In the days when numbers were small, White's proposal for organization was that it should be as simple as possible,[3] but even in the early 1850s his

---

[1]Ibid.

[2]Cf. above, p. 122. One is reminded of the Whites' role on their annual Eastern tours in persuading the local churches to disfellowship certain members, suppressing unauthorized preachers, and instructing members in the doctrinal tenets of Sabbatarian Adventism. The credentials held by the travelling brethren represented their general authority over less experienced members.

[3]Cf. above, p. 191.

recommendations for overall supervision of the church went beyond the congregational style accepted by the majority of Adventists at Albany in the spring of 1845.[1]

The right to discipline and to receive new members, however, has always remained the prerogative of the local Seventh-day Adventist congregation. One might cite the constitution for state conferences recommended by the first General Conference session. The responsibility of the local conference was defined as "general watch-care over all matters pertaining to the interests of the cause within the bounds of the Conference."[2] The duties of the churches to the conference involved the regular reporting of financial matters, membership gains and losses, and requests for ministerial labor. No reference is made to involvement by the conference in disciplinary concerns. Several years before the organization of conferences, local congregations, often with the advice of a visiting minister, voted as a congregation on matters of discipline.[3]

Pragmatic Considerations

Three practical principles stand out in the development of Seventh-day Adventist organization: necessity, simplicity, and efficiency.

---

[1]Cf. above, pp. 84-85.

[2]Byington and Smith, "Report of General Conference," p. 205.

[3]See above, pp. 122-123. The SDA Church Manual (1981), retains the same principle. Neither the conference, nor minister of the church, nor church board can disfellowship or receive into membership. Only the church as a body may do so (p. 238). Provision is made whereby an entire church may be expelled from the "sisterhood of churches" for apostasy or rebellion, but only by the conference in session (p. 249).

White declared on several occasions that church order
developed through "the sheer necessity of the case."[1] Organization
was established in order to secure unity of doctrine and action
and to fortify the church against "outside influences."[2] It seems
that Seventh-day Adventist leaders, White in particular, initiated
and extended plans for the organization of the denomination in
response to the exigencies of the time. His pragmatic approach is
revealed in the context of the debate in 1860 over the choice of a
name. "All means, which according to sound judgment, will advance
the cause of truth, and are not forbidden by plain scripture
declarations, should be employed."[3] Eleven years later, he contended
that the success of organization was due to the fact that "the
machinery works well."[4]

We do not mean to imply that there were no underlying biblical or theological motivations for the actions taken by the church,
but it was the occurrence of immediate practical necessities that led
the church to study the biblical norm and express a more explicit
theological rationale. One should not be surprised to discover this
fact. Christian doctrine has often taken shape under the pressure of

---

[1]See above, p. 190.

[2][White], "Conference Address" (1873), p. 180. White does
not give any examples of these influences. One assumes he had in
mind occasions when General Conference organization had enabled the
church to meet perceived threats of heresy or schism (cf. above,
p. 170).

[3]White, "Making Us a Name," RH, April 26, 1860, p. 180.

[4][White], "Mutual Obligation," RH, October 17, 1871, p. 140.
The same pragmatism may be seen in contemporary Seventh-day Adventist
writings. Cf., e.g., "Church Government," SDA Encyclopedia (1976),
10:300, which states: "Only a primitive organization existed in the

existing needs, whether they be threats from without (such as persecution) or challenges from within (heresy or schism).[1]

White commented in September 1860 that he had been urging church organization for eight years. Throughout that time, he said, "we have recommended the simplest form possible."[2] He continued to apply the same principle of simplicity to Seventh-day Adventist order at each stage in the development of church organization till the end of his life. Thus, ten years after the formation of the General Conference he wrote, in the same vein: "And as numbers have increased, and missionary fields have opened before us, we have all come to prize our simple and, to a human view, complete organization."[3] A few months before his death in 1881, White expressed a similar favorable opinion of the Seventh-day Adventist system:

> Those who drafted the form of organization adopted by S.D. Adventists labored to incorporate into it, as far as possible, the simplicity of expression and form found in the New Testament.

---

early Christian church, for the obvious reason that organization came only when the growth of the church demanded it." Cf. also the suggestion that some policies of the Seventh-day Adventist Church "came into being under the pressure of necessity" (W. P. Bradley, "How a Policy Is Made," RH, December 4, 1969, p. 18).

[1]While we do not agree with all of their premises or conclusions, the studies of Maurice Wiles (The Making of Christian Doctrine [Cambridge: University Press, 1967]), and Robert L. Wilken (The Myth of Christian Beginnings [Garden City, N.Y.: Doubleday & Co., 1971]) provide stimulating insights into some of the factors in the development of doctrine in the early Christian church. For an evangelical discussion on the subject, see Peter Toon, The Development of Doctrine in the Church (Grand Rapids, Mich.: William B. Eerdmans Pub. Co., 1979).

[2]White, "'I Want the Review [sic] Discontinued,'" p. 148.

[3]White, "Organization" (1873), p. 60.

The more the spirit of the gospel manifested, and the more simple, the more efficient the system.[1]

White was apparently aware of some inherent dangers in any form of organization. He expressed the opinion on one occasion that two extremes must be avoided--"anarchy" on the one hand, and "popery" on the other.[2] He, and probably other Seventh-day Adventist leaders who had experienced opposition and rejection as members of the Millerite movement, were conscious of the tendency for humans to regard organization as an end in itself. The Millerites considered the rigid adherence to church creeds by the hierarchies of the various denominations which had evicted them to be responsible for the failure of the message of Christ's return to obtain a more favorable hearing.[3] Seventh-day Adventists, believing themselves to be the true successors of the Millerites and instilled with the same urgency to proclaim the imminent Second Advent were, in their early history at least, fearful that any organization that went beyond the bare minimum required for unity of doctrine and action would return them to the "Babylonish state" of the established churches.[4]

---

[1]White, "Organization and Discipline," p. 9. Other comments by White on the simplicity of church organization may be found in "Business Proceedings of the B.C. Conference," RH, October 9, 1860, p. 162; [White], "Organization" (1871), p. 76; [White], "Conference Address" (1873), p. 180; White, "Permanency of the Cause," p. 28; James White, "Spirit of Prophecy," RH, January 22, 1880, p. 52; White, "Christ and His Ministers," p. 248.

[2]White, "Extremes," pp. 140-141. Cf. above, p. 130.

[3]One is reminded of G. Storrs's anti-organizational attitude in particular. See above, p. 53.

[4]See above, pp. 196-201, for additional discussion on the impact of Seventh-day Adventist eschatology on its organizational principles.

On several occasions, White associated simplicity with two other ideals--completeness and efficiency.[1] His intention may be understood by referring to G. I. Butler's analogy of the church as an army.

> Perhaps the most complete system of organization that exists anywhere among men is found in the army. Every man has his special duty assigned him and just how he shall do it. One mind, perhaps, moves a million men. At a word they are all in motion. The perilous and fearful responsibilities of war make it necessary that power shall be exercised by one man, because it is found to be most effective [emphasis supplied].[2]

Essentially, his argument was that especially challenging and demanding circumstances--such as the prospect of Christ's Second Coming and the work yet to be accomplished before that event-- required that the church be marshalled for quick and effective action. There was little question in his mind that a one-man government is more efficient than a democracy.

While White opposed the concept of one-man rule,[3] the "perfection and efficiency of our organization" was a theme often expressed in his writings.[4] The form organization took was to some extent a secondary consideration to its efficiency and the first

---

[1]See, e.g., [White], "Conference Address" (1873), p. 180; White, "Permanency of the Cause," p. 28; White, "Organization" (1873), pp. 60-61; White, "Organization and Discipline," pp. 8-9.

[2]Butler, "Thoughts on Church Government," RH, August 18, 1874, p. 68. It is significant that Butler used this analogy of the army to propose the pre-eminent authority of White himself (see above, p. 175). Butler added that the rebellion by the South in the recent American Civil War could not have been put down without efficient organization.

[3]See above, p. 178.

[4]See, e.g., [White], "Conference Address" (1873), p. 184; above, pp. 171-175.

concern of Seventh-day Adventism, from his point of view, was that there is "a great work" to do in "a short time."[1] It is likely that this principle of efficiency reflected not only the priority of completing an unfinished task, but also the pragmatic "pioneer spirit" for which North America was noted and which was particularly prominent among those who followed the frontier westward in the 19th century, as many Seventh-day Adventist leaders did.

The Development of Church Order After 1881

It is perhaps worthwhile, having described the development of Seventh-day Adventist organization up to 1881 in the previous chapter and examined the theological, biblical, and pragmatic foundations of such organization in the preceding pages, to reflect briefly on the implications of the decisions made by Seventh-day Adventist pioneers for events in later years.

For the most part, the centralized organization established in 1863 proved successful in preserving the doctrinal unity of the church and in promoting efficient implementation of its mission during White's lifetime. Could the same system of order serve an international church as effectively?

The Reorganization of the
General Conference, 1901

Official Seventh-day Adventist overseas missions which began in Europe in 1874 had expanded by the turn of the century so that the major areas of the world (except China) had been entered by Seventh-day Adventist workers. By 1901 there were fifty-seven local

---

[1]White, "Conference Address" (1859), p. 21.

conferences, forty-one mission territories, nearly 1,600 evangelistic workers, and 78,188 members.[1] The growth of the church and the number and size of its institutions made apparent the need for reappraisal of its organization. Seventh-day Adventist leaders, meeting at the 1901 General Conference session, accepted the desirability of reorganization at the urging of Ellen G. White, who addressed the delegates at the opening meeting.[2] It is clear from a reading of her appeal and from the response of the conference that she played a much more crucial role in organizational matters at this juncture than she did in 1863.[3]

Ellen G. White urged the leaders of the church and of its numerous "quasi-independent organizations"[4] to yield their personal ambitions for power and influence in the interest of unity. She

---

[1]Schwarz, Light Bearers, p. 267.

[2]A definitive history of the development of church organization during the 1880s and 1890s and of the pivotal 1901 General Conference has yet to be written. The best source of information on the session is the daily bulletin of the Conference (Seventh-day Adventist General Conference, General Conference Bulletin Thirty-fourth Session [Battle Creek, Mich.: General Conference of Seventh-day Adventists, 1901], pp. 17-488). Other sources on the 1901 General Conference include: Jorgensen, "Investigation of Administrative Reorganization" (1949); Anderson, "The History and Evolution of Seventh-day Adventist Church Organization" (1960); Crisler, Organization, pp. 135-176; Schwarz, Light Bearers, pp. 267-281; Maxwell, Tell It to the World, pp. 251-261.

[3]On Ellen G. White's role in the early development of Seventh-day Adventist order, see above, pp. 191-192.

[4]Schwarz, Light Bearers, p. 269. Schwarz lists the International Tract and Missionary Society, the Sabbath School Association, the Seventh-day Adventist Publishing Association, the Pacific Seventh-day Adventist Publishing Association, the Seventh-day Adventist Educational Society, the Health Reform Institute, and the American Health and Temperance Society as organizations "allied with, but not subject to" the General Conference.

called for an end to dissension and strife, the conversion of the
leaders of the church, and reformation within the ranks of the
movement.[1] In view of the expansion of the work of the church, she
pressed for more consultation and wider distribution of management.
"Never should the mind of one man or the minds of a few men be
regarded as sufficient," she declared.[2] Perhaps her greatest concern
at this time was the rivalry between ministerial and medical
missionary workers. Neither group seemed willing to relinquish any
of its jurisdiction. She countered this kind of spirit with the
contention that God had not put "kingly power" in the hands of one or
two leaders.[3]

In response to Ellen G. White's admonition the conference
delegates set about the task of reorganization. The two new major
features introduced in 1901 were union conferences and an increase in
the size of the General Conference executive committee, so that each
of the formerly semi-independent organizations could be represented
at the highest decision-making level as departments of the General
Conference, and at the same time be under its overall
administration.[4] The changes made in 1901 represented dispersal of

---

[1]General Conference Bulletin (1901), p. 25.

[2]Ellen G. White, MS 43, 1901. These comments were made to a
special group of leaders at Battle Creek on April 1, 1901, the day
before the opening of the session (cf. Olson, Through Crisis to
Victory, pp. 180-182). Ellen G. White's address to the assembled
delegates on the first day of the General Conference session was on
the same subject and is recorded in the General Conference Bulletin
(1901), pp. 23-27.

[3]Ibid., p. 26.

[4]On the major changes introduced in 1901, see "Organization, Development of, in SDA Church," SDA Encyclopedia (1976),

authority on one hand and increased centralization on the other.[1]
One of the primary purposes for the establishment of union
conferences was to allow key decisions to be made by those with more
immediate knowledge of a local area than was possible for the General
Conference officers at Battle Creek. The formation of departments
represented greater centralization of the various concerns to enable
the church to carry out its mission more effectively.[2]

A. G. Daniells, the newly elected General Conference chairman,[3] cited the duty of the church to proclaim the Second Coming of
Christ as the primary motivation for reordering the church. "Our
field is the world," he observed, but added that unless definite
changes were made in the way in which the church carried out its
mission it would take "a millennium to give this message."[4] He also
expressed the opinion that too many were "spending their energies in

10:1050-1053; Jorgensen, "Investigation of Administrative Reorganization" (1949), pp. 31-33; Olson, Through Crisis to Victory, pp. 187-
189.

[1]Cf. Schwarz, Light Bearers, p. 279.

[2]On the newly formed departments in 1901 and 1903, see
General Conference Bulletin (1901), pp. 228-229; Jorgensen, "Investi-
gation of Administrative Reorganization" (1949), pp. 40-55; Schwarz,
Light Bearers, pp. 278-279.

[3]In an attempt to make the leadership of the church more
democratic, Daniells was appointed as chairman of the General
Conference Committee in 1901 rather than as "president." The
experiment was deemed to be unsuccessful, and after two years the
title of "president" was officially restored (see General Conference
Bulletin [1903], p. 145).

[4]General Conference Bulletin (1901), pp. 47-48. A. G.
Daniells was elected partly because of his experience as president of
the Australasian Union Conference, which had adopted the union
structure in 1894. The success of the experiment encouraged the
church to draw on the Australian pattern for the world field.

institutions" rather than being directly engaged in evangelistic work.[1]

Behind the decisions taken in 1901 lay the conviction that time was short in which to complete the mission of the church.[2] Daniells, appealing for harmony, asserted that the Second Coming of Christ had been delayed by the failure of God's people to work together.[3] Ellen G. White, urging the delegates to the 1901 session to surrender self-interest, declared: "There is a great work to be done, and my heart is panting and longing for the salvation of souls."[4]

This brief sketch of events around the turn of the century reveals some significant developments in Seventh-day Adventist church order as compared to the original General Conference organization in 1863 and to the situation that obtained in 1881. The most obvious change (as already noted) was the introduction of the union conference, a new administrative level between local conferences and the General Conference. After 1901, the union became the constituent part of the General Conference instead of the local conference.[5] While this difference was important, it represented a modification or addition to the already existing structure, rather than an entirely new organizational approach.[6] The consolidation of the several

---

[1]Ibid., p. 50.

[2]See above, pp. 196-201, on the Seventh-day Adventist sense of mission.

[3]General Conference Bulletin (1901), p. 47.

[4]Ibid., p. 26.   [5]Ibid., pp. 169-170.

[6]Cf. above, pp. 171-172.

semi-independent organizations into departments of the General Conference was probably equally important to the formation of Union conferences.[1] The problems associated with numerical growth and geographical expansion could hardly have been entirely foreseen by White and his colleagues, but their practical approach to matters of church order enabled them to introduce a system sufficiently flexible to encompass later circumstances.

One finds a common thread running through organizational development among early Seventh-day Adventists and during the reorganization of 1901. As White appealed for efficient and simple organization because there was "a great work to do in a short time,"[2] so also Daniells and Ellen G. White urged the church to work in greater harmony in order to hasten the return of Christ. It is doubtful that unity could have been maintained and enhanced in 1901 had it not been for the conviction that the remnant church was invested with a unique message and mission that outweighed in importance the personal ambitions and interests of individual members. The influence of Ellen G. White and the respect with which she was regarded were also crucial factors.

The emergence of problems of "kingly power," especially in the decade before 1901, may have grown out of a situation that already obtained during White's lifetime. One is reminded, for example, of Butler's somewhat extreme stand on the authority of

---

[1]The discussion on the feasibility of departmental organization may be found in the General Conference Bulletin (1901), pp. 228-229.

[2]Cf. above, p. 200.

church leaders. Although his view was eventually rejected by the church and relinquished by Butler himself, he still brought a forceful and authoritarian style to his presidency.[1] White, too, believed that the General Conference executive should maintain direct jurisdiction over every part of the work.[2] Perhaps in consequence, as the number of conferences and institutions multiplied and such oversight became impossible for a committee of a few men, the leaders of some church entities took upon themselves ever increasing authority. It is not surprising that a system of polity designed to serve a small, relatively homogeneous community should require some adjustment to care for the administration of a larger, more widely flung group.

The experience of the church in 1901 serves as a useful checkpoint to measure the effectiveness of Seventh-day Adventist church order as originally formulated. Possibly its greatest strength lay in its suitability to a movement which prized doctrinal unity and was committed to accomplishing its task as efficiently as possible. One also wonders if a less flexible system (such as congregational or presbyterian) could have served a growing church in a changing world as effectively.

Seventh-day Adventist Order in the Present and Future

If the Seventh-day Adventist Church underwent significant changes between 1844 and 1901, it has undergone a far more radical transformation since the latter date. Membership is now over 4.5

---

[1]Cf. above, pp. 175-178.   [2]Cf. above, pp. 179-182.

million and the denomination is presently working in 184 countries, according to official reports. Perhaps more importantly, about 85 percent of the membership resides outside North America, mostly in the Third World.[1] The church is cosmopolitan in every sense. One may find rich and poor, educated and unschooled, professional people and laborers, in the Seventh-day Adventist community. Not only has the church changed, but the world in which it must carry out its mission has altered too. The dilemmas facing the Seventh-day Adventist Church in its early years are still the same, but they are greatly augmented in the 1980s.

Unity in the face of such diversity is no easy accomplishment, but it is essential that the church remain structurally one if it is to carry out its world-wide mission. An invaluable aid to this end would seem to be an understanding of the church's history; in particular, its organization. Flexibility is important, as has been indicated; but whatever innovations may be introduced to meet modern exigencies, it is vital that continuity be maintained with the past.

The earlier discussion on the theological and biblical foundations of church order has revealed at least two key principles which ought to remain constant.[2] First, at the forefront of Seventh-day Adventist theological self-understanding is the conviction that the everlasting gospel of salvation in Jesus Christ and the three angels' messages must be preached to all the world. Structural and

---

[1]Yost, "Membership and Financial Statistics," p. 28.

[2]See above, pp. 195-201, 228-231.

doctrinal unity are not only prerequisites for effective proclamation, they are in fact part of the gospel that is preached.
One is reminded of Ellen G. White's statement that unity within the
church is a "powerful evidence in favor of the Christian religion."[1]
New approaches to organization, therefore, should be welcomed if they
are seen to build up the witness of the church.

Second, in the formulation or modification of denominational
structure it is important to be sensitive to the pastoral role of the
church. Christians have at least a twofold concern--to reach those
"outside" the fellowship of the community of faith and to care for
the spiritual needs of the members.[2] This latter responsibility may
tend to be neglected as every effort is made to reach the unchurched.
As has been indicated,[3] White and some of his associates came to
recognize the servanthood of church leaders and laid increasing
stress upon the essential role of ministers as under-shepherds of
Christ's church. Early Sabbatarian Adventists described themselves
as "the little flock"[4] because of their sense of alienation from the
seemingly hostile established churches of the day. Such a phrase can
hardly have precisely the same meaning for the Seventh-day Adventist
Church today as "one of the most international of Protestant

---

[1] Ellen G. White, "Unity and Love," p. 513.

[2] Both "outreach" and pastoral ministries may well entail
caring for the social and physical needs of people as part of the
work of the gospel.

[3] See above, pp. 185, 228-231.

[4] Cf. above, p. 117.

churches."[1] However, the need exists within every Christian community to extend pastoral concern to its members. Alienation from
other Christian bodies may not be as keenly felt today as 140 years
ago; but as the Seventh-day Adventist Church continues to grow, the
danger increases that the individual may feel insignificant in the
face of the complexity of the organization of the church.

In order to maintain doctrinal unity in the church it would
seem that a centralized structure is needed. In contrast, pastoral
care for the individual and the outreach of the church is best seen
as the function of the local congregation. The most effective cure
for a feeling of unimportance among members is to recapture the full
meaning of the doctrine of the priesthood of all believers (cf. 1 Pet
2:9). Such a belief implies that all members of the church should
share in its mission and ministry. These two ideas (the centrality
of organization and the local congregation as "the bulwark of
Adventist mission and ministry"[2]) must be kept in creative tension.
Exaggeration of either aspect may lead to distortion of the church's
message and mission. For example, in the interest of efficiency,
there may well be a temptation to cut short consultation and
decision-making processes and concentrate authority in a few leaders.
The challenges of dissidents within the church and the threat of

---

[1]Russell Staples, "The Face of the Church to Come," RH,
January 2, 1986, p. 8.

[2]Gottfried Oosterwal, "The SDA Church in the 1980's." Paper
presented at a theological consultation for Seventh-day Adventist
Administrators and Religion Scholars, Glacier View, Colorado, August
15-19, 1980, p. 77. Oosterwal, a Seventh-day Adventist missiologist,
adds: "This is not a plea for congregationalism; not at all! Only a
call to recognize the local church as the basis of the church's
mission and ministry."

schism may be seen as good reasons to increase the powers of those on higher administrative levels. Such temptations should be resisted, as also moves toward congregationalism (perhaps in the name of greater autonomy) should be withstood.

Under the blessing of God, Seventh-day Adventists anticipate continued growth in the years ahead. What form is this expansion likely to take and what will be the implications for church order?[1] It has been estimated (probably conservatively) that membership will increase to about ten million by the year 2000, and that there may well be about four million members in South and Inter-America and almost three million in sub-Saharan Africa by that time.[2] The Seventh-day Adventist Church will become increasingly a Third World church and less a North American or European one. Churches in major regions of the world may well adopt their own ways of worship and forms of organization in keeping with the cultures of the area in question, while affirming the oneness of the Seventh-day Adventist message and mission.[3]

Several significant developments have been suggested which may come about as a result of the growth of the church and the demographic changes mentioned above. Seventh-day Adventist

---

[1]Three Seventh-day Adventist writers--Oosterwal, Staples, and Raoul Dederen--have recently reflected on what the church might be like in the future. See Gottfried Oosterwal, "Mission Still Possible," Ministry, December 1986, pp. 4-8; Staples, "The Face of the Church to Come," pp. 8-10; Raoul Dederen, "Tomorrow's Church, Truly a 'Remnant,'" RH, January 9, 1986, pp. 8-10.

[2]Staples, "The Face of the Church to Come," p. 8.

[3]Cf. Dederen, "Tomorrow's Church," p. 10.

missiologists, in particular, have pointed out some of the implications of expansion in the under-developed and developing countries of the world. The magnitude of the church in these parts of the world, compared to its relative smallness in wealthier areas, means that the Third World church will need to become more self-sufficient financially.[1] Russell Staples has indicated that the church in the poorer parts of the world may need to adopt a "tentmaking" or self-supporting ministry alongside, if not instead of, the full-time salaried workers.[2]

The Seventh-day Adventist Church in the future may well place less priority upon the establishment of institutions. It has been argued that the premature building of elaborate organizational structures, before the church in a given area has sufficient resources to support them, may hinder the work of preaching the gospel.[3] A reduction in financial support for the work of the church outside North America would not necessarily have a negative impact on the effectiveness of its mission. Borge Schantz suggests that reduced Western financial support for the Third World church would probably lead to increased stewardship in areas of the developing world where the Seventh-day Adventist Church is established, enabling the church in these regions to become self-sufficient financially and

---

[1]Staples, "The Face of the Church to Come," p. 9.

[2]Ibid.

[3]Oosterwal, "The SDA Church in the 1980's" (1980), p. 40. Cf. Schantz, "Development of SDA Missionary Thought" (1983), pp. 744-745. Schantz asks if existing institutions should be kept running if not contributing to the growth of the church.

allowing Western money to be diverted to unentered areas.[1]

Gottfried Oosterwal distinguishes between "church-oriented" and "world-oriented" mission.[2] The aim of church-oriented mission, he suggests, is

> . . . to add as many people as possible to the church, to expand and strengthen its organizational structures, and to establish institutions. All these give the church presence, stability, and continuity, and make further mission possible.[3]

In contrast, world-oriented mission, according to Oosterwal, is decentralized and spontaneous. It encourages the active participation of all believers in the evangelization of the unreached. The church is the instrument and tool of such mission, rather than its aim and focus. A world-oriented mission, he adds, is essential if the masses who have never heard the everlasting gospel are to be reached.[4]

At the center of the above proposals for the Seventh-day Adventist Church in the future lies a concern that church structure should promote the participation of the whole people of God in ministry.[5] It may well be a natural inclination to extend and make more complex the forms of organization and to increase centralization in the interests of unity and efficiency. The experience of Seventh-day Adventists in 1901 has shown that increased centralization is not

---

[1]Schantz, "Development of SDA Missionary Thought" (1983), p. 910. For a contemporary appraisal of Seventh-day Adventist mission finance, see pp. 855-912.

[2]Oosterwal, "Mission Still Possible," pp. 5-6.

[3]Ibid., p. 5.   [4]Ibid., p. 7.

[5]See, e.g., Dederen, "Tomorrow's Church," p. 10; Oosterwal, "The SDA Church in the 1980's" (1980), p. 77.

necessarily the best response to growth in membership. At that time, unions were introduced to disperse some decision-making powers from headquarters. Perhaps today, and in the future, there should be a renewed emphasis upon the local congregation as the foundation of mission and ministry.

Early Seventh-day Adventists were sufficiently flexible in their approach to church order to accept innovation if the situation required it. It could be that, as the church becomes more predominantly a Third World movement, some of the typically Western concepts of organization should be modified, if not changed.[1] In determining which aspects of church order are subject to adjustment and which are not, the centralized government of Seventh-day Adventism must be recognized as vital for maintaining doctrinal unity, coordinating the whole mission of the church, and lending weight to its sense of identity. Within the limits implied by these underlying considerations, Seventh-day Adventists should seek to discern which specific forms of church order are historically or culturally conditioned and therefore subject to modification. It is hoped that this study of the development of Seventh-day Adventist organization and its theological and biblical foundations will provide insights relevant to today's church.

---

[1]Cf. Oosterwal, "The SDA Church in the 1980's" (1980), pp. 39-40.

BIBLIOGRAPHY

BIBLIOGRAPHY

Primary Sources

Published Materials

Books and Pamphlets

Andrews, J. N. The Three Messages of Revelation XIV, 6-12. Battle
    Creek, Mich.: Seventh-day Adventist Pub. Assn, 1877.

Baird, Robert. Religion in America, or an Account of the Origin,
    Relation to the State and the Present Condition of the
    Evangelical Churches in the United States, with Notice of the
    Unevangelical Denominations. 1st ed., 1843. New York, 1856.

Bates, Joseph. Autobiography. Battle Creek, Mich.: Seventh-day
    Adventist Pub. Assn, 1868.

_____. A Seal of the Living God. New Bedford, Mass.: By the
    Author, 1849.

_____. The Seventh-day Sabbath, A Perpetual Sign, from the
    Beginning, to the Entering into the Gates of the Holy City,
    According to the Commandment. 2nd ed., rev. and enl. New
    Bedford, Mass.: Benjamin Lindsey, 1847.

_____. A Vindication of the Seventh-day Sabbath and the
    Commandments of God: With a Further History of God's Peculiar
    People, from 1847 to 1848. New Bedford, Mass.: Benjamin
    Lindsey, 1848.

_____. A Vision. New Bedford, Mass.: Benjamin Lindsey, 1847.

Bliss, Sylvester. Memoirs of William Miller. Boston: J. V. Himes,
    1853.

Butler, G. I. Leadership. [Battle Creek, Mich.: General Conference
    of Seventh-day Adventists, 1873.]

Finney, Charles G. Lectures on Systematic Theology. South Gate,
    Calif.: Colporter Kemp, 1944. (Originally published in 1878.)

_____. Lectures to Professing Christians. Oberlin, Oh.: James
    Steele, 1880.

287

_____. Views of Sanctification. Oberlin, Oh.: James Steele, 1840.

The First Report of the General Conference of Christians Expecting the Advent of the Lord Jesus Christ. Held in Boston, Oct. 14, 15, 1840. Boston: J. V. Himes, 1841.

Frisbie, J. B. Order in the Church of God. Battle Creek, Mich.: Review and Herald Pub. Assn, 1859.

Goss, Charles C. Statistical History of the First Century of American Methodism. New York: Carlton & Porter, 1866.

Litch, Josiah. The Probability of the Second Coming of Christ about A.D. 1843. Shown by a Comparison of Prophecy with History, Up to the Present Time, and an Explanation of Those Prophecies Which Are Yet to Be Fulfilled. Boston: David H. Ela, 1838.

Loughborough, J. N. The Church: Its Organization, Order, and Discipline. Washington, D.C.: Review and Herald Pub. Assn, 1907.

_____. The Great Second Advent Movement: Its Rise and Progress. Washington, D.C.: Review and Herald Pub. Assn, 1905.

_____. Rise and Progress of the Seventh-day Adventists. Battle Creek, Mich.: General Conference Association of the Seventh-day Adventists, 1892.

Miller, William. Evidence from Scripture and History of the Second Coming of Christ about the Year A.D. 1843, and of His Personal Reign of 1000 Years. Brandon, Vt.: Vermont Telegraph Office, 1833.

_____. Evidences from Scripture and History of the Second Coming of Christ, about the Year 1843: Exhibited in a Course of Lectures. Troy, N.Y.: Kemble & Hooper, 1836.

_____. Views of the Prophecies and Prophetic Chronology Selected from Manuscripts of William Miller; With a Memoir of His Life. Edited by Joshua V. Himes. Boston: Moses A. Down, 1841.

_____. Wm. Miller's Apology and Defence. Boston: J. V. Himes, 1845.

Preble, Thomas M. A Tract, Showing That the Seventh Day Should Be Observed As the Sabbath, Instead of the First Day; "According to the Commandment." Nashua, N.H.: Murray and Kimball, 1845.

Proceedings of the Second Session of the General Conference of Christians Expecting the Advent of Our Lord Jesus Christ, Held in Lowell, Mass., June 15, 16, 17, 1841. Second Advent Tracts, No. VIII. [Boston: J. V. Himes, 1841.]

Scudder, M. L. _American Methodism_. Hartford, Conn.: S. S. Scranton & Co., 1867.

Simpson, Matthew. _A Hundred Years of Methodism_. New York: Phillips & Hunt, 1881.

[Smith, Uriah; Amadon, G. W.; and Walker, E. S.] _A Vindication of the Business Career of Elder James White_. Battle Creek, Mich.: Seventh-day Adventist Pub. Assn, 1863.

Summerbell, N. _History of the Christian Church_. Cincinnati: Office of the Christian Pulpit, 1873.

Wellcome, I. C. _History of the Second Advent Message and Mission, Doctrine and People_. Yarmouth, Me.: I. C. Wellcome, 1874.

White, Ellen G. _The Acts of the Apostles_. Mountain View, Calif.: Pacific Press Pub. Assn, 1911.

_____. _Early Writings_. 5th ed. Washington, D.C.: Review and Herald Pub. Assn, 1963.

_____. _Fundamentals of Christian Education_. Nashville, Tenn.: Southern Pub. Assn, 1923.

_____. _The Great Controversy_. Mountain View, Calif.: Pacific Press Pub. Assn, 1888.

_____. _Life Sketches of Ellen G. White_. Mountain View, Calif.: Pacific Press Pub. Assn, 1915.

_____. _The Remnant Church_. Mountain View, Calif.: Pacific Press Pub. Assn, 1950.

_____. _The Story of Patriarchs and Prophets_. Mountain View, Calif.: Pacific Press Pub. Assn, 1958.

_____. _Supplement to the Christian Experience and Views of Ellen G. White_. Rochester, N.Y.: James White, 1854.

_____. _Testimonies for the Church_. 9 vols. Mountain View, Calif.: Pacific Press Pub. Assn, 1948.

_____. _Testimony for the Church_. No. 6. Battle Creek, Mich.: Review and Herald Pub. Assn, 1861.

_____. _Testimonies to Ministers_. Mountain View, Calif.: Pacific Press Pub. Assn, 1962.

White, James, _Life Incidents, in Connection with the Great Advent Movement, As Illustrated by the Three Angels of Revelation XIV_. Battle Creek, Mich.: Seventh-day Adventist Pub. Assn, 1863.

White, James, and White, Ellen G. Life Sketches, Ancestry, Early Life Christian Experience, and Extensive Labors of Elder James White and His Wife, Ellen G. White. Battle Creek, Mich.: Seventh-day Adventist Pub. Assn, 1888.

White, James; White, Ellen G.; and Bates, Joseph. A Word to the "Little Flock." Brunswick, Me.: James White, May 1847. Facsimile reproduction, Washington, D.C.: Review and Herald Pub. Assn, [1944].

Periodicals and Newspapers

Advent Herald. Boston: 1844-1855.

Advent Mirror. Boston: January 1845.

Advent Review and Sabbath Herald. Saratoga Springs, N.Y.: August 5, 1851-March 23, 1852; Rochester, N.Y.: May 6, 1852-October 30, 1855; Battle Creek, Mich.: December 4, 1855-August 1881.

Advent Shield and Review. Boston: May 1844 and January 1845.

Bible Examiner. New York: September 24, 1844.

Day-Star. Cincinnati: March 11, 1845-March 14, 1846.

Day-Star. Extra. Cincinnati: February 7, 1846.

Jubilee Standard. New York: April 3, 17, 24, May 22-July 10, 31, August 7, 1845.

Midnight Cry. New York: November 17, 1842-1845. (Name changed to Morning Watch, January 2, 1845.)

Morning Watch. New York: 1845 (Merged with Advent Herald on August 13, 1845).

Present Truth. Middletown, Conn.: July-September 1849; Oswego, N.Y.: December 1849-May 1850; Paris, Me.: November 1850.

Second Advent Review, and Sabbath Herald. Paris, Me.: November 1850-June 1851. (Formed by merging of Present Truth and Advent Review in November 1850. Name changed to Advent Review and Sabbath Herald, August 5, 1851.)

Signs of the Times. Boston: March 20, 1840-1844. (Name changed to Advent Herald, February 14, 1844.)

True Midnight Cry. Haverhill, Mass.: August 22, 1844.

Vermont Telegraph. Brandon, Vt.: November 6, 1832-March 12, 1833.

Voice of Truth and Glad Tidings of the Kingdom at Hand. Rochester, N.Y.: 1844-1845.

Western Midnight Cry. Cincinnati: 1844-1845. (Name changed to *Day-Star*, February 18, 1845.)

Articles

Andrews, J. N. "The Call to the Christian Ministry." RH, June 29, 1869, p. 4.

_____. "Duty Toward Those That Have the Rule." RH, September 16, 1873, p. 108.

_____. "General Conferences." RH, July 15, 1862, p. 52.

_____. "Organization." RH, September 17, 1861, p. 124.

_____. "The Review Office." RH, August 21, 1860, p. 108.

_____. "Thoughts on Revelation XIII and XIV." RH, May 19, 1851, pp. 81-86.

_____. "The Three Angels of Rev XIV, 6-12." 7-part series in RH, February 6, 1855, pp. 169-171; February 20, 1855, pp. 177-178; March 6, 1855, pp. 185-187; March 20, 1855, pp. 193-196; April 3, 1855, pp. 201-204; April 17, 1855, pp. 209-212; May 1, 1855, pp. 217-218.

[_____]. "The Wants of the Cause of Christ." RH, July 6, 1869, p. 12.

Andrews, J. N.; Cottrell, R. F.; and Smith, Uriah. "The Office." RH, December 5, 1854, pp. 124-125.

Baker, Rufus. "Necessity of Church Order." RH, October 1, 1861, p. 142.

Bates, Joseph. "Church Order." RH, August 29, 1854, pp. 22-23.

_____. "The Laodicean Church." RH, November 1850, pp. 7-8.

Bates, Joseph, and Smith, Uriah. "Business Proceedings of the Battle Creek Conference." RH, April 16, 1857, p. 188.

_____. "Business Proceedings of the General Conference of June 3-6, 1859." RH, June 9, 1859, pp. 20-21.

_____. "Business Proceedings of the Michigan State Conference." RH, October 14, 1862, pp. 156-157.

_____. "Doings of the Battle Creek Conference, October 5 and 6, 1861." RH, October 8, 1861, pp. 148-149.

"Battle Creek." RH, February 5, 1880, p. 89.

[Bliss, Sylvester]. "The Downfall of Great Babylon." ASR, May 1844, pp. 112-120.

"The Boston Tabernacle." ST, June 14, 1843, p. 119.

Brown, F. G. "Reasons for Withdrawing from the Church." MC, April 4, 1844, p. 301.

"Business Proceedings of the B.C. Conference." 3-part series in RH, October 9, 1860, pp. 161-163; October 16, 1860, pp. 169-171; October 23, 1860, pp. 177-179.

"Business Proceedings of the B.C. Conference." RH, April 30, 1861, p. 189.

"Business Proceedings of the Eighth Annual Session of the General Conference of S.D. Adventists." RH, March 22, 1870, pp. 109-110.

"Business Proceedings of the Twelfth Annual Meeting of the S.D.A. General Conference." RH, November 25, 1873, p. 190.

Butler, G. I. "The Death of Elder White." RH, August 16, 1881, pp. 120-121.

_____. "Leadership." RH, November 18, 1873, pp. 180-181.

_____. "Ordination." RH, February 13, 1879, pp. 50-51.

_____. "Stability a Characteristic of Our Work." RH, April 15, 1873, p. 140.

_____. "Thoughts on Church Government." 8-part series in RH, July 28, 1874, pp. 52-53; August 4, 1874, pp. 60-61; August 18, 1874, pp. 68-69; August 25, 1874, pp. 76-77; September 1, 1874, p. 85; September 8, 1874, pp. 92-93; September 15, 1874, p. 101; September 22, 1874, p. 109; September 29, 1874, p. 116; October 13, 1874, pp. 124-125.

Byington, John, and Smith, Uriah. "Fourth Annual Session of General Conference." RH, May 22, 1866, pp. 196-197.

_____. "Report of General Conference of Seventh-day Adventists." RH, May 26, 1863, pp. 204-206.

Caldwell, Luther. "I Will Spue Thee Out of My Mouth." MC, December 14, 1843, p. 149.

Chandler, S. C. "Conference at Jamaica, Vt." MC, June 20, 1844, p. 391.

"The Conference." ST, September 1, 1840, p. 84.

Cornell, M. E. "Making Us a Name." RH, May 29, 1860, pp. 8-9.

Cottrell, R. F. "Making Us a Name." RH, March 23, 1860, pp. 140-141.

_____. "A Response." RH, May 3, 1860, p. 188.

_____. "System--Order." RH, October 21, 1862, pp. 165-166.

_____. "What Are the Duties of Church Officers?" RH, October 2, 1856, p. 173.

Crosier, O. R. L. "The Law of Moses." D-S, Extra, February 7, 1846, pp. 37-44.

D. "More Ultraism." ST, July 20, 1842, p. 126.

Dickinson, Prescott; Clapp, Frederick; Hatstat, William M.; Nichols, Stephen; Lang, John; Wood, Micajah; Hamlin, Joseph G.; Augustus, John; and Himes, Joshua V. "To the Public." ST, May 10, 1843, pp. 73-75.

Editorial. "Address to the Public." AH, November 13, 1844, pp. 108-112.

_____. "The Advent Herald." AH, October 30, 1844, pp. 92-93.

_____. "The Advent Question." AH, November 27, 1847, pp. 132-133.

_____. "Boston Second Advent Conference." ST, June 1, 1842, pp. 68-69.

_____. "The Church at the First Advent." MC, April 25, 1844, p. 326.

_____. "The Conference." AH, February 14, 1844, pp. 8-9.

_____. "The Conference." RH, June 9, 1859, p. 20.

_____. "The Late Movement." AH, November 6, 1844, pp. 102-103.

_____. "'The Lord's Day.'" 2-part series in MC, September 5, 1844, pp. 68-69; September 12, 1844, pp. 76-77.

_____. "Low-Hampton Conference." AH, January 15, 1845, pp. 182-183.

_____. _MC_, September 21, 1843, p. 33.

_____. "Mission to Europe." _AH_, October 2, 1844, p. 68.

_____. "Our Duty." _ST_, November 30, 1842, p. 86.

_____. "The Scale Turned." _AH_, October 9, 1844, p. 76.

_____. _ST_, June 21, 1843, p. 123.

_____. "The Tide Turning." _AH_, December 11, 1844, p. 141.

_____. "To Correspondents." _ST_, August 23, 1843, p. 5.

_____. "To Those Who Are Looking for the Appearing of Our Lord Jesus Christ, in His Glory." _AH_, October 30, 1844, p. 96.

_____. "You Are Breaking Up the Churches." _MC_, December 14, 1843, p. 148.

Fitch, Charles. "Come out of Her, My People." _MC_, September 21, 1843, pp. 33-36.

Fleming, L. D. "Enquiry." _MC_, February 8, 1844, p. 228.

"Fourth Annual Session of General Conference." _RH_, May 22, 1866, pp. 196-197.

Frisbie, J. B. "Church Order." _RH_, December 26, 1854, pp. 147-148.

_____. "Church Order." 4-part series in _RH_, June 19, 1856, pp. 62-63; June 26, 1856, pp. 70-71; July 3, 1856, pp. 78-79; July 10, 1856, p. 86.

_____. "Church Order." _RH_, October 23, 1856, p. 198.

_____. "Deacons." _RH_, July 31, 1856, p. 102.

_____. "Gospel Order." _RH_, January 9, 1855, pp. 153-155.

"General Conference Statistics, 1880." _RH_, October 28, 1880, p. 280.

Hale, Apollos. "Editorial Correspondence." _AH_, September 10, 1845, p. 40.

Hale, Apollos, and Turner, Joseph. "Has Not the Savior Come as the Bridegroom?" _AM_, January 1845, pp. [1-4].

Hamilton, D. H. "Result of the Second Advent Conference in Prospectville." _ST_, October 19, 1842, p. 38.

Haskell, S. N. "Responsibility of Christ's Ministers." _RH_, June 17, 1880, p. 395.

Himes, Joshua V. "The Advent Herald." AH, October 16, 1844, p. 81.

_____. "The Advent Herald." AH, October 30, 1844, pp. 92-93.

[_____]. "The Closing Up of the Day of Grace." ST, August 1, 1840, pp. 69-70.

_____. "The Crisis Has Come!" ST, August 3, 1842, pp. 140-141.

_____. "Editorial Correspondence." AH, February 5, 1845, p. 205.

_____. "Editorial Correspondence." MC, June 27, 1844, p. 399.

_____. "Editorial Correspondence." MW, April 3, 1845, p. 110.

_____. "Editorial Correspondence. Separation from the Churches." AH, September 18, 1844, p. 53.

[_____]. "The General Conference." ST, November 1, 1840, p. 113.

_____. "Memoir of William Miller." MC, November 17, 1842, pp. 1-2.

[_____]. "Our Course." ST, November 15, 1840, pp. 126-127.

_____. "Provision for the Destitute." MC, October 31, 1844, p.140.

Himes, Joshua V., and Bliss, Sylvester. "The Time of the Advent." AH, October 9, 1844, p. 80.

[Jacobs, Enoch]. "Intolerance." WMC, December 30, 1844, p. 30.

[_____]. "The Time." WMC, November 29, 1844, p. 20.

Litch, Josiah. "Babylon's Fall--the Sanctuary Cleansed." ST, July 26, 1843, pp. 165-166.

_____. "Fall of the Ottoman Power in Constantinople." ST, August 1, 1840, p. 70.

_____. "The Nations." ST, February 1, 1841, pp. 161-162.

[_____]. "The Rise and Progress of Adventism." ASR, May 1844, pp. 46-93.

Litch, Josiah; Himes, Joshua V.; and Clark, William. "Circular. Address of the Second General Conference on the Second Appearing of Our Lord Jesus Christ, Convened at Lowell, Mass., June 15, 16 and 17, 1841." ST, August 2, 1841, pp. 69-70.

"Look at Facts." D-S, reprinted in ST, October 19, 1842, p. 34.

Loughborough, J. N. "Anarchy or Order--Which?" RH, May 28, 1901, pp. 346-347.

_____. "Eastern Tour." RH, November 13, 1860, pp. 204-205.

_____. "The Image of the Beast." RH, January 15, 1861, pp. 69-70.

Loughborough, J. N.; Hull, Moses; and Cornell, M. E. "Conference Address. Organization." RH, October 15, 1861, pp. 156-157.

[Marsh, Joseph]. "The Albany Conference." VT, May 21, 1845, pp. 61-62.

_____. "Come out of Babylon!" VT, September 11, 1844, pp. 126-128.

[_____]. "Door of Mercy." VT, February 26, 1845, pp. 18-19.

_____. "Existence of Creeds a Reason Why We Should Not Go Back to the Church." VT, April 30, 1845, pp. 33-35.

Miller, William. "An Address to the Believers in Christ of All Denominations." AH, February 14, 1844, p. 9.

_____. "An address to the Believers in Christ, of All Denominations." MC, February 22, 1844, pp. 420-421.

_____. "The Albany Conference." AH, June 4, 1845, p. 129.

_____. "Miller's Lectures--No. 1." ST, July 1, 1840, pp. 49-51.

Miller, William; Bliss, Sylvester; and Hale, Apollos. "Advent Conference in Boston." MW, June 19, 1845, pp. 197-200.

Miller, William; Litch Josiah; Himes, Joshua V.; Jones, Henry; and Ward, Henry Dana. "General Conference of Christians Expecting the Second Advent of Our Lord Jesus Christ." ST, April 15, 1841, p. 12.

[Minor, C. S.] "Life from the Dead. No. 3." MC, April 11, 1844, pp. 309-310.

Morse, G. Washington. "Items of Advent Experience during the Past Fifty Years.--No. 4." RH, October 16, 1888, pp. 642-643.

Munger, Hiram. "Affairs at Chicopee." AH, June 19, 1844, pp. 158-159.

"Mutual Conference of Adventists at Albany." MW, May 8, 1845, pp. 149-152.

"Mutual Conference of Adventists at Albany." AH, May 14, 1845, pp. 105-108.

"Mutual Conference of Adventists at Albany." VT, May 21, 1845, pp. 57-59.

Nevin, John W. "The Sect System." Mercersburg Review 1 (1849):499-500.

Plumb, David. "Babylon." MC, February 1, 1844, pp. 218-219.

"Proceedings of the Conference on the Second Coming of Our Lord Jesus Christ, Held in Boston, Mass., October 14, 15, 1840." ST, November 1, 1840, pp. 113-116.

"Proceedings of the Eleventh Annual Meeting of the General Conference of S.D. Adventists." RH, March 18, 1873, p. 108.

"Proceedings of the Fourteenth Annual Session of the S.D. Adventist General Conference." RH, August 26, 1875, p. 59.

"Report of the Third Annual Session of the General Conference of S.D. Adventists." RH, May 23, 1865, pp. 196-197.

"Second Advent Conference." ST, July 15, 1841, p. 61.

Smith, Uriah. "Business Meeting of the Church in Battle Creek." RH, March 31, 1863, p. 141.

_____. "General Conference Statistics, 1880." RH, October 28, 1880, p. 280.

_____. "The Seventh-day Adventists: A Brief Sketch of Their Origin, Progress, and Principles." 4-part series in RH, November 3, 1874, pp. 148-149; November 10, 1874, p. 156; November 17, 1874, p. 164; November 24, 1874, p. 171.

_____. "To the Friends of the Review." RH, December 4, 1855, p. 76.

Snook, B. F. "General Conferences." RH, July 29, 1862, p. 72.

_____. "Organization." RH, September 24, 1861, p. 132.

[Snow, S. S.] "The Laodicean Church." JS, June 12, 1845, p. 108.

Stockman, L. S. "Ecclesiastical Trial." AH, February 14, 1844, p. 13.

Storrs, George. "Come out of Her My People." MC, February 15, 1844, pp. 237-238.

_____. "'Go Ye out to Meet Him.'" Bible Examiner, September 24, 1844, p. [1].

Waggoner, J. H. "To All the Brethren." RH, September 24, 1861, p. 132.

Waggoner, J. H.; White, James; Loughborough, J. N.; Shortridge, E. W.; Bates, Joseph; Frisbie, J. B.; Cornell, M. E.; Hull, Moses; and Byington, John. "Conference Address. Organization." RH, June 11, 1861, pp. 21-22.

Ward, Henry Dana; Jones, Henry; and Russel, Philemon R. "Circular: The Address of the Conference on the Second Advent of the Lord, Convened at Boston, Mass., October 14, 1840." ST, November 1, 1840, pp. 116-117.

White, Ellen G. "Communication from Sister White." RH, August 27, 1861, pp. 100-102.

_____. "'He Went Away Sorrowful, For He Had Great Possessions.'" RH, November 26, 1857, pp. 18-19.

_____. "Order in the Church." RH, April 15, 1880, p. 241.

_____. "Testimony for the Church No. 5." RH, June 16, 1859, p. 32.

_____. "Unity and Love." RH, August 12, 1884, pp. 513-514.

_____. "Unity of the Church." RH, February 19, 1880, pp. 113-114.

[White, James]. "The Angels of Rev. XIV." 4-part series in RH, August 19, 1851, p. 12; September 2, 1851, p. 20; December 9, 1851, pp. 63-64; December 23, 1851, pp. 69-72.

[_____]. "An Appeal to the General Conference Committee on Behalf of New England." RH, October 6, 1863, p. 148.

[_____]. "The Association." RH, June 2, 1863, p. 4.

[_____]. "The Battle Creek Church." RH, November 5, 1861, p. 180.

_____. "Borrowed Money." RH, February 23, 1860, p. 108.

[_____]. "A Brief Sketch of the Past." RH, May 6, 1852, p. 5.

_____. "The Cause." RH, August 13, 1857, p. 116.

[_____]. "The Cause." RH, October 29, 1861, p. 172.

_____. "The Cause of God." RH, December 2, 1880, p. 360.

_____. "Christ and His Ministers." RH, April 19, 1881, p. 248.

[_____]. "Church Order." RH, January 23, 1855, p. 164.

_____. "A Complaint." RH, June 16, 1859, p. 28.

_____. "Conference." RH, November 12, 1857, pp. 4-5.

_____. "Conference Address." RH, June 9, 1859, pp. 21-23.

[_____]. "Conference Address." RH, May 20, 1873, pp. 180-181, 184.

[_____]. "Correction." RH, October 14, 1862, p. 160.

_____. "Dangers to Which the Remnant Are Exposed." RH, March 3, 1853, pp. 164-165.

_____. "Eastern Tour." RH, October 14, 1852, p. 96.

_____. "Eastern Tour." RH, September 20, 1853, pp. 84-85.

_____. "Eastern Tour." RH, October 18, 1853, p. 117.

[_____]. "Eastern Tour." RH, November 15, 1853, pp. 148-149.

[_____]. "Eastern Tour." RH, September 3, 1861, p. 108.

[_____]. "Eastern Tour." RH, November 24, 1863, p. 204.

[_____]. "Eastern Tour." RH, November 14, 1871, p. 172.

_____. [Editorial Correspondence]. RH, April 7, 1851, p. 64.

_____. "Extremes." RH, March 24, 1859, pp. 140-141.

_____. "The Faith of Jesus." RH, August 19, 1852, pp. 60-61.

[_____]. "General Conference." RH, April 28, 1863, p. 172.

[_____]. "General Conferences." RH, July 1, 1862, p. 37.

_____. "Gospel Order." 4-part series in RH, December 6, 1853, p. 173; December 13, 1853, p. 180; December 20, 1853, pp. 188-190; December 27, 1853, pp. 196-197.

[_____]. "Gospel Order." RH, March 28, 1854, pp. 76-77.

[_____]. "Gospel Union." RH, November 25, 1851, p. 56.

_____. "'I Want the Review Discontinued.'" RH, September 25, 1860, p. 148.

_____. "Leadership." RH, December 1, 1874, pp. 180-181.

_____. "Leadership." RH, May 23, 1878, p. 164.

_____. "Making Us a Name." RH, March 29, 1860, p. 152.

_____. "Making Us a Name." RH, April 26, 1860, pp. 180-182.

_____. "Moving West." RH, May 7, 1857, p. 5.

[_____]. "Mutual Obligation." 4-part series in RH, June 6, 1871, p. 196; June 13, 1871, p. 204; June 20, 1871, p. 4; October 17, 1871, p. 140.

_____. "New Fields." RH, October 6, 1859, p. 156.

[_____]. "Order in the Church of God." RH, December 12, 1871, p. 204.

_____. "Organization." RH, June 19, 1860, p. 36.

[_____]. "Organization." RH, July 16, 1861, pp. 52-53.

_____. "Organization." RH, August 27, 1861, p. 100.

[_____]. "Organization." RH, October 1, 1861, pp. 140-141.

[_____]. "Organization." RH, October 22, 1861, p. 164.

[_____]. "Organization." RH, January 7, 1862, p. 44.

[_____]. "Organization." RH, September 30, 1862, p. 140.

[_____]. "Organization." RH, April 19, 1864, p. 164.

[_____]. "Organization." RH, August 22, 1871, p. 76.

_____. "Organization." RH, August 5, 1873, pp. 60-61.

_____. "Organization." RH, June 24, 1880, p. 8.

_____. "Organization and Discipline." RH, January 4, 1881, pp. 8-9.

_____. "Our Present Position." RH, December 1850, pp. 13-14.

[_____]. "Our Tour East." RH, November 25, 1851, p. 52.

_____. "Our Visit to Vermont." RH, February 1851, pp. 45-46.

[_____]. "The Paper." RH, May 6, 1852, p. 8.

_____. "Permanency of the Cause." RH, July 8, 1873, pp. 28-29.

_____. "Present Truth, and Present Conflicts." 4-part series in RH, November 8, 1870, pp. 164-165; November 15, 1870, pp. 172-173; November 22, 1870, pp. 180-182; November 29, 1870, pp. 188-189.

[_____]. "Publications." RH, March 1851, pp. 53-54.

[_____]. "Remarks." RH, September 24, 1861, pp. 134-135.

_____. "Re-Ordination." RH, August 6, 1867, p. 120.

_____. "The Seven Churches." RH, October 16, 1856, pp. 188-189, 192.

_____. "Signs of the Times." RH, September 13, 1853, pp. 73-76.

_____. "Spirit of Prophecy." RH, January 22, 1880, pp. 50-52.

_____. "A Test." RH, October 16, 1855, pp. 61-62.

_____. "Things in Maine." RH, November 26, 1867, pp. 377-379.

_____. "The Third Angel's Message." PT, April 1850, pp. 65-69.

_____. "Thoughts on Revelation 14." In A Word to the "Little Flock," pp. 10-11. Brunswick, Me.: James White, May 1847. Facsimile reproduction, Washington, D.C.: Review and Herald Pub. Assn, [1944].

_____. "Tract and Missionary Work." RH, November 5, 1872, p. 164.

_____. "Unity and Gifts of the Church." 4-part series in RH, December 3, 1857, p. 29; December 10, 1857, p. 37; December 31, 1857, pp. 60-61; January 7, 1858, pp. 68-69.

[_____]. "Western Tour." RH, July 4, 1854, p. 172.

_____. "Western Tour." RH, October 30, 1860, pp. 188-189.

_____. "Yearly Meetings." RH, July 21, 1859, p. 68.

White, James; Andrews, J. N.; Waggoner, J. H.; Bell, G. H.; and Smith, Uriah. "Course of Study for Ministers." RH, May 10, 1870, p. 164.

White, James, and Smith, Uriah. "Ministers' Lecture Association." RH, April 12, 1870, pp. 132-133.

Letters

Andrews, J. N., to James White. RH, March 24, 1863, p. 132.

Brinkerhoff, W. A., to James White. RH, July 25, 1865, p. 64.

Brown, Freeman G., to Sylvester Bliss. AH, December 4, 1844, p. 135.

Butler, E. P., to Joseph Marsh. RH, January 1851, pp. 38-39.

Case, J. F., to [Uriah Smith]. RH, December 4, 1856, pp. 38-39.

Cook, J. B., to G. Storrs. MC, November 23, 1843, p. [120].

Cottrell, R. F., to Uriah Smith. RH, June 5, 1860. p. 20.

_____, to James White. RH, June 19, 1860, p. 36.

_____, to James White. RH, September 24, 1861, p. 132.

_____, to James White. RH, October 8, 1861, p. 151.

Gurney, H. S., to James White. RH, December 27, 1853, p. 199.

Harmon, Ellen G., to Enoch Jacobs. D-S, January 24, 1846, pp. 31-32.

_____, to Enoch Jacobs, D-S, March 14, 1846, p. 7.

Holt, G. W., to James White. RH, January 31, 1854, p. 15.

Hull, Moses, to James White. RH, March 24, 1863, p. 132.

Hutchins, A. S., to Uriah Smith. RH, September 18, 1856, p. 158.

_____, to James White. RH, October 8, 1861, p. 151.

_____, to James White. RH, March 24, 1863, p. 132.

Ingraham, William S., to James White. RH, September 24, 1861, p. 134.

Kellogg, John P., to James White. RH, January 24, 1854, p. 7.

Lewis, P. P., to Uriah Smith. RH, August 18, 1859, p. 103.

Miller, William, to Sylvester Bliss. AH, February 12, 1845, pp. 2-3.

_____, to "My Dear Brother." MW, March 20, 1845, pp. 91-92.

_____, to Joshua V. Himes. AH, November 27, 1844, pp. 127-128.

_____, to Joshua V. Himes. AH, December 11, 1844, p. 142.

_____, to Joshua V. Himes. MC, December 14, 1843, p. [145].

_____, to Joshua V. Himes. MC, February 1, 1844, p. 221.

_____, to Joshua V. Himes. MC, October 12, 1844, pp. 121-122.

_____, to Joshua V. Himes. MW, June 12, 1845, pp. 190-192.

_____, to Joshua V. Himes. ST, September 1, 1840, pp. 81-82.

_____, to Joshua V. Himes. ST, October 15, 1841, p. 105.

_____, to Joshua V. Himes and Sylvester Bliss. AH, December 18, 1844, p. 147.

_____, to I. E. Jones. AH, December 25, 1844, pp. 154-155.

_____, to Joseph Marsh. VT, reprinted in D-S, March 11, 1845, p. 13.

_____, to My Dear Brother. MW, March 20, 1845, pp. 91-92.

_____, to the Second Advent Brethren. JS, April 17, 1845, pp. 41-42.

_____, to the Second Advent Conference held at Portland, Me., October 12, 1841. ST, November 1, 1841, p. 117.

_____, to N. Southard. MC, November 23, 1843, pp. [117-118].

Pickands, J. D., to S. S. Snow. JS, June 19, 1845, pp. 119-120.

Rogers, J. C., to James White. RH, August 11, 1853, p. 52.

Sanborn, I., to James White. RH, March 24, 1863, p. 132.

Shimper, Mrs. F. M., to James White. RH, August 19, 1851, p. 15.

Snook, B. F., to James White. RH, March 24, 1863, p. 132.

_____, to James White. RH, July 25, 1865, pp. 63-64.

Snow, S. S., to N. Southard. MC, February 22, 1844, pp. 243-244.

_____, to N. Southard. MC, June 27, 1844, p. 397.

Waggoner, J. H., to James White. RH, March 24, 1863, p. 132.

_____, to Uriah Smith. RH, November 20, 1856, p. 24.

White, Ellen G., to Eli Curtis. A Word to the "Little Flock." Brunswick, Me.: James White, May 1847, pp. 11-14. Facsimile reproduction, Washington, D.C.: Review and Herald Pub. Assn, [1944].

_____, to Dear Brethren and Sisters. <u>PT</u>, August 1849, pp. 21-24.

White, James, to Enoch Jacobs. <u>D-S</u>, September 6, 1845, pp. 17-18.

_____, to Enoch Jacobs. <u>D-S</u>, September 20, 1845, pp. 25-26.

_____, to Enoch Jacobs. <u>D-S</u>, January 24, 1846, p. 30.

Wilcox, E. H., to Joshua V. Himes. <u>ST</u>, July 6, 1842, p. 110.

Z., to Joshua V. Himes. <u>MW</u>, February 27, 1845, p. 70.

Other Manuscripts

Nott, Eliphalet. <u>A Sermon Preached Before the General Assembly of the Presbyterian Church in the United States of America . . . May 19, 1806</u>. Philadelphia: Printed by Jane Aitken, 1806.

Unpublished Materials

Unless otherwise stated, all unpublished letters and manuscripts are located in the Ellen G. White Estate Branch Offices, Andrews University, Berrien Springs, Mich.

Letters

Butler, G. I., to J. N. Andrews, May 25, 1883.

White, Ellen G., to Brethren of the General Conference, B-32a, December 19, 1892.

_____, to Managers of the Battle Creek Sanitarium, October 16, 1890.

_____, to Ellet J. Waggoner, W-27a, December 27, 1892.

White, James, to J. C. Bowles, October 17, 1849.

_____, to J. C. Bowles, November 8, 1849.

_____, to Brother Collins, August 26, 1846.

_____, to Brother Dodge, August 20, 1855.

_____, to Brother Howland, March 14, 1847.

_____, to Brother and Sister Collins, September 8, 1849.

_____, to Brother and Sister Hastings, April 27, 1848.

_____, to G. I. Butler, July 13, 1874.

_____, to Dear Brethren in Christ, November 11, 1851.

_____, to Dear Children, May 3, 1879.

_____, to Dear Children, May 11, 1879.

_____, to the Hastingses, August 26, 1848.

_____, to the Hastingses, March 22, 1849.

_____, to Leonard W. Hastings, March 18, 1850.

_____, to Sister Hastings, August 22, 1847.

_____, to J. N. Loughborough, July 19, 1878.

_____, to Ellen G. White, April 16, 1880.

_____, to Ellen G. White, February 7, 1881.

_____, to William C. White, July 5, 1874.

_____, to William C. White, May 4, 1880.

Other Manuscripts

Edson, Hiram. MS (Incomplete). "Experience in the Advent Movement," n.d.

White, Ellen G. MS 3, 1849.

_____. MS 11, 1850.

_____. MS 1, 1865.

_____. MS 4, 1883.

_____. MS 26, 1889.

_____. MS 165, 1898.

_____. MS 177, 1899.

_____. MS 30, 1900.

_____. MS 43, 1901.

_____. "To Those Who Are Receiving the Seal of the Living God." Broadside, January 31, 1849.

Location of Primary Sources

Archives of the General Conference of Seventh-day Adventists. Washington, D.C.

Ellen G. White Estate. Washington, D.C.

Ellen G. White Estate Branch Office. Andrews University. Berrien Springs, Mich.

Ellen G. White Estate Branch Office. Newbold College. Bracknell, Berks., England.

Heritage Room, A Seventh-day Adventist Archive. Andrews University. Berrien Springs, Mich.

Secondary Sources

Published Materials

Books and Pamphlets

Ahlstrom, Sydney E. A Religious History of the American People. New Haven, Conn.: Yale University Press, 1972.

Anderson, Godfrey T. Outrider of the Apocalypse: Life and Times of Joseph Bates. Mountain View, Calif.: Pacific Press Pub. Assn, 1972.

Armstrong, M. W.; Loetscher, Lefferts A.; and Anderson, C. A., eds. The Presbyterian Enterprise: Sources of American Presbyterian History. Philadelphia: Westminster Press, 1956.

Armstrong, O. K., and Armstrong, Marjorie. The Baptists in America. Garden City, N.Y.: Doubleday & Co., 1979.

Atkins, Gaius G., and Fagley, Frederick L. History of American Congregationalism. Boston: Pilgrim Press, 1952.

Baumer, Franklin L. Modern European Thought: Continuity and Change in Ideas, 1600-1950. New York: Macmillan Pub. Co., 1977.

Baxter, Norman A. History of the Freewill Baptists: A Study in New England Separatism. Rochester, N.Y.: American Baptist Historical Society, 1957.

Billias, George A., and Grob, Gerald N., eds. American History: Retrospect and Prospect. New York: Free Press, 1971.

Blackman, Milton V., Jr. Christian Churches of America: Origins and Beliefs. Provo, Utah: Brigham Young University Press, 1976.

Boorstin, Daniel J. The Americans. 3 vols. New York: Random House, 1965. Vol. 2: The National Experience.

Bucke, Emory S., ed. The History of American Methodism. 3 vols. New York: Abingdon Press, 1964.

Burrage, Champlin. The Early English Dissenters in the Light of Recent Research, 1550-1641. 2 vols. New York: Russell & Russell, 1912; reprint ed., 1967.

Bush, L. Russ, and Nettles, Tom J. Baptists and the Bible. Chicago: Moody Press, 1980.

Calvin, John. Institutes of the Christian Religion. 2 vols. Grand Rapids, Mich.: William B. Eerdmans Pub. Co., 1962.

Chilson, Adriel, ed. Miracles in My Life. Angwin, Calif.: Heritage Publications, n.d.

Clebsch, William A. From Sacred to Profane America: The Role of Religion in American History. New York: Harper & Row, 1968.

Committee on Problems in Bible Translation. Problems in Bible Translation. Washington, D.C.: Review and Herald Pub. Assn, 1954.

The Confession of Faith; the Longer and Shorter Catechisms.   N.p.: Publications Committee of the Free Presbyterian Church of Scotland, 1976.

Crisler, Clarence C. Organization: Its Character, Purpose, Place, and Development in the Seventh-day Adventist Church. Washington, D.C.: Review and Herald Pub. Assn, 1938.

Cross, F. L., ed.   The Oxford Dictionary of the Christian Church. Rev. ed. London: Oxford University Press, 1974.

Cross, Whitney R. The Burned-over District: The Social and Intellectual History of Enthusiastic Religion in Western New York, 1800-1850. New York: Harper & Row, 1965.

Damsteegt, P. Gerard. Foundations of the Seventh-day Adventist Message and Mission. Grand Rapids, Mich.: William B. Eerdmans Pub. Co., 1977.

Dexter, Henry M. Congregationalism of the Last Three Hundred Years As Seen in Its Literature.   Boston, 1880; reprint ed., Westmead, Farnborough, Hants., England: Gregg International Publishers, 1970.

Douglas, J. D., and Cairns, Earle E., eds. The New International Dictionary of the Christian Church.   Rev. ed. Grand Rapids, Mich.: Zondervan Pub. House, 1978.

Edwards, Rex. _Every Believer a Minister_. Mountain View, Calif.: Pacific Press Pub. Assn, 1979.

Firth, Robert E., ed. _Servants for Christ: The Adventist Church Facing the '80s_. Berrien Springs, Mich.: Andrews University Press, 1980.

Froom, L. E. _Movement of Destiny_. Washington, D.C.: Review and Herald Pub. Assn, 1971.

_____. _The Prophetic Faith of Our Fathers: The Historical Development of Prophetic Interpretation_. 4 vols. Washington, D.C.: Review and Herald Pub. Assn, 1946-1954.

Gale, Robert. _The Urgent Voice_. Washington, D.C.: Review and Herald Pub. Assn, 1975.

Gaustad, Edwin S. _A Religious History of America_. New York: Harper & Row, 1966.

_____, ed. _The Rise of Adventism_. New York: Harper & Row, 1974.

Haller, William. _The Rise of Puritanism_. New York: Harper & Row, 1938.

Hasel, Gerhard F. _The History and Theology of the Remnant Idea from Genesis to Isaiah_. 3rd ed. Berrien Springs, Mich.: Andrews University Press, 1980.

_____. _Understanding the Living Word of God_. Mountain View, Calif.: Pacific Press Pub. Assn, 1980.

Hastings, James, ed. _Encyclopedia of Religion and Ethics_. Vol. 4. New York: Charles Scribner's Sons, 1914.

Henderson, G. D. _Presbyterianism_. Aberdeen: University Press, 1954.

Hewitt, Clyde E. _Midnight and Morning: An Account of the Adventist Awakening and the Founding of the Advent Christian Denomination, 1831-1860_. Charlotte, N.C.: Venture Books, 1983.

Higham, John. _Send These to Me: Jews and Other Immigrants in Urban America_. New York: Atheneum, 1975.

Hofstadter, Richard. _Anti-intellectualism in American Life_. New York: Alfred A. Knopf, 1963.

Hudson, Winthrop S. _Religion in America: An Historical Account of the Development of American Religious Life_. 2nd ed. New York: Charles Scribner's Sons, 1973.

Hyde, Gordon M., ed. A Symposium on Biblical Hermeneutics. Washington, D.C.: General Conference of Seventh-day Adventists, 1974.

Jackson, Samuel MaCauley, ed. The New Schaff Herzog Encyclopedia of Religious Knowledge. Vol. 3. New York: Funk and Wagnalls Co., 1909.

Johnson, Charles A. The Frontier Camp Meeting: Religion's Harvest Time. Dallas: Southern Methodist University Press, 1955.

Kromminga, Diedrich H. The Millennium in the Church. Grand Rapids, Mich.: William B. Eerdmans Pub. Co., 1945.

Latourette, Kenneth S. A History of the Expansion of Christianity. Vol. 4: The Great Century, A.D. 1800 - A.D. 1914. London: Eyre and Spottiswoode, 1941.

Lindén, Ingemar. The Last Trump: An Historico-genetical Study of Some Important Chapters in the Making and Development of the Seventh-day Adventist Church. Frankfurt am Main: Peter Lang, 1978.

McLoughlin, William G., Jr. Modern Revivalism. New York: Ronald Press Co., 1959.

_____. New England Dissent, 1630-1833: The Baptists and the Separation of Church and State. 2 vols. Cambridge, Mass.: Harvard University Press, 1971.

Maxwell, C. Mervyn. Tell It to the World. Rev. ed. Mountain View, Calif.: Pacific Press Pub. Assn, 1977.

Miller, Perry. Orthodoxy in Massachusetts, 1630-1650. Cambridge, Mass.: Harvard University Press, 1933.

_____. Roger Williams: His Contribution to the American Tradition. Indianapolis: Bobbs-Merrill & Co., 1953.

_____, ed. The American Puritans: Their Prose and Poetry. Garden City, N.Y.: Doubleday Anchor Books, 1956.

Milner, Benjamin C., Jr. Calvin's Doctrine of the Church. Leiden: E. J. Brill, 1970.

Montgomery, Oliver. Principles of Church Organization and Administration. Washington, D.C.: Review and Herald Pub. Assn, 1942.

Morgan, Edmund S. Visible Saints: The History of a Puritan Idea. New York: University Press, 1963.

Morison, Samuel E. The Oxford History of the American People. New York: Oxford University Press, 1965.

Morrill, Milo T. A History of the Christian Denomination in America, 1794-1911 A.D. Dayton, Oh.: Christian Pub. Assn, 1912.

Morris, Leon. Ministers of God. London: Inter-Varsity Fellowship, 1964.

Neufeld, Don F. Seventh-day Adventist Encyclopedia. Rev. ed. Commentary Series, vol. 10. Washington, D.C.: Review and Herald Pub. Assn, 1976.

Nichol, Francis D. The Midnight Cry. Washington, D.C.: Review and Herald Pub. Assn, 1944.

Niebuhr, H. Richard, and Williams, Daniel D., eds. The Ministry in Historical Perspectives. New York: Harper and Bros., 1956.

Niesel, Wilhelm. The Theology of John Calvin. Translated by Harold Knight. Guildford, England: Lutterworth Press, 1956; reprint ed., Grand Rapids, Mich.: Baker Book House, 1980.

Ochs, Daniel A., and Ochs, Grace L. The Past and the Presidents. Nashville, Tenn.: Southern Pub. Assn, 1974.

Olsen, M. Ellsworth. A History of the Origin and Progress of Seventh-day Adventists. Washington, D.C.: Review and Herald Pub. Assn, 1925.

Olson, A. V. Through Crisis to Victory, 1888-1901. Washington, D.C.: Review and Herald Pub. Assn, 1966.

Pessen, Edward. Jacksonian America: Society, Personality and Politics. Rev. ed. Harewood, Ill.: Dorsey Press, 1978.

Randall, John H., Jr. The Making of the Modern Mind. Cambridge, Mass.: Houghton Mifflin Co., 1940.

Read, Walter E. The Bible, the Spirit of Prophecy, and the Church. Washington, D.C.: Review and Herald Pub. Assn, 1952.

Robinson, Virgil. James White. Washington, D.C.: Review and Herald Pub. Assn, 1976.

Rouner, Arthur A., Jr. The Congregational Way of Life. Englewood Cliffs, N.J.: Prentice-Hall, 1960.

Rowe, David L. Thunder and Trumpets: Millerites and Dissenting Religion in Upstate New York, 1800-1850. Chico, Calif.: Scholars Press, 1985.

Rutman, Darrett B. American Puritanism: Faith and Practice. Philadelphia: J. B. Lippincott Co., 1970.

Sandeen, Ernest R. The Roots of Fundamentalism: British and American Millenarianism, 1800-1930. Chicago: University Press, 1970.

Schaff, Philip. The Creeds of Christendom. 3 vols. New York: Harper & Bros., 1877.

_____. The Creeds of Christendom. 3 vols. 4th ed., rev. and enl. New York: Harper & Bros, 1919.

Schlesinger, Arthur M., Jr. The Age of Jackson. New York: Book Find Club, 1945.

Schneider, Herbert W. The Puritan Mind. Ann Arbor, Mich.: University of Michigan Press, 1958.

Schwarz, Richard W. Light Bearers to the Remnant. Mountain View, Calif.: Pacific Press Pub. Assn, 1979.

Schweizer, Eduard. Church Order in the New Testament. London: SCM Press, 1961.

Seventh-day Adventist Church Manual. [Washington, D.C.]: General Conference of Seventh-day Adventists, 1981.

Seventh Day Baptist General Conference, comp. Seventh Day Baptists in Europe and America. 2 vols. Plainfield, N.J.: Seventh Day Baptist General Conference, 1910.

Simpson, Alan. Puritanism in Old and New England. Chicago: University Press, 1955.

Smith, H. Shelton; Handy, Robert T.; and Loetscher, Lefferts A. American Christianity: An Historical Interpretation with Representative Documents. 2 vols. New York: Charles Scribner's Sons, 1960.

Smith, James W., and Jamison, A. Leland, eds. Religion in American Life. 4 vols. Princeton: University Press, 1961. Vol. 1: The Shaping of American Religion.

Smith, Timothy L. Revivalism and Social Reform: American Protestantism on the Eve of the Civil War. New York: Abingdon Press, 1957.

Spalding, A. W. Origin and History of Seventh-day Adventists. 4 vols. Washington, D.C.: Review and Herald Pub. Assn, 1961-1962.

Spicer, W. A. *Gospel Order: A Brief Outline of the Bible Principles of Organization*. Washington, D.C.: Review and Herald Pub. Assn, n.d.

Strand, Kenneth A., ed. *The Sabbath in Scripture and History*. Washington, D.C.: Review and Herald Pub. Assn, 1982.

Sweet, William Warren. *Methodism in American History*. Nashville, Tenn.: Abingdon Press, 1961.

_____. *Religion on the American Frontier, 1783-1850: A Collection of Source Materials*. Vol. 1: *The Baptists*. New York: Henry Holt & Co., 1931. Vol. 2: *The Presbyterians*. New York and London: Harper & Bros., 1936. Vol. 3: *The Congregationalists*. Chicago: University Press, 1939. Vol. 4: *The Methodists*. Chicago: University Press, 1946.

Taylor, E. R. *Methodism and Politics*. New York: Russell & Russell, 1975.

Telford, John, ed. *The Letters of the Reverend John Wesley, A.M.* 8 vols. London: Epworth Press, 1931.

Toon, Peter. *The Development of Doctrine in the Church*. Grand Rapids, Mich.: William B. Eerdmans Pub. Co., 1979.

_____. *Puritanism and Calvinism*. Swengel, Penn.: Reiner Publications, 1973.

Torbet, Robert G. *A History of the Baptists*. Philadelphia: Judson Press, 1950.

Trinterud, Leonard J. *The Forming of an American Tradition: A Re-Examination of Colonial Presbyterianism*. Philadelphia: The Westminster Press, 1949; reprint ed., New York: Books for Libraries Press, 1970.

Tyler, Alice F. *Freedom's Ferment: Phases of American Social History to 1860*. Minneapolis: University of Minnesota Press, 1944.

Van Deusen, Glyndon G. *The Jacksonian Era, 1828-1848*. New York: Harper & Bros., 1959.

Vande Vere, Emmet K. *Rugged Heart: The Story of George I. Butler*. Nashville, Tenn.: Southern Pub. Assn, 1979.

Vedder, Henry C. *A Short History of the Baptists*. Philadelphia: American Baptist Publication Society, 1907.

Walker, Williston. *Creeds and Platforms of Congregationalism*. New York: 1893; reprint ed., Boston: Pilgrim Press, 1960.

Wallenkampf, Arnold V., and Lesher, W. Richard, eds. The Sanctuary and the Atonement: Biblical, Historical, and Theological Studies. Washington, D.C.: Review and Herald Pub. Assn, 1981.

Walters, Ronald G. American Reformers, 1815-1860. New York: Hill and Wang, 1978.

Weisberger, Bernard A. They Gathered at the River: The Story of the Great Revivalists and Their Impact upon Religion in America. New York: Harper & Row, 1965.

White, Arthur L. Ellen G. White. Vol. 5: The Early Elmshaven Years. Washington, D.C.: Review and Herald Pub. Assn, 1981.

_____. Ellen G. White: Messenger to the Remnant. Washington, D.C.: Review and Herald Pub. Assn, 1954.

_____. Ellen G. White: Messenger to the Remnant. Rev. ed. Washington, D.C.: Review and Herald Pub. Assn, 1969.

White, Morton. Science and Sentiment in America: Philosophical Thought from Jonathan Edwards to John Dewey. New York: Oxford University Press, 1972.

_____, ed. Documents in the History of American Philosophy, from Jonathan Edwards to John Dewey. New York: Oxford University Press, 1972.

Wiles, Maurice. The Making of Christian Doctrine. Cambridge: University Press, 1967.

Wilken, Robert L. The Myth of Christian Beginnings. Garden City, N.Y.: Doubleday & Co., 1971.

Winslow, Ola E. Master Roger Williams. New York: Macmillan Publishing Co., 1957.

Wood, James E., Jr., ed. Baptists and the American Experience. Valley Forge, Penn.: Judson Press, 1976.

Periodicals

Adventist Heritage. Loma Linda, Calif.: July 1974.

American Quarterly. Philadelphia, Penn.: 1969.

British Advent Messenger. Grantham, Lincs., England: 1974.

Church History. Chicago: December 1954.

General Conference Bulletin. Battle Creek, Mich.: 1901-1903.

Spectrum. Takoma Park, Maryland: March 1984.

The Thomist. Washington, D.C.: January 1975.

Articles

Agnew, Theodore, L. "Methodism on the Frontier." In The History of
American Methodism, 1:488-545. 3 vols. Edited by Emory S.
Bucke. New York: Abingdon Press, 1964.

Ahlstrom, Sydney E. "Theology in America: A Historical Survey." In
Religion in American Life. 4 vols. Edited by James W. Smith
and A. Leland Jamison. Princeton: University Press, 1961.
Vol. 1: The Shaping of American Religion, pp. 233-321.

Anderson, Godfrey T. "Make Us a Name." Adventist Heritage, July
1974, p. 30.

"Andrews University." Seventh-day Adventist Encyclopedia. 1976
ed. 10:45-52.

Arthur, David T. "Millerism." In The Rise of Adventism, pp. 154-
172. Edited by Edwin S. Gaustad. New York: Harper & Row,
1974.

"Battle Creek Sanitarium." Seventh-day Adventist Encyclopedia. 1976
ed. 10:135-140.

Beach, B. B. "Windows of Vulnerability." RH, August 2, 1984, pp. 3-
5.

Bradley, W. P. "How a Policy Is Made." RH, December 4, 1969, p. 18.

Burdick, William L. "The Eastern Association." In Seventh Day
Baptists in Europe and America, 2:587-716. 2 vols. Compiled
by Seventh Day Baptist General Conference. Plainfield, N.J.:
Seventh Day Baptist General Conference, 1910.

Butler, Jonathan M. "Adventism and the American Experience." In The
Rise of Adventism, pp. 173-206. Edited by Edwin S. Gaustad.
New York: Harper & Row, 1974.

"A Call for an Open Church." Spectrum 14 (March 1984):14-53.

Carner, Vern; Kubo, Sakae; and Rice, Curt. "Bibliographical Essay."
In The Rise of Adventism, pp. 207-317. Edited by Edwin S.
Gaustad. New York: Harper & Row, 1974.

"A Century of Adventism in the British Isles." British Advent
Messenger. Centennial Historical Special, 1974.

"Church Elder." Seventh-day Adventist Encyclopedia. 1976 ed. 10: 299-300.

"Church Government." Seventh-day Adventist Encyclopedia. 1976 ed. 10:300.

Colvin, George. "Explaining Participation: A Commentary." Spectrum 14 (March 1984):36-39.

Cooke, Jacob E. "The Federalist Age: A Reappraisal." In American History: Retrospect and Prospect, pp. 85-153. Edited by George A. Billias and Gerald N. Grob. New York: Free Press, 1971.

Corliss, John O. "The Message and Its Friends--No. 2: Joseph Bates As I Knew Him." RH, August 16, 1923, p. 7.

Cottrell, Raymond F. "The Sabbath in the New World." In The Sabbath in Scripture and History, pp. 244-263. Edited by Kenneth A. Strand. Washington, D.C.: Review and Herald Pub. Assn, 1982.

_____. "The Varieties of Church Structure." Spectrum 14 (March 1984):40-53.

"Cottrell, Roswell F." Seventh-day Adventist Encyclopedia. 1976 ed. 10:354.

Dederen, Raoul. "Tomorrow's Church, Truly a 'Remnant'." RH, January 9, 1986, pp. 8-10.

"Division." Seventh-day Adventist Encyclopedia. 1976 ed. 10:393-394.

Douglas, Walter B. T. "The Church: Its Nature and Function." In Servants for Christ: The Adventist Church Facing the '80s, pp. 53-85. Edited by Robert E. Firth. Berrien Springs, Mich.: Andrews University Press, 1980.

Fiorelli, Lewis S. "Expectancy of an Imminent Parousia and Concern with Church Order: An Inverse Relationship?" The Thomist 39 (January 1975):1-23.

"Frisbie, Joseph Birchard." Seventh-day Adventist Encyclopedia. 1976 ed. 10:484.

Gallagher, Jonathan. "The Delay of the Advent." Ministry, June 1978, pp. 4-6.

Gaustad, Edwin S. "Baptists and the Making of a New Nation." In Baptists and the American Experience, pp. 39-53. Edited by James E. Wood, Jr. Valley Forge, Penn.: Judson Press, 1976.

"Great Britain and Northern Ireland, Development of SDA Work."
    Seventh-day Adventist Encyclopedia. 1976 ed. 10:528-531.

Harmon, Nolan B. "Structural and Administrative Changes." In The
    History of American Methodism, 3:1-58. 3 vols. Edited by
    Emory S. Bucke. New York: Abingdon Press, 1964.

Hudson, Winthrop S. "A Time of Religious Ferment." In The Rise of
    Adventism, pp. 1-17. Edited by Edwin S. Gaustad. New York:
    Harper & Row, 1974.

Kirby, Gilbert W. "Congregationalism." New International Dictionary
    of the Christian Church. 1978 ed., pp. 251-253.

Lake, Donald M. "Saybrook Platform (1708)." New International
    Dictionary of the Christian Church. 1978 ed., p. 881.

"Loughborough, John Norton." Seventh-day Adventist Encyclopedia.
    1976 ed. 10:815-816.

McLoughlin, William G., Jr. "Revivalism." In The Rise of Adventism,
    pp. 119-150. Edited by Edwin S. Gaustad. New York: Harper &
    Row, 1974.

"Marion Party." Seventh-day Adventist Encyclopedia. 1976 ed.
    10:853-854.

Mathews, Donald G. "The Second Great Awakening as an Organizing
    Process, 1780-1830: An Hypothesis." American Quarterly 21
    (1969):23-43.

Maxwell, C. Mervyn. "Joseph Bates and SDA Sabbath Theology." In The
    Sabbath in Scripture and History, pp. 352-363. Edited by
    Kenneth A. Strand. Washington, D.C.: Review and Herald Pub.
    Assn, 1982.

_____. "Sanctuary and Atonement in SDA Theology: An Historical
    Survey." In The Sanctuary and the Atonement: Biblical,
    Historical, and Theological Studies, pp. 516-544. Edited by
    Arnold V. Wallenkampf and W. Richard Lesher. Washington, D.C.:
    Review and Herald Pub. Assn, 1981.

Mead, Sidney E. "Denominationalism: The Shape of Protestantism in
    America." Church History 23 (December 1954):291-320.

"Messenger Party." Seventh-day Adventist Encyclopedia. 1976 ed.
    10:870-871.

"Methodist Churches." Oxford Dictionary of the Christian Church.
    1974 ed., pp. 908-910.

"Millerite Movement." Seventh-day Adventist Encyclopedia. 1976 ed.
    10:892-898.

Neufeld, Don F. "Biblical Interpretation in the Advent Movement." In A Symposium on Biblical Hermeneutics, pp. 109-125. Edited by Gordon M. Hyde. Washington, D.C.: General Conference of Seventh-day Adventists, 1974.

Oosterwal, Gottfried. "Mission Still Possible." Ministry, December 1986, pp. 4-8.

"Open and Shut Door." Seventh-day Adventist Encyclopedia. 1976 ed. 10:1034-1037.

"Ordination." Seventh-day Adventist Encyclopedia. 1976 ed. 10: 1037-1040.

"Organization, Development of, in SDA Church." Seventh-day Adventist Encyclopedia. 1976 ed. 10:1042-1054.

Reid, George W. "Time to Reorder the Church?" RH, July 28, 1983, pp. 14-15.

Reid, W. S. "Presbyterianism." New International Dictionary of the Christian Church. 1978 ed., pp. 800-802.

"Remnant Church." Seventh-day Adventist Encyclopedia. 1976 ed. 10:1200-1201.

"Sabbath." Seventh-day Adventist Encyclopedia. 1976 ed. 10:1250-1253.

Sandeen, Ernest R. "Millennialism." In The Rise of Adventism, pp. 104-118. Edited by Edwin S. Gaustad. New York: Harper & Row, 1974.

"Savoy Declaration." Oxford Dictionary of the Christian Church. 1974 ed., p. 1239.

"Session Actions: Fundamental Beliefs of Seventh-day Adventists-- Church Manual Revision." RH, May 1, 1980, p. 27.

"Seventh-Month Movement." Seventh-day Adventist Encyclopedia. 1976 ed. 10:1338.

Smith, Timothy L. "Social Reform." In The Rise of Adventism, pp. 18-29. Edited by Edwin S. Gaustad. New York: Harper & Row, 1974.

Staples, Russell. "The Face of the Church to Come." RH, January 2, 1986, pp. 8-10.

Summerbell, J. J. "Christians." The New Schaff-Herzog Encyclopedia of Religious Knowledge. 1909 ed. 3:45-46.

Task Force Report. "A Call for an Open Church." Spectrum 14 (March 1984):18-24.

Task Force Report. "Defining Participation: A Model Conference Constitution." Spectrum 14 (March 1984):25-35.

"Three Angels' Messages." Seventh-day Adventist Encyclopedia. 1976 ed. 10:1483-1484.

"Tract and Missionary Societies." Seventh-day Adventist Encyclopedia. 1976 ed. 10:1495-1497.

"Union." Seventh-day Adventist Encyclopedia. 1976 ed. 10:1514.

Walker, Williston. "Congregationalism." Encyclopaedia of Religion and Ethics. 1914 ed. 4:19-25.

Walters, James W. "The Need for Structural Change." Spectrum 14 (March 1984):14-17.

Warner, Madeline. "The Changing Image of the Millerites in the Western Massachusetts Press." Adventist Heritage 2 (Summer 1975):5-7.

"Wheeler, Frederick." Seventh-day Adventist Encyclopedia. 1976 ed. 10:1584.

"White, James Springer." Seventh-day Adventist Encyclopedia. 1976 ed. 10:1598-1604.

Yost, F. Donald. "Membership and Financial Statistics." RH, July 4, 1985, p. 28.

Unpublished Materials

Manuscripts

Anderson, Carl D. "The History and Evolution of Seventh-day Adventist Church Organization." Ph.D. dissertation, American University, 1960.

Arthur, David T. "'Come Out of Babylon': A Study of Millerite Separatism and Denominationalism, 1840-1865." Ph.D. dissertation, University of Rochester, 1970.

_____. "Joshua V. Himes and the Cause of Adventism, 1839-1845." M.A. thesis, University of Chicago, 1961.

Bradford, Charles E. "A Theology of Church Organization and Administration." Paper presented at a theological consultation for Seventh-day Adventist Administrators and Religion Scholars, Glacier View, Colorado, August 15-19, 1980.

Dick, Everett N. "The Adventist Crisis of 1843-1844." Ph.D. dissertation, University of Wisconsin, 1930.

Gallagher, Jonathan. "Believing Christ's Return: An Interpretative Analysis of the Dynamics of Christian Hope." Ph.D. dissertation, University of St. Andrews, 1982.

Graham, Roy E. "Ellen G. White: An Examination of Her Position and Role in the Seventh-day Adventist Church." Ph.D. thesis, University of Birmingham, 1977.

Graybill, Ronald D. "The Power of Prophecy: Ellen G. White and the Women Religious Founders of the Nineteenth Century." Ph.D. dissertation, Johns Hopkins University, 1983.

Harkness, Reuben E. E. "Social Origins of the Millerite Movement." Ph.D. dissertation, University of Chicago, 1927.

Jorgensen, G. "An Investigation of the Administrative Reorganization of the General Conference of Seventh-day Adventists as Planned and Carried Out in the General Conference of 1901 and 1903." M.A. thesis, SDA Theological Seminary, 1949.

Martinborough, Gordon O. "The Beginnings of a Theology of the Sabbath among American Sabbatarian Adventists, 1842-1850." M.A. thesis, Loma Linda University, 1976.

Olson, Robert W. "The 'Shut Door' Documents." Ellen G. White Estate, Washington, D.C., April 11, 1982.

Oosterwal, Gottfried. "The SDA Church in the 1980's." Paper presented at a theological consultation for Seventh-day Adventist Administrators and Religion Scholars, Glacier View, Colorado, August 15-19, 1980.

Poehler, Rolf J. "'. . . and the Door Was Shut': Seventh-day Adventists and the Shut-Door Doctrine in the Decade after the Great Disappointment." Research paper. February 1978. Ellen G. White Estate Branch Office. Andrews University. Berrien Springs, Mich.

Rowe, David L. "Thunder and Trumpets: The Millerite Movement and Apocalyptic Thought in Upstate New York, 1800-1845." Ph.D. dissertation, University of Virginia, 1974.

Schantz, Borge. "The Development of Seventh-day Adventist Missionary Thought: Contemporary Appraisal." 2 vols. Ph.D. dissertation, Fuller Theological Seminary, 1983.

Veltman, Fred. "The Role of Church Administrators and Theologians." Paper presented at a theological consultation for Seventh-day Adventist Administrators and Religion Scholars, Glacier View, Colorado, August 15-19, 1980.

Microfilm

The Millerites and Early Adventists. Ann Arbor, Mich.: University
    Microfilms International, 1978.